Spices and Herbs
Lore & Cookery

Elizabeth S. Hayes

Illustrations by
J.M. Yeatts

D1531384

Dover Publications, Inc.
New York

TO MY MOTHER who distilled her infinite wisdom into several pure component parts so that one of these should arouse within me an unquenchable thirst for useful knowledge of fragrance and the delicate art of seasoning with spices and herbs. Only after this knowledge was acquired did she help me with my charts, which have led to so many delicious and fascinating flavors.

Published in Canada by General Publishing Company, Ltd., 30 Lesmill Road, Don Mills, Toronto, Ontario.
Published in the United Kingdom by Constable and Company, Ltd., 10 Orange Street, London WC2H 7EG.

This Dover edition, first published in 1980, is an unabridged republication of the work originally entitled *Spices and Herbs around the World*, published by Doubleday and Co., N. Y., in 1961. A list of suppliers has been included and the original full-color frontispiece omitted.

International Standard Book Number: 0-486-24026-6
Library of Congress Catalog Card Number: 80-66063

Manufactured in the United States of America
Dover Publications, Inc.
180 Varick Street
New York, N.Y. 10014

CONTENTS

THE SETTING, 11

PART ONE: ASSEMBLY OF THE SPICES

1. *Assembly of the spices*   15

2. *Nature's spicy stories (with recipes)*   20

   PEPPER, 20   CARDAMON, 43
   CLOVES, 24   VANILLA, 45
   CINNAMON, 27   TURMERIC, 49
   NUTMEG AND MACE, 30   SAFFRON CROCUS, 51
   ALLSPICE, 33   CAPERS, 54
   BAY, 37   CAPSICUM, 55
   GINGER, 39   PAPRIKA, 56
   WILD GINGER, 41

3. *A time for pleasure and contentment*   58

4. *Spice chart: how the spices are used*   59

PART TWO: BEVERAGES AND SEASONINGS OTHER THAN SPICES OR HERBS (with recipes)

5. *Beverages*   65

   COFFEE, 65
   TEA, 73
   COCOA, 79
   BEVERAGE CHART: HOW THE BEVERAGES ARE USED, 82

6. *Salt*   83

7. *Sugar*   86

   SUGAR BEET, 87

8   *Contents*

PART THREE: ASSEMBLY OF THE HERBS

8. *Dedication of Gerard's* Herball   91
9. *Assembly of the herbs*   94
   A FEW FACTS ABOUT HERB COOKING, 97
10. *Herbs tell their stories (with recipes)*   99
    AMBROSIA, 99
    ANGELICA, 101
    ANISE, 103
    BALM, 105
    BERGAMOT, 106
    BETONY, 107
        WOOD BETONY, 108
        PAUL'S BETONY, 109
    BORAGE, 110
    BURNET, 111
    CALAMUS, 112
    CAMOMILE, 113
    CARAWAY, 114
    CATNIP, 116
    CHERVIL, 117
    CHICORY, 118
    CHIVES, 120
    CLARY, 122
    CORIANDER, 123
    COSTMARY, 125
    CRESSES, 126
        UPLAND CRESS, 127
        WATER CRESS, 128
        GARDEN CRESS, 129
    CUMIN, 129
    DANDELION, 131
    DILL, 133
    FENNELS, 136
    FENNEL FLOWER, 138
    FEVERFEW, 139
    GARLIC, 140
    GERANIUM-SCENTED LEAVES, 142
        ROSE GERANIUM, 142
        LEMON GERANIUM, 143
    GERMANDER, 144
    HOP, 145
    HOREHOUND, 146
    HORSE-RADISH, 148
    HYSSOP, 149

LAVENDER, 151
LEEK, 153
LEMON VERBENA, 154
LOVAGE, 155
POT MARIGOLD, 156
MARJORAMS, 157
MAY APPLE, 160
MINTS, 161
  PEPPERMINT, 162
  SPEARMINT, 163
  APPLE MINT, 164
MUSTARDS, 166
  BLACK OR BROWN MUSTARD, 166
  WHITE OR YELLOW MUSTARD, 167
NASTURTIUM, 167
ORÉGANO, 169
PARSLEY, 171
PENNYROYAL, 173
PEPPER TABASCO, 174
  SMALL RED CHILI, 175
POPPY, 179
RHUBARB, 180
ROCAMBOLE, 182
  LESSER-LEAVED GARLIC, 183
ROSEMARY, 184
ROSES, 185
RUE, 188
SAGE, 189
SANTOLINAS, 191
SAVORY, 192
SESAME, 196
SHALLOT, 199
SORREL, 200
  FRENCH SORREL, 200
  GARDEN SORREL, 201
  WOOD SORREL, 202
SWEET BASIL, 203
SWEET CICELY, 205
SWEET WOODRUFF, 206
TANSY, 207
TARRAGON, 208
THYME, 209
WINTERGREEN, 211
YARROW, 213

11. *Herb chart: how the herbs are used*   215
  CHIEF HERBS USED IN COOKERY, 224

OUTSTANDING ROBUST HERBS FOR COOKERY, 224
MOST COMMONLY USED COMBINATIONS OF FINES HERBES, 224

12. *Some facts about growing herbs*   225
PERENNIALS, 225
ANNUALS AND BIENNIALS, 226
HERB GROWING CHARTS, 227
SUGGESTED PATTERNS FOR GROWING, 240
    Model perennial herb garden, 240
    Model annual herb garden, 241
    Small herb garden—pyramid, 242
    Small herb garden, 242
    Small herb garden—wheel, 243
    Semi-formal "wayside" herb garden, 243
    Terrace and border garden, 244
    Garden wall boxes, 245
    Window garden, 245
    Enlarged herb garden, 246

13. *Yesterday, today, and tomorrow*   247
HINTS FOR PREPARING AND DRYING HERBS, 247
HINTS FOR FREEZING AND THAWING HERBS, 247

14. *Rules for judging herb exhibits*   249

15. *Tussie mussies*   253

ACKNOWLEDGMENTS, 255

BIBLIOGRAPHY, 257

INDEX, 261

The setting

Go, little book, and wish to all
Flowers in the garden, meat in the hall,
A bin of wine, a spice of wit,
A house with lawn enclosing it,
A living river by the door,
A nightingale in the sycamore!

ROBERT LOUIS STEVENSON

Mankind has been drawn by the exotic lure of spices and herbs since before recorded history. No other commodities of commerce have had such an all-encompassing place in history, adventure, legend, and lore. In ancient times they stirred the imagination of kings and ambitious adventurers to seek sea routes to Asia in an effort to reach the riches that were waiting for a taker. Thus, the New World was found.

Queens from vivacious Cleopatra to formal Elizabeth added luster to their lives by experimenting with fascinating, fragrant concoctions and embrocations. The great writers down through the ages have found the mysteries of spices and herbs to be delightful subjects. Theophrastus of Greece wrote *On the History of Plants* and *On the Causes of Plants*. Dioscorides of Greece was next to contribute to the field of horticulture. Galen, also of Greece, was a physician who wrote of medicinal plants and invented the formula for cold creams. Pliny, a Roman, found time to study and write about the virtues of frail and perishable plants. John Gerard from London spent more than thirty-six years in growing, classifying, and writing about plants from all parts of the world. John Parkinson, also from London, made a great contribution through his *Theatre of Plants*, published in 1640.

Collinson of London corresponded with Custis of Williamsburg and Bartram of Philadelphia, who were the earliest American writers on botany. Their love of horticulture taught the meaning and necessity of plant exchange between countries and individuals.

The beautiful *Song of Solomon* and the nostalgic writings of Shakespeare are filled with references to sweet-smelling spices and herbs that pervade many of America's gardens to this day.

The dreams and ideals of the first settlers were expressed through their gardens and terraced walks, in which their heritage and vistas of the past were evident.

My father, Edgar W. Smith, was a timber surveyor and contractor. As a result, it was my good fortune to grow up with nature. When he was growing up the kitchen herb garden was a must for every family, and he taught me how to plant my first herb garden on his plantation. It was planted in a wheel from one of his wagons. An interest in having my own garden has been with me since childhood.

After joining a garden club I became interested in collecting data on spices and herbs. The material was useful on garden club and television programs and in garden therapy work: sweet-scented herb gardens added enrichment to the life of shut-ins, the aged, and the blind.

Practically all authorities agree that retired people become such enthusiastic gardeners because of the future outlook, for "Gardening is a constant succession of new beginnings." The "Pleasure Garden" for fragrance and flavor has become one of the most popular of their planting and growing programs.

This is not a technical book. It is a book of stories built on a foundation of history and an endless number of books. The compiled material took book form so that the history, romance, adventure, legend, and lore of fragrance, flavor, and beauty—our heritage of spices and herbs—might be shared with many, many others.

E. S. H.

1. Assembly of the spices

> *All that mankind has done, thought, gained or been: it is lying in magic preservation in the pages of books.*
> *They are the chosen possessions of men.*
>
> THOMAS CARLYLE

Have you ever imagined the magnitude of thought that went into the planning of the very first garden? The Garden of Eden must have been like this:

FIRST, there must have been all the shades of green to rest the eyes . . . and then all the colors of the rainbow to lift the spirits.

SECOND, there must have been fragrance—beautiful, subtle, and inviting; beckoning us to come forward in a delightful state of anticipation to seek the treasures that were there for the finding.

THIRD, there must have been the tantalizing sight of mouth-watering fruit—sun-ripened peaches and cherries hanging like precious jewels on the boughs—to give exotic flavors.

In the first garden there was made to grow every tree that was beautiful to look upon, . . . bearing an abundance of fruit good to eat. There were clear waters, lilies of the field, and sweet-smelling herbs.

Through the misty curtains of the past we glimpse the earliest spice and herb gatherers, who must truly have been the children of nature: enjoying the songs of birds, the life-giving sunshine, the slopes, the hills, the mountains and all of the floor levels of the earth, the refreshing rains, the streams, the rivers, and the star-studded roof of the heavens. As they rested they must have pondered over the wondrous treasures whose fragrance emanated from the temples of the gods or enveloped the bubbling kettles of witchcraft.

The real pleasures and most rewarding experiences of the spice and herb gatherers must have been in taking their treasures to the market places and seeing the people flock to the markets seeking a multitude of delights that would add luster to their living.

From Arabia came the camel caravans, whose merchants worked feverishly to load their camels for the long, arduous, and dangerous trek to faraway places with their precious merchandise. Spices were the basis of our earliest trade and commerce. The ancients sold ointments and oils for very large sums of money to the wealthy ruling classes, who wanted soothing balms and sweet fragrances to fill their homes. The first gifts of the Wise Men were frankincense from the East African *Boswellia* tree; myrrh from the Arabian and East African *Balsamodendron myrrha* shrub; and other sweet smelling herbs brought in vases and cups made from the ornamental murra stone from ancient Rome.

Romantic associations are attached to many of our spices. The bay tree (*Laurus nobilis*), Dr. John Lindley tells us, is sometimes called Apollo's laurel. In *Chambers's Cyclopaedia of English Literature* (1853) Warton tells a romantic little story that is truly a treasure:

> *The daughter of the king of Hungary having fallen into melancholy, in consequence of the loss of her lover, the squire of low degree, her father thus endeavours to console her. The passage is valuable, "because," says Warton, "it delineates in lively colours, the fashionable diversions and usages of ancient times."*

Extract from *The Squire of Low Degree:*

Tomorrow ye shall in hunting fare
Be seated in a velvet chair—
Ye shall have harp and song

And other mirths among.
Ye shall have Rumney and Malespine
And other Vernage wine [a drink made of wine, honey, and spices]
When ye are laid in a bed so soft,
A cage of gold will be hung aloft—
With long paper fair burning
And cloves that be sweet smelling.
Frankincense and olibanum
That where ye sleep the taste will come—
And if ye no rest can take,
All night minstrels for ye shall wake.

The clove tree is another treasure that should be dear to all of us because of its fragrance and flavor. Gerard has said, "Tho this description be very brief—it has none that can compare—their smell is so pleasing it is like the pepper-nut more fragile—it is grown in the Indian ground but was brought to us from the Eastern Spice Islands for the smell."

The island of Zanzibar, just off the east coast of Africa, used to be noted as a center of the slave trade but since this is now a thing of the past its great claim to fame is cloves. Its symmetrical, shiny green, and red-stemmed clove trees are second only to those of the Far Eastern Spice Islands. The spicy stimulating odor overhangs the island. Dr. David Livingstone started from Zanzibar to try to find the Mountain of the Moon. His body is buried in England but his heart was laid away in the African wilderness. It was here that he cried out in a resounding voice against the slave trade.

The ancients spoke eloquently of the cinnamon tree. They described its beautiful leaves, and how the bark, when taken off and cast on the ground in the heat of the sun, gave off a warm sweetness of smell. They also mentioned the nutmeg tree, which makes a goodly show when well laden with fruit. They pointed out that nutmeg would sweeten the breath if held in the mouth and much chewed upon.

Most spices, at least the earliest known ones, were indigenous to China. They were taken into India by camel caravans over back-breaking land routes that varied in level from the lowest steppe to the highest mountain. From India they were taken to Arabia and Egypt. Not until the Crusades brought East and West face to face in the Holy Land did European appetites quicken at the pungent Eastern flavors. To satisfy this new European desire and demand for these exotic flavors from the East, ships began plying the Mediterranean, carrying spices to the large metropolitan seaports along the southern coast of Europe. It was natural that Venice, with its cosmopolitan tastes and huge shipping interests, should control this trade. Venice maintained a monopoly on spice shipping until Portugal found new sea routes to the East.

These new routes were found because of the constant battling for control of trade on the seas. Competition brought about more shipbuilding and created an ever-growing interest among the navigators and explorers of many countries such as Magellan from Portugal and Columbus, the Italian navigator. Most of this trade was in spices!

The next glimpse between the unfurled curtains was of ships sailing down through the next hundred and fifty years, their explorers and navigators searching their charts and setting their courses for the unknown. Literally they searched each wave for a clue to the lands beyond the horizons. In looking for new sea routes to the East, Columbus discovered America.

The drama for which the stage was set by Columbus is portrayed in some verses written in the eighteenth century by George Berkeley, a bishop to whom the Pope assigned "every virtue under Heaven."

> *The Muse, disgusted at an age and clime*
>   *Barren of every glorious theme,*
> *In distant times now waits a better time,*
>   *Producing subjects worthy fame.*
>
> *In happy climes, where from the genial sun*
>   *And virgin earth, such scenes ensue,*
> *The force of art by nature seems outdone,*
>   *And fancied beauties by the true:*

In happy climes, the seat of innocence,
  Where nature guides and virtue rules.
Where men shall not impose for truth and sense
  The pedantry of courts and schools:

There shall be sung another golden age,
  The rise of empire and of arts,
The good and great inspiring epic rage,
  The wisest heads and noblest hearts.

Not such as Europe breeds in her decay;
  Such as she bred when fresh and young,
When heavenly flame did animate her clay
  By future poets shall be sung.

Westward the course of empire takes its way;
  The four first acts already past,
A fifth shall close the drama with the day;
  Time's noblest offspring is the last.

The early use of spices and herbs is most intriguing, but one side of the spice picture seems to have escaped many of us. While we tend to think only in terms of flavorings and seasonings, history and legend tell of many other uses in medieval times. These included the preserving of food and the preparation of dyes, perfumes, medicines, and confections.

In our modern use of scintillating spices and herbs we are becoming more aware of our priceless heritage of fragrance and flavor. It is hoped that the story unfolded on the previous pages will inspire others to become more aware of the wondrous beauty, exciting fragrance, and exotic flavors that surround us in all phases of the commercial world of today. For spices and fragrant perfumes, we go to the merchants, but for the unlimited varieties of herbs, we should go to the seedsman, the nurseryman, and the garden shop where these lovely gifts of nature can be obtained. By growing them in our gardens we can add exciting fun and enjoyment to our everyday living.

2. Nature's spicy stories

PEPPER
Piper nigrum

The spiciest of all spices—that's pepper. It is the most important and authoritative of all. We know it carries itself with great authority because it asserts itself immediately when we bring it too close to our nostrils. As a seasoning it is second only to salt, its twin. It is on practically every table in the world and is used at every meal. Pepper makes almost everything taste better.

Nothing has had a more romantic history than pepper. The pepper shrub originally came from the Malabar district on the west coast of India, but today eighty per cent of the pepper supply comes from the Netherlands Indies. Sarawak, in the northern part of Borneo, is one of the chief producers and Chinese farmers grow most of Sarawak's pepper. Apparently the Chinese first came to this area more than a thousand years ago to work in the rice fields, but the rice crop proved to be unprofitable. Those who did not turn to trade became rubber or pepper growers. Their pepper gardens average only about five acres, for the British discouraged large estates.

The Greeks were using pepper as early as the fourth century B.C., but in ancient and medieval times only the rich could afford it. It came from the Far East by caravan, and to reach Europe it had to be transported halfway around the world over the most tortuous routes imaginable. The expense was so great that a pound of pepper was considered to be "fit for a king."

It seems that pepper is one of two things that people all around the world have had to have. Unlike salt, it is not essential to life itself, but it is certainly essential to a good disposition. Since it is so important, it was quite natural that pepper should have been used as money. Taxes and tribute have been paid with pepper. When Alaric the Goth besieged Rome, the ransom demanded from the city was five thousand pounds of gold, thirty thousand pounds of silver, and three thousand pounds of pepper. The Romans had the gold and the silver, but they had a very difficult time getting together the pepper portion of the ransom. Toward the end of the tenth century English landlords charged a rent tax of one pound of pepper a year. It was a valuable part of the spoils obtained by victorious soldiers. The very high price set on pepper was one of the reasons Portugal sought (and found) a water route to India. The cost of pepper in Europe dropped tremendously when the way was found around the Cape of Good Hope.

Here is what Gerard says about pepper in his great *Herball*: "The Plant that beareth the blacke pepper groweth up like a vine, amongst bushes and brambles, where it naturally groweth but where it is manured it is fowne at the bottom of tree Janfel and the Date tree, whereon it taketh hold and clymbeth up even unto the top, as doth the vine, ramping and taking hold with his clasping tendrels of any other thing. All pepper heateth, provoketh, digesteth, draweth, disperseth, and clenseth the dimness of the sight, as Dioscorides noteth."

Pepper comes from the fruit or seeds of a climbing shrub that will grow wild. However, most of it is cultivated on plantations where shrubs are grown from seeds or cuttings. The shrub yields fruit in three years and reaches top yield in seven years. Black pepper is made by drying unripe berries until they are black. White pepper is made by grinding only the seeds taken from the berry.

Black pepper is much stronger than white pepper. The next time you pass a container of black pepper, shake some out on your hand and you will notice that there are white grains mixed with the black grains. Most black pepper is marketed for home use as a mixture. White pepper is used to buffer, or gentle, the piercing flavor of pure black pepper.

To get the most enjoyment out of pepper, use a grinder and grind the berries fresh for every meal. Its fragrance and flavor, just after grinding, will give you a new taste thrill.

A quaint "Item for Housekeepers" (in a Manchester, New Hampshire, newspaper, 1866) says: "Scatter ground black pepper over your furs and flannels when you lay them away for the summer and the moths will never trouble them."

So that's pepper, a part of our way of life.

Here are two recipes using pepper. It is hoped that you will try both of them. If you can try only one, however, do not miss the experience of tasting Black-Seeded Simpson Salad.

WHITE PEPPER POTATO SOUP
"par excellence"

> *4 large potatoes*
> *2 large onions*
> *½ teaspoon salt*
> *1¼ cups water*
> *1 quart milk*
> *1 pint heavy cream*
> *3 tablespoons flour*
> *¼ pound butter*
> *½ teaspoon white pepper*
> *½ teaspoon paprika*

Peel and cube potatoes and onions. Add salt and 1 cup water (hold ¼ cup), simmer until tender. Drain off water, add milk and cream. Mix flour and ¼ cup cold water to a thin smooth paste, add to soup, and simmer on low heat until thickened. Pour into cream soup bowls. Cut butter into 8 cubes and add 1 cube to each soup bowl. Sprinkle *generously* with white pepper and garnish with paprika. Serves 8.

BLACK-SEEDED SIMPSON SALAD

> *½ gallon garden lettuce leaves*
> *4 crisp green onions*
> *4 fresh eggs*
> *3 tablespoons bacon drippings*
> *2 tablespoons brown sugar*
> *½ teaspoon salt*
> *¼ teaspoon red pepper*
> *¼ teaspoon black pepper*
> *¾ cup cider vinegar*
> *¼ cup water*

Wash and crisp lettuce leaves. Slice onions in thin slices, green tops and all. The eggs should be hard-boiled and set aside. Line a large wooden salad bowl with one layer of frilled lettuce, leaving a ruffle of leaves above the top of the bowl. Tear lettuce in chunks (by hand), add a layer of lettuce, onion slices, boiled egg slices—layer on layer until bowl is filled. Garnish with egg slices.

DRESSING: Heat heavy iron skillet. Add bacon drippings, brown sugar, salt, red pepper, black pepper, vinegar, and water and simmer 1 minute. Pour hot dressing over salad. Cover with a large plate to keep steam in. Appetizing and delicious. Serves 6.

CLOVES
*Caryophyllus
aromaticus*

Everywhere there was an indescribably piquant, pungent, and
sweet fragrance, saturating every breath of moisture-laden air
rising above the waves of the blue-green sea. As the ship sailed with
the breeze, sailors knew they were getting close to the isle of
Amboina, thirty miles long and only half as wide. Everywhere on
the isle are tiny brilliant blossoms, poised like precious jewels in a
dense setting of deep, rich green. It was from here that the sweet
fragrance borne on the land breeze let the sailors know they had
arrived at the "Garden of Spices."

By all size comparisons, the isle of Amboina is small. The
romantic history of this small isle would fill several books, some
pleasing and some not so pleasing. In the search for "bouquet"
(fragrance and flavor) lives were lost, hardships overcome, wars
fought, and even the survival of nations hung on a handful of spice.
Great wealth was gained and lost but lasting satisfaction became a
part of living because of the acquisition of this *bouquet de piquancy*.

The bouquet was desperately needed by many countries, among
which was medieval England, whose winter diet consisted of coarse
meal and salted meat, as cold storage was unknown. Before the winter was over, much of this bare mealtime fare was half spoiled. To
cut down on the spoilage and make the food more palatable, those
with money were quite willing to pay fantastic sums for small
amounts of cloves (along with other members of the "Big Four"—
pepper, cinnamon, and nutmeg). They were worth more than their
weight in gold. As a result, even the smallest nations, with no natural
sources of great wealth, became rich and powerful beyond belief
simply by controlling the spice trade. Portugal, the Netherlands, and

England did so and are still reaping benefits because the spices have remained invaluable, even in these "deepfreezer" days!

Now another look at Amboina, which with a few close-by smaller islands makes up the "clove garden." Amboina is one of the true spice islands, one of the Moluccas, which are in turn a part of the great Australasian island group. The Moluccas are located east of the Celebes and separate them from New Guinea. Amboina was the first and only home of the rare spicy delicacy, the clove, until it was finally transplanted to Zanzibar and the West Indies. Although it has been witness to many a bloody battle in the past, Amboina is now a quiet, methodical Dutch town, where English traders are welcome, and it is still the center of the clove world.

A little more about the clove tree. It has been said that nutmegs have to smell the sea and the clove has to see it, to grow to maturity properly. This saying has been borne out through centuries as the clove tree prospered in salt air. It is truly a magnificent tree, an evergreen that sometimes grows to a height of forty feet and blooms the whole year round. The flower buds are a pale color at first; they turn gradually to green and then to bright red. At this stage they are ready for picking. Drying to a dark brown hue prevents them from decaying. They then shrivel to the brownish-black and spicy tidbits we know as cloves. They are about half an inch long and the knob of one end contains unopened flower petals in the form of a ball. The clove looks like a nail and because of this it was given its name from the French word *clou*, meaning nail.

In addition to their very widespread use in our food, cloves have always occupied an important place in the "world of perfumery." The oils extracted from the clove are indeed precious to the scent maker. Cloves have also found themselves in demand by the "concocter of confections," and the field of medicine has utilized them here and there in many varied ways. The best-known use of cloves in medicine is as a soother for toothache. For this, oil of clove is used. The oil is obtained by repeated distillation in water.

The flowers of the clove tree, which grows only in the East and West Indies, were first used for decoration. They were used by ancient China in 266 B.C., when the emperor ordered his courtiers to hold cloves in their mouths while in his presence. Cloves were used by Romans, Greeks, and Persians as a base in many of their love philters.

To have the scent of cloves in our own gardens, we can grow clove pinks and clove gillyflowers. The Arabs of North Africa, more than two thousand years ago, used the petals of spicy pinks to give a pleasing taste to the bitter herb tonics they used to abate fever. Pinks were also used as a medium of exchange when the Arabs crossed the Mediterranean to Spain. A different species of pinks was used by early Romans in the chaplets they wore at banquets.

BEAU BRUMMELL POMANDERS

Traditional spice-scented pomanders are quaint and delightful to hang in the closet the year round.

> 2 *small thin-skinned oranges*
> 1 *box powdered cinnamon*
> 1 *small box powdered orris root*
> 1 *box powdered angelica root*
> 2 *large boxes whole cloves*

Mix cinnamon, orris root, and angelica. Use fork with sharp tines to make holes all over oranges. Put cloves into each hole. Roll clove-covered oranges in mixed spices and let stand overnight. Roll again in spices until no moisture shows. Stand on paper towels for about a week and dust frequently with spices.

THELMA'S CLOVE PICKLE
Watermelon Rind

> 10 *pounds watermelon rind*
> 1 *quart sugar*
> 1 *quart white vinegar*
> 40 *drops oil of cinnamon*
> 40 *drops oil of cloves*

Peel, cut, wash, and cover rind with cold water for 24 hours. Second day, drain and rewash. Cover with cold water and simmer for 10 minutes. Drain, cover again with cold water, and drain. Put rind in kettle, add sugar, vinegar, and oils. Color with green vegetable color and stir often for 3 days. Bring to a boil and allow to boil for 10 minutes after it starts to bubble. Put in jars or crocks. Not necessary to seal.

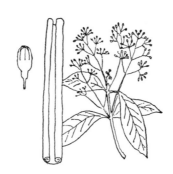

CINNAMON
Cinnamomum
zeylanicum
of the laurel family

In a far-off place man found a tree that now has the botanical name of *Cinnamomum zeylanicum*. It is native to the Far East, particularly to Ceylon and India. The tree is unusual in that it has a double bark . . . and from the inner bark comes the distinctive and distinguished "bouquet" we know as cinnamon.

It has been used since biblical times, first in combination with myrrh and aloes as a body scent or perfume (Proverbs 7:17); it was also burned in the temples of the gods as an incense.

It is believed that Galle, the oldest Ceylon seaport, was the Tarshish of the Bible and belonged to the Phoenician traders. Here it might have been that King Solomon obtained his pearls and other riches.

Ceylon has been the cinnamon capital of the world from biblical times until today. Cinnamon was the deadly lure of Ceylon's European conquerors. First came the Portuguese in 1505; they monopolized the cinnamon trade until 1658, when the Dutch decided to take over. The Dutch had a magnificent reign until 1796 when the English found that they were missing out on a very profitable trade. They wrested control from the Dutch and managed to hold on until 1948, when Ceylon was granted dominion status.

Incidentally, the British, when they first took over the island, were able to do what neither the Portuguese nor the Dutch could accomplish—they liquidated the kingdom of Kandy high up in the mountains. As an aid, they used a weapon of "psychological warfare"; the devout Singhalese believed that whoever held Buddha's sacred tooth was the island's rightful ruler, so the British captured the tooth and brought the whole kingdom under their control.

When the enterprising Dutch were in control, the penalty for the illegal sale of even a single stick of cinnamon was death. This penalty remained in effect until the Dutch gave in to the English. The control of the spice trade was of such importance that England formed the East India Company to undermine the Dutch. This company was all-powerful. It had trading centers in all important seaports of the world, including Boston, then the hub of the Massachusetts Colony, Britain's newly found source of wealth in America. By operating as one huge unit, the East India Company was able to exert its influence all over the globe, applying a little pressure here and there and making uncomfortable situations for its competitors.

As one leaves Colombo, Ceylon's capital, it is necessary to pass through the "City of Gardens," a beautiful collection and a summary of the world's best in fragrance and flavor. These gardens are intended to be a reminder that for many centuries the spice trade, and especially cinnamon, was Ceylon's greatest source of wealth.

Cinnamon is another "island plant," like cloves and nutmeg. It does best near the ocean with its salty breezes. It is a spice from the true spice islands and sailors, when near the islands, always know where they are by the fragrance wafting outward to them.

The cinnamon tree is a beautiful thing. It is an evergreen with gorgeous leaves, not unlike the orange tree, but it has the deep dark green color of the bay tree. The flowers are a white delight and they turn into sparkling round berries that resemble those of a ripe olive tree. When the berries are chafed between the hands a fragrance that cannot be adequately described fills the air. Trying to imagine this fragrance without experiencing it is like learning a song without singing it. Like the cork tree, the trunk or woody body is covered with double bark. When the whole bark is stripped from the tree and the inner bark is placed on the ground under the hot sun, it curls and folds into itself and looks like a roll of wrapping paper. Experience has shown that it is at its best when it has dried to a light brown color. Every three years the ritual of debarking the cinnamon tree is carried out and with great pleasure, because it means that money or some medium of exchange will be forthcoming. Cinnamon deserves its seat of honor in every spice cabinet.

From the English the early American colonists learned the use of cinnamon in their "winter warmers." These were hot drinks made from rum, boiling water, spices, butter, and cinnamon sticks. They were served in tankards or mugs, always before an open fire.

EARLY AMERICAN HOT BUTTERED RUM
Great Winter Warmer

> *2 ounces Puerto Rican rum*
> *1 teaspoon sugar*
> *1 stick cinnamon*
> *pinch of nutmeg*

Place ingredients in preheated mug. Fill with boiling water. Drop in generous glob of butter. Dip a cube of sugar in rum and light. Float flaming cube on top. Relax before open fire.
Drink!

CINNAMON CRÈME DEBANANE

> *2 bananas*
> *4 tablespoons butter*
> *¾ cup brown sugar*
> *1 teaspoon cinnamon*
> *1 ounce rum*
> *½ ounce crème debanane*

Our Latin-American friends start this luscious dessert by peeling 2 bananas and then cutting them into 4 strips. In a large pan, so as not to crowd bananas, melt the butter, add brown sugar and cinnamon. When the sugar has melted and the mixture begins to thicken, place bananas in the pan and cook until soft. Remove from fire, add rum and crème debanane. Ignite and serve while hot. Serves 4. A perfect dessert with your coffee.

NUTMEG AND MACE
Myristica moschata

Here is a "companion pair"—brothers under the skin that come from a paradisaical setting to find their way into many of our culinary delights. There must be nutmeg trees in Paradise because they pass the entrance requirements for beauty and bounty.

Of the more than eighty species of nutmeg trees and shrubs, the most common is a luxuriant evergreen with branches from the bottom to the top of its straight trunk—it grows to a height of about twenty-five feet. During the blooming season it is covered with small yellow flowers that generate a fragrance similar to that of lilies of the valley. The tree blooms and bears continuously the year round, yielding a yellow fruit about the size of a pear. The color harmony is almost matchless, with spots of yellow waving in the wind among broad leaves that are a deep, dark, glossy green on top and lined with silver on the bottom.

The nutmeg tree is another island tree that grows primarily in the Netherlands Indies, the West Indies, and on the island of Penang, which is just off the west coast of the Malay Peninsula. The Banda Islands in the Molucca group are the most famous for the quality of their nutmeg-bearing products.

This tree should be called the nutmeg and mace tree. The reason will be obvious as the harvesting and processing steps are described. The fruit is picked when fully ripe and the outer husk is removed. This husk is the first "goody" obtained from the fruit. It is preserved in syrup and looked upon in the Netherlands Indies as a rare delicacy. Mace, the woven scarlet fruit fiber, is under the outer husk and inside the mace is the musky little nutmeg seed surrounded by its aril. The aril withers away, leaving the nut or nutmeg so well known to commerce. It is normally about one inch long and oval-shaped. The mace and nuts are both dried, first on a fire and then in the sun. The drying period is generally a month. The mace is finely ground on the spot but the nuts are exported whole to retain their flavor. Oil of mace and nutmeg butter are made from nuts of inferior quality, which are ground to extract the oil.

The history of nutmeg and mace is tied to that of the over-all spice trade, which has been described previously. The first mention of nutmeg appeared in the twelfth century when it was described as a street fumigant. It was usually laid in piles and burned when some person of high esteem was expected to visit the city. Not much was known of nutmeg, however, until the sixteenth century, when the Dutch started to exploit the newly found sea route to the Far East, where fragrant and flavorsome riches and treasures lay waiting. When the Dutch ran across the Moluccas they organized them into a tight, closely guarded unit that systematically produced for them. Originally the Banda Islands (part of the Moluccas) were made the sole home of the nutmeg tree so as to restrict its growth and thereby make it more valuable in the field of commerce. The seed-carrying birds, however, did not "know" about these restrictions!

Several medicinal uses for nutmeg are listed in reference books, among them one described as a cure for insomnia. Very probably the nutmeg, with its unusually different bouquet, simply erased cares and worries from the mind of the insomnia sufferer, thus making it possible to drift quietly off to dreamland.

One of my earliest memories of shopping for my mother concerns nutmeg. She would send me to the store with a nickel to buy three nutmegs that were later grated on a tiny nutmeg grater and used on baked custards, which were served in individual brown custard cups. This brings to mind a quotation:

Be as rough as a nutmeg grater and rogues will obey you well.

ORAN HILL

So that is nutmeg—it lives in its mace until it is ready to find its place, along with the mace, in your spice cabinet.

NUTMEG . . . with its aromatic pungency!

and MACE . . . with its tender, sweet mildness!

TRADITIONAL EGGNOG

6 fresh eggs
¾ cup sugar
1 pint heavy cream
1 pint milk
1 pint straight bourbon
1 ounce Jamaica rum
ground nutmeg

Beat egg yolks separately. Add ½ cup sugar to yolks. Beat egg whites very stiff. Add ¼ cup sugar to egg whites. Fold in cream, milk, bourbon, and rum. Serve very cold with grated nutmeg on the top of each cup. Makes 5 pints.

MACE SAUCE FOR FRUIT DISHES

1 cup sugar
2 tablespoons cornstarch
¼ teaspoon salt
1 teaspoon mace
2 cups water
2 tablespoons butter

Blend sugar, cornstarch, salt, and mace. Add water and cook over low heat until thick and clear. Add butter. Serve over fruit rolls, pie, or pudding.

MACE MEXICAN WEDDING CAKES
by Sally

> ½ *cup butter*
> 1 *teaspoon vanilla*
> ½ *cup sugar*
> 2 *cups sifted flour*
> 1 *teaspoon mace*
> 1 *cup chopped walnuts*
> 6 *tablespoons confectioners' sugar*

Cream butter, vanilla, and sugar. Stir in flour, mace, and chopped nuts. Mix well. Drop small balls on well-greased cooky sheet. Bake 10 to 12 minutes at 400° F. Remove from oven and roll in confectioners' sugar while still warm. Store overnight before serving. Makes 3 to 4 dozen cakes.

ALLSPICE
Pimenta officinalis
of the myrtle family

Allspice is truly a wondrous creation of nature. The fruit is about the size of a black currant and resembles a peppercorn. So aptly named, it combines the overtones of fragrance and flavor that make cinnamon, cloves, and nutmeg among the jewels of food flavorings. Allspice means exotic bouquet—a bouquet with the full-bodied pleasantness of the clove, the soothing velvet of the nutmeg, and the rich aroma of cinnamon. All of these can be readily found by putting a small amount of ground allspice on your hand and wafting it under your nose. The fragrance of the three is there as though it were a physical mixture.

The allspice tree is a beautiful tropical American evergreen that resembles the clove tree and the nutmeg tree. The berries are picked while still green and then are sun-dried for about one week or until they turn a dark reddish brown. Allspice is known throughout the spice trade as pimento and this should not be confused with pimiento, which is a species of red pepper used as a garnish.

The finding of allspice was part of the history connected with the intriguing story of the discovery, development, and socialization of the West Indies. Allspice is the only major spice grown exclusively in the Western Hemisphere. Today practically all of the world's production comes from Jamaica, but it is also grown in Mexico, Guatemala, Honduras, Brazil, and the Leeward Islands.

For the newcomer to the wonderful experience of seasoning with the spices, there could be no better starting point than allspice.

ALLSPICE WASSAIL BOWL

> 1 *gallon apple cider*
> 1 *cup dark brown sugar* (*packed*)
> 1 *can frozen lemon concentrate*
> 1 *can frozen orange juice concentrate*
> 1 *tablespoon whole cloves*
> 1 *tablespoon allspice*
> 1 *tablespoon ground nutmeg*
> 24 *cinnamon sticks*

In large kettle, combine cider, brown sugar, undiluted lemon juice, and undiluted orange juice. Tie cloves and allspice in cheesecloth. Add to cider along with nutmeg. Cover and simmer for 20 minutes. Remove and discard clove bag. Serve hot in mugs with a cinnamon stick in each mug. Makes 24 mugs.

BETH'S SPICE CAKE

> 1 cup butter
> 2 cups sugar
> 4 large eggs
> 1½ cups applesauce
> 3 cups sifted cake flour
> 1½ teaspoons soda
> ½ teaspoon ginger
> ½ teaspoon cloves
> ½ teaspoon allspice
> 2 squares unsweetened chocolate

Cream butter and sugar. Add eggs and applesauce. Sift flour, soda, and all the spices together, and add gradually to cake mixture. Melt chocolate over hot water and add to cake for a lovely rich color. Makes 3 large 9-inch layers. Bake at 375° F. for 20 minutes. Ice with mocha icing.

MOCHA ICING

> 1 box confectioners' sugar
> ⅛ stick butter
> ½ cup strong black coffee

Put sugar into a large mixing bowl. Melt butter and gradually add coffee and melted butter alternately until mixture is the right spreading consistency. Ice tops and sides of cake and decorate with English or black walnut halves. Luscious and lovely!

ALL-SPICED BLUEBERRY PIE

> 1 cup sugar
> 2 tablespoons minute tapioca
> ¼ teaspoon cinnamon
> ¼ teaspoon cloves
> ¼ teaspoon allspice
> 4 cups freshly picked blueberries

Mix sugar, tapioca, cinnamon, cloves, and allspice and mix with blueberries in a large bowl.

PASTRY

Prepare pastry for a double-crust pie:
> 1½ cups flour
> ½ teaspoon salt
> ½ teaspoon baking powder
> ½ cup shortening
> 4 tablespoons cold water

Sift flour, salt, and baking powder together. Use pastry cutter to cut shortening into the mixture. Cut until the whole resembles a coarse meal. Gradually add cold water to make stiff dough. Chill dough. Cut off enough pastry for the under crust. Use a 9-inch pan. Roll pastry to about ¼ inch in thickness and a little larger than the pan. Pierce top crust with fork several times. Bake at 450° F. for 30 minutes, then reduce heat and bake 10 minutes longer. Serves 6 to 8.

BAY
Laurus nobilis
of the laurel family

The bay tree is so steeped in history that it is difficult to find its equal. This was the tree most celebrated by ancient poets. Ovid tells with great beauty the fable about Daphne's transformation into a laurel tree to save her from the pursuit of Apollo, who adopted the tree as his own:

> *Because thou canst be*
> *My mistress, I espouse thee for my tree,*
> *Be thou the prize of honor and renown;*
> *The deathless poet and the poem crown.*
> *Thou shalt the Roman festivals adorn,*
> *And, after poets, be by victors worn.*

OVID

The leaves of the bay tree were considered to be suitable for crowns because of their dedication to the gods of poetry and music. Poets (and they were held in especially high esteem in ancient times) were crowned with "fashioned" bay leaves. Later the laurel crowns were placed upon the heads of triumphant warriors and victors in the Olympic games. Doctors were also honored by having the laurel crown placed upon their heads. Poets, warriors, and kings still receive the laurel crown in poetry, on statues, and on coins. In addition, court poets, at least until recent years, were honored with the title of laureate.

Besides having a kingly history, the bay tree looks kingly. In southern climates it will exceed thirty feet in height. It is a beautiful evergreen with deep, rich green leaves that are highly but pleasantly aromatic. The bay tree is of the same family as the sassafras and camphor trees, both of which are noted for their aromatic qualities. It does better in the subtropics where the older trees (but only the older ones) bear beautiful yellow flowers and red to black cherry-shaped fruit. The tree is very common throughout the Far East, and there are entire forests of bay trees in the Canary Islands. It can be cultivated, however, in southern Europe and has been completely naturalized in Italy and France. Even in southern England it has been possible to grow one variety successfully, and it is one of England's most beautiful evergreens, though it will never yield the lovely flowers so common to the tree in the subtropics.

The leaves of the bay tree are laden with a luscious aromatic oil that is much used in medicine as well as cookery. The leaves, when bruised between the fingers, give off a pleasant odor. When burned, they give a wonderful, grateful incense. For cooking purposes, bay leaves are used in dried form for both fragrance and flavor.

The husks of the berries contain a great quantity of volatile oil that is very aromatic. Also the kernels, when pressed, furnish an oil that is much used for embrocations. This oil is greenish in color and faintly resembles in odor that of the bay leaf. Bay rum is the name given to a toilet preparation made by mixing oil of bay with diluted alcohol and adding oil of allspice and oil of orange peel; originally bay rum came from the West Indies. Toilet waters prepared from the one and only bay rum are still used today, and on an ever-widening scale, by discriminating people.

A BAY-FLAVORED CHOWDER OF LAMB KIDNEYS

½ *pound butter*
12 *large sweet onions*
12 *lamb kidneys*
¼ *teaspoon paprika*

2 tablespoons flour
2 pints light cream
¼ cup dry vermouth
3 sprigs fresh parsley
¼ teaspoon thyme
1 bay leaf
1 clove bud
1 tablespoon lemon juice
1 tablespoon sweet butter
½ teaspoon salt
¼ teaspoon pepper

Put butter into large deep fryer. Slice onions into butter, cook until tender and gold, not brown. Quarter lamb kidneys, add to onions and butter, cook and keep turning for about 5 minutes. Add paprika and flour, stir, and turn gently. Pour 1 pint cream over kidneys and onions, add vermouth, parsley, thyme, bay leaf, clove bud. Cover and simmer about 30 minutes. Add the other pint of cream during the cooking period. When done add lemon juice, 1 tablespoon sweet butter, and salt and pepper. The chowder should be thin like oyster stew. Serve piping hot. Serves 6.

GINGER
Zingiber
officinale

Much romantic tradition and history center about ginger. It has been used since the remotest time and in many different ways. It had several medicinal uses long before it became known as a food "pepper upper." Ginger has been chewed as an aid to digestion, to improve the disposition, and to sooth a toothache. Today at least six beverages owe their tantalizing flavor to ginger. A fisherman's tale says that, when ginger is chewed and the juice is applied to the bait, the fish really flock to the hook.

Ginger is a pungent rootstock indigenous to India and China. Today it is grown as an important commercial crop in West Africa, the West Indies, Central America, and Jamaica. It was the first oriental spice to be grown in the New World. In the Middle Ages it was second only to pepper in value, and even as late as the seventeenth century the price of a pound of ginger was the same as the price of a sheep. Marco Polo saw the growing plant and noted this fact in his journal in the year A.D. 1280.

Jamaica ginger is the most valuable of all ginger grown in the world today. It is marketed in two forms: preserved (or green) and dried and cured. Ground ginger (dried and cured) can be obtained in two forms—when the skin is left on the root it is called "black ginger"; with the skin removed, we have "white ginger." The plant usually grows to a height of approximately two feet and the essence of fragrance is to be found in the cured roots and especially in the creamy flowers. Ginger has so fascinated people through the ages that many places and things have ginger associated with their names. One of these is "The Land of Green Ginger"—the name of a street in Hull, England. It was here that a preserve known as green ginger was made from ginger and lemon juice. It was so delectable to the people of the neighborhood that they decided to name a street after it.

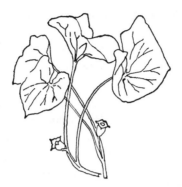

WILD
GINGER

Separate and aside from ginger is wild ginger (*Asarum cana-dense*). Although it is said to be native to Europe and Asia, the first American colonizers found the Indians growing it. They used wild ginger mainly to make hominy grits, one of their basic foods, more palatable. Wild ginger can be grown in your kitchen herb garden if you can provide deep shade, plenty of water, and rich humus. It is a handsome plant with kidney-shaped leaves and luxuriant, brownish-purple flowers that grow very close to the ground, as though afraid of getting too far away from their natural environment. Of interest is the fact that the flower peeps out of the ground even before the first leaf appears.

Ginseng has often been mistaken for ginger. It is most famous for its medicinal properties, but it has a gingerlike fragrance and flavor and its rootstock is so like that of ginger that it has often been difficult to distinguish them. Similar to both ginger and ginseng is the spikenard plant, best remembered for the "very precious" ointments made from it during biblical times. Despite their similarity, the spikenard is only a distant relative of ginseng, and ginseng has the same relation to ginger.

Webster must have really known his ginger. His definition says in part that ginger is the spice "to put life and vigor into." Its heart-shaped foliage, creamy flowers, and quaint little roots make ginger an important part of our heritage of fragrant beauty.

GINGER 'N' HONEY CRUMB CAKE

> 3 cups sifted cake flour
> 1 teaspoon salt
> ½ teaspoon soda
> ½ teaspoon baking powder
> ½ teaspoon ground cloves
> 1 teaspoon ground ginger
> ½ cup shortening
> 1 cup sugar
> 1 cup boiling water
> 1 cup strained honey
> ½ cup thin strips crystallized
>   or candied ginger

Sift together flour, salt, soda, baking powder, and spices. Combine with shortening and sugar. Mix to a crumbling consistency. Set aside ½ cup crumbs for top of cake. Combine boiling water and honey. Add to the rest of the crumb mixture, beat until smooth. Sprinkle the half cup of crumbs over the top. Bake in loaf pan at 375° F. for about 40 minutes. Decorate top of cake with the thin sliced candied ginger while the cake is still hot. Serves 8.

GINGER-TOMATO PRESERVES

> 2 pounds ripe tomatoes
> 2 pounds tart apples
> 6 cups sugar
> ½ teaspoon salt
> 2 lemons (medium)
> 2 cups water
> 1 cup seedless raisins
> 1 cup chopped walnuts
> ¼ cup chopped candied ginger

Scald and peel tomatoes, cut in very small pieces, and place in large kettle. Peel and core apples, cut in small pieces, and add to tomatoes. Add sugar and salt. Stir over medium heat until sugar dissolves. Simmer until mixture thickens. Cook until fruit is transparent and syrup is thick. Slice lemons very thin, remove seeds, cut each slice in eight sections, and add water. Cook over medium heat until rind is very tender. Add to tomatoes. Add raisins, walnuts, and ginger and cook about 15 minutes longer. Pack in scalded jars at once, and cover with ¼-inch layer hot paraffin. Serve with pork dinners. For holiday gifts, wrap and tie with red ribbon bow.

CARDAMOM
Elettaria
cardamomum
maton
of the Zingiberaceae
family

"Grains of Paradise" is a description given to the seeds chewed as a confection by the Arabs in ancient times. The pungent, aromatic cardamom was first used about the eighth century and was a native of India. It is said to have been imported into Europe about the year A.D. 1214.

Gerard's description is fascinating: "There be divers sorts of Graines, some long, others Peare-fashioned; some greater, and others lesser." Of the husk, or cod, he says, "The Cod wherein the hot spice lies, which we call Graines; in shops, Grana Paradisi: it growes, by the report of the Learned, upon a low herby plant; the leaves are some foure inches long, and three broad, with somewhat a thicke middle rib, from which runs transverse fibres, they much in shape resemble those of Cloves. The fruit is like a great cod or huske, in shape like a fig when it groweth upon the tree, but of colour russet, thrust full of small seeds or grains of a darke reddish colour of an exceeding hot taste." Then Gerard describes the virtues: "The graines chewed in the mouth draw forth from the head and stomacke waterish and pituitous humors. They also comfort and warm the weake cold and feeble stomack, help the ague, and rid the shaking fits, being drunk with Sacke."

Cardamom is cultivated today in India, Ceylon, Guatemala, Mexico, Thailand, and Central America. The seeds have a versatile affinity that leads to a broad range of uses from the daintiest dessert to sausage and curry powder.

The Arabs' love of coffee is legend. The brew of Oman and most of Arabia is said to be bitter and black, often flavored with cardamom, and served in cups like little crucibles.

CHRISTMAS CARDAMOM CAKE

1 cup sugar
½ cup melted butter
4 eggs, well beaten
4 cups sifted cake flour
pinch of salt
4 teaspoons baking powder
½ cup milk
1½ cups chopped dates
1½ cups chopped cherries, orange
 and lemon peel
½ teaspoon ground cardamom seed

Bake Christmas cake as the sun rises. If you wait until sunset cake will be sad.

Combine sugar, butter, and eggs. Beat until smooth. Sift together flour, salt, and baking powder. Add alternately with milk to first mixture. Add dates, fruit peel, and cardamom seeds. Fold in thoroughly. Pour into well-greased pound cake pan, bake at 325° F. about 1½ hours.

CARDAMOM-FLAVORED GRAPE PIE

4 cups grapes
¾ cup sugar
⅛ teaspoon cardamom seed
1 tablespoon minute tapioca
1 tablespoon grated orange rind
½ teaspoon lemon juice
pastry for 2-crust pie
whipped cream

Stew grapes and slip the pulp out of the skins; set skins aside and cook pulp until seeds loosen. Remove seeds and combine pulp, skins, sugar, cardamom seed, tapioca, orange rind, and lemon juice. Pour into a 9 inch pastry-lined pan and cover with old-fashioned pastry lattice. Bake about 30 minutes at 375° F. and serve warm with whipped cream.

VANILLA
Vanilla planifolia
of the orchid family

In the days of Marco Polo sailors talked about the mysterious, enchanted island of Madagascar. They told of a land of dense jungles, towering mountains, and beautiful flowers among which was an exotic, climbing, shimmering golden orchid with oblong and fleshy leaves measuring four inches when mature. The aerial roots and slender stems twine around trees and the flowering branches produce as many as twenty orchids in a cluster. The pods, which contain an abundance of seed, are six to ten inches long and from these pods we obtain vanilla.

The Spanish explorer Cortez was astonished to see the great Aztec ruler Montezuma drink a beverage of chocolate flavored with vanilla beans. Among all the treasures of Aztec art, gold, and silver returned to Spain, the vanilla beans proved to be no less valuable and appreciated for their delectable flavor. Just enough of them reached Europe to suggest their worthiness but it was many years before the mystery of this temperamental plant was unraveled. A membrane separates the stamen from the pistil so that it cannot fertilize itself. As a result, only one flower in more than a hundred ever matures into a pod under natural conditions. The wind or rare visits of insects were its only sources of pollination until the nineteenth century. About 1835, orchid growers in Madagascar were taught to transfer pollen by hand.

It was here that bean "rustling" became a problem. Just before harvest time the rustlers would raid the vines. The growers had to start branding the beans just as cattle are branded. The brands were made by using cork and sharp pins to make distinctive patterns that left permanent scars on the green beans.

The beans are harvested about seven months after pollination and then carefully cured, for they are tasteless and odorless until the bouquet inherent in the bean is brought out through fermentation, which causes the formation of a volatile oil called *vanillin*. Curing consists of warming the beans in the sun, after which they are put into "sweat boxes" where fermentation occurs. These two steps are carried out alternately until the optimum amount of oil is formed. To produce the world's most popular flavor for confections, beverages, and food dishes, the vanillin is dissolved in alcohol. Its popularity extends even to the manufacture of perfumes.

A little town called Antalaha in Madagascar is the capital of the world's production of vanilla beans. Next in line are Mexico and the Netherlands Indies. They are cultivated on a minor scale in Central America, the West Indies, and Tahiti.

DEEP SOUTH ICE CREAM

> 3 *pints light cream*
> 1 *cup sugar*
> *pinch of salt*
> 2 *fresh eggs, beaten*
> 2 *teaspoons vanilla extract*

Scald cream in double boiler. Add sugar, salt, and eggs. Cool, then add vanilla extract. Freeze in hand-turned freezer, using 8 parts ice, 1 part coarse salt. Makes 2 quarts.

VANILLA ICEBOX CAKE

> 1 *stick butter*
> 1 *cup powdered sugar*
> 3 *egg yolks, beaten*
> 1 *teaspoon vanilla extract*
> 1½ *ounces unsweetened chocolate, melted*
> ½ *cup coconut-angel flakes or frozen*
> ½ *cup chopped pecans*
> 6-ounce *package vanilla wafers, crushed*
> 3 *stiffly beaten egg whites*
> 1 *cup heavy cream, whipped*
> 2 *tablespoons powdered sugar*
> ½ *teaspoon vanilla extract*

Cream butter and sugar together, add egg yolks and 1 teaspoon vanilla extract. Add chocolate, coconut, pecans and vanilla wafers. Fold in egg whites and pack in buttered baking dish, 3 by 8 by 10 inches. Chill in refrigerator overnight. Top with whipped cream that has been sweetened with the 2 tablespoons powdered sugar and flavored with ½ teaspoon vanilla extract. Delicious! Serves 9.

FLOATING ISLAND

> *3 eggs, separated*
> *6 tablespoons sugar*
> *¼ teaspoon salt*
> *2½ cups milk*
> *¼ cup sugar*
> *2 tablespoons cornstarch*
> *¼ teaspoon salt*
> *½ teaspoon vanilla extract*
> *¼ teaspoon almond extract*
> *dash of nutmeg*
> *2 cups well-drained fruit*

Beat egg whites until stiff. Gradually add the 6 tablespoons sugar and ¼ teaspoon salt, beating until mixture holds its shape. Pour milk into 10-inch skillet; heat. Drop egg-white mixture on milk by tablespoonfuls; cook in simmering milk until set. Carefully remove meringues to tray. Cool at room temperature, then refrigerate.

Strain milk—there should be 2 cups. Combine ¼ cup sugar, cornstarch, and ¼ teaspoon salt. Gradually add milk. Cook in double boiler over hot water, stirring until slightly thickened. Beat egg yolks; add to hot mixture gradually. Cook over hot water, stirring until mixture coats spoon. Cool, add vanilla extract, almond extract, and nutmeg. Chill before serving. Serve with meringues on top and add fresh fruit or berries. Serves 6 to 8.

ORANGE JIFFY GEMS

> *1 box Golden Yellow Jiffy Cake Mix*
> *(Chelsea Milling Co.)*
> *½ cup fresh orange juice*
> *1 egg, unbeaten*
> *½ teaspoon vanilla extract*

Stir ¼ cup orange juice into mix and beat 150 strokes by hand. Add egg and beat 75 strokes. Stir in remaining juice and vanilla extract and beat 75 strokes.

Grease doll-size muffin pans generously. Dust with sifted corn-starch. Fill pans barely half full. Bake at 350° F. about 15 minutes, or until a delicate brown. Remove gems from pan, cool. Insert fork into gem and dip bottom side into ORANGE SYRUP. Hold gem over pan until excess syrup drops off. Place gems on wax paper to drain. Store in airtight tins. Delicious to serve with COFFEE ROYALE.

ORANGE SYRUP

> 1 *cup fresh orange juice*
> 2 *cups sugar*
> 2 *tablespoons grated orange rind*

Combine orange juice, sugar, and orange rind in deep saucepan. Stir over low heat until sugar is dissolved. Boil until you have a thick syrup.

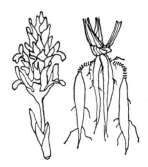

TURMERIC
Curcuma longa
of the ginger family

Turmeric is one of the ancient spices that were well known in biblical days. It was used then as a perfume as well as a spice and has always been an important part of the fabulous spice trade. It is native to Indonesia and China, but today India, Haiti, Jamaica, and Peru grow it as an important crop and export quantities to the United States. India has under cultivation vast fields of turmeric with eye-catching fragrant flowers that have pinkish tops and cool yellow blossoms in the middle. The leaves and stems are a deep rich green. Just as in the case of ginger, turmeric is grown for the roots, which grow to the same size but are far sweeter, more delicate, and have greater fragrance than ginger. The roots of turmeric have a clean, fresh, distinctive aroma. They can be purchased either in whole root form or powdered.

Turmeric lends itself nicely to combination with other spices. It is one of the chief ingredients of curry powder, which has been called the "salt of the Orient." Many people prefer turmeric to saffron as a food coloring. This lovely spice is used to impart the appealing color and mouth-watering delicate taste to mustard sauce and powdered mustard.

Turmeric is one of the more versatile spices. Not only is it used in perfumery, flavoring, and seasoning, it has a place in the huge chemical industry where it is used in a test to detect the presence of alkalis. The natives of India and China use it in dyeing.

CURRIED LAMB WITH MACARONI

1 pound lamb, cubed
½ pound macaroni
2 tablespoons butter
2 tablespoons flour
2 tablespoons curry powder
1 teaspoon salt
¼ teaspoon pepper
2 cups milk

Sauté cubes of lamb in butter. Cover and steam until tender. Cook macaroni in boiling salted water until done. Drain. In a saucepan melt 2 tablespoons butter, add flour, curry powder, salt, and pepper, and blend thoroughly. Add milk gradually, stirring constantly, and cook until a smooth slightly thick sauce results. In casserole put alternate layers of macaroni, lamb, and curry sauce. Repeat until all is used. Cover and bake at 350° F. for 45 minutes. Serves 4.

TURMERIC GARDEN SALAD

1 head green cabbage
4 large white onions
2 green sweet peppers
2 red sweet peppers
1 bunch bleached celery

Chop cabbage and slice onions in thin rings. Cut peppers in thin strips about 1 inch long. Dice celery. Put in large salad bowl and chill.

TURMERIC DRESSING

2 cups sugar
2 cups mild white vinegar
1 tablespoon salt
1 teaspoon celery salt
4 tablespoons flour
1 teaspoon turmeric

Combine above ingredients and cook, stirring until thickened. May be served as a *hot* dressing over the garden salad or stored and chilled. Serves 8.

SAFFRON
CROCUS
Crocus sativus
of the crocus family

People of the Mediterranean regions valued the saffron crocus for all its virtues long before the Phoenicians carried it over their trade routes to spreading civilizations. Steeped in romance since Queen Nefertiti's time, the saffron crocus has been dedicated to the sun; it was cultivated in King Solomon's garden; Cleopatra used it in some of her favorite cosmetics; early Egyptians used it in their religious ceremonies; and it has been said that in ancient Ireland a king's mantle was dyed with the crocus.

It is the world's most expensive spice, since seventy-five thousand blossoms are required to produce one pound of saffron powder. Because it has always been so costly, the temptation to adulterate it has been great. In Nuremberg in the fifteenth century, dishonest dealers were burned at the stake together with their adulterated saffron.

The crocus is apparently responsible for the crocodile's name. It is said that the crocodile was named for the lovely purple crocus because the only sincere tears he ever shed were forced from him by the blissful fragrance of the saffron crocus.

Paracelsus, one of the early famous physicians, used saffron in concocting all of his medicines. It was used as a specific remedy for gout, whose pain and inflammation it had the power to alleviate, and it was used also for rheumatism.

It was prized as a cosmetic and perfume many centuries ago in Babylon, and even today its delicate piquancy is used in perfumery.

The saffron crocus grows in the flowery meadows of Kashmir's "Happy Valley," where the climate is temperate and lovely and the soil is rich. The rulers of Kashmir have loved and planted this valley like a vast garden from end to end. It is also grown in Italy, France, and Spain, from which countries more than three thousand pounds of saffron crocus are imported into the United States each year. The Spanish are particularly fond of its pungent flavor and rich coloring qualities for their paella and fancy sauces.

Gerard's description of the saffron crocus is excellent: "The floure doth first rise out of the ground nakedly in September, and the long small grasse leaves shortly after the floure, never bearing floure and leafe at once. The which to express, I thought it convenient to set downe two figures before you, with this description, viz. The root is small, round, and bulbous. The floure consisteth of six small blew leaves tending to purple, having in the middle many small yellow strings or threds; among which are two, three, or more thicke chives of a fierie colour somewhat reddish, of a strong smell when they be dried, which doth stuffe and trouble the head. The first picture setteth forth the plant when it beareth floures, and the other expresseth nothing but leaves."

To enjoy this classic beauty with its pleasantly bitter flavor, plant your corms in late spring or early summer and blooms will appear in October.

SAFFRON RICE AND CHICKEN

> 2 *frying chickens*
> 1 *cup olive oil*
> 1 *onion*
> 2 *cloves garlic*
> 1 *6-ounce can tomatoes*
> 6 *cups water*
> 1 *bay leaf*
> 2 *teaspoons salt*
> 2 *cups rice*
> ¼ *teaspoon saffron*
> 1 *green pepper*
> 1 *2-ounce can petits pois (small*
>   *green peas)*
> 2 *pimientos*

Cut chicken into pieces and fry in olive oil in large Dutch oven. Add onion and garlic. When tender, add tomatoes and water and simmer for 5 minutes, then add bay leaf, salt, rice, saffron, and green pepper. Stir carefully and bake at 350° F. for 20 minutes. Serve piping hot, garnished with petits pois and pimientos. Serves 6.

CAPERS
Capparis spinosa
of the Capparidaceae
family

Here are faithful companions that have been with us for a long
time, and will be with us probably until eternity, for capers wear
well. They have a wonderful aromatic flavor that comes from the
unopened flower buds, just as in the case of cloves.

Capers are truly sensitive: the flowers open as the sun strikes
and close as the sun sets, so the buds must be gathered very early in
the morning between daybreak and sunrise. These flowers bloom on
a prickly plant called the caperbush, which grows wild on the mountain slopes bordering the Mediterranean Sea, especially in Italy,
Spain, and southern Greece.

The largest single use for capers is as a seasoning for sauces.
These sauces usually accompany sea foods but they may be used
succulently on meats as well.

CAPERS CRAB MEAT SALAD

> *6 medium tomatoes*
> *⅓ cup French dressing*
> *2 cups flaked crab meat*
> *½ cup diced celery*
> *6 tablespoons mayonnaise*
> *¼ cup capers*
> *paprika*
> *water cress*

Scald, peel, and chill tomatoes, then hollow out to form cups.
Marinate inside of tomatoes with French dressing for 30 minutes.

Mix crab meat, celery, and French dressing gently so the crab meat will not be broken. Stuff tomatoes and garnish with mayonnaise, capers, and paprika. Place on crystal salad plates on a bed of water cress. Piquant flavor with a flourish! Serves 6.

CAPSICUM
Genus Capsicum
of the potato family

    The Spanish call this spice *ají*. On Columbus' second visit to South America his ship's physician wrote in his journal that the Indians ate a root called *ñame* (yam) and seasoned it with a spice called *ají* or capsicum.

    When one mentions capsicum, the word "capsaicin" should be mentioned immediately, for this is the spice that creates the famous bouquet of the capsicums. Capsicum is a genus of South American and Asiatic annual subshrubbery plants of the potato family. Many species are cultivated for their fruits, which in some cases grow six to ten inches long. The fruits are fleshy, of many colors, and contain capsaicin, as do the seeds.

    It is now time to point out that the capsicums are pepper plants but they have nothing to do with black or white pepper, used every day by almost everyone at every meal. Of all the peppers belonging to the genus Capsicum, it appeared logical to cover here only those that can be cultivated in almost every country in the world, and to cover pepper tabasco and the small red chili in Chapter 10. Actually, cayenne pepper is the only important and widely used pepper in the category just mentioned.

    Of a very unusual nature, it has been called the purest and most certain stimulant. In times past it was used internally and externally as a local irritant. The health suggestion was, "Take a hot bath every day, while in the bath drink a cup of capsicum tea, after the bath rub down with capsicum cayenne."

Cayenne pepper has been called the most pungent of all spices. The good chef keeps cayenne at his finger tips as an indispensable flavoring for meats and gravies. Although it must be used with restraint, the right amount will add flavor interest to eggs, sauces, fish, and vegetables. It is an ingredient of pork sausage seasoning and, of course, a part of curry powder.

YAM CRISPS

4 medium yams
½ cup brown sugar
½ cup Zwieback crumbs
¼ teaspoon ground capsicum
½ cup butter

Cook yams in their jackets, cool, peel, and cut in strips 1 by 2 inches. Mix brown sugar, Zwieback crumbs, and capsicum. Dredge yam strips. Fry to a crisp light brown in butter. Watch and turn often as they burn easily. Serve hot. Serves 2.

PAPRIKA
Capsicum annuum
of the potato family

The early explorers found *Capsicum annuum* growing in Central America. It was so attractive from all standpoints that they carried it back to southern Europe, where the plants flourished in

Spain and Italy. They are also native to India and New Guinea. The capsicums were better known in an earlier day as ginny peppers. There are many varieties, and the fruits are called cods. Some cods grow upright, others hang down, some are extremely hot, others are mild and sweet. The color range is from rich dark green to yellow and bright red. The paprika plant looks like a tomato or bell pepper plant with its fruit growing down. It is dearly loved for its mildness and rich color. Like saffron, it was valued as a coloring agent.

We import large quantities of mild paprika from Spain; smaller amounts of a hotter variety come from Hungary and Yugoslavia. Paprika is also grown in California, where modern tunnel drying systems greatly speed the drying of the fruit. Europeans generally dry the fruit, or cods, in the sun.

There is scarcely a spice shelf anywhere that does not hold paprika, to use as a garnish or flavoring for many foods. Large quantities are used to give color to meat products and in the preparation of condiments, catsup, and chili sauce. It is a part of the pepper mixture that is an important ingredient in curry powder. At America's drive-in eating places paprika has become a "must" for the younger set's popular dish, french fried potatoes. The mild pleasant aroma and agreeably mild sweet taste, as well as the bright red color, make the french fries flavorful and gives them zestful eye appeal.

It has been said that the use of paprika is valuable in maintaining good sight and that it helps to prevent night blindness.

PAPRIKA BUTTER

> *6 tablespoons butter*
> *½ teaspoon onion powder*
> *1 teaspoon paprika*
> *¼ cup chopped chives*

Sauté onion powder in 2 tablespoons butter until a golden brown. Cool and add paprika. Cream the remaining butter and add. Shape into balls and roll in chopped chives. Use on broiled fish, poultry, or baked potatoes.

3. A time for pleasure and contentment

Good health, good feeling, and a zest for living are ours for the asking. Along with restful sleep, eating is at the top of the list of things necessary to good health. Just eating, however, is not enough. Mealtime should be a time for real pleasure, a time for relaxation; a time for light and lilting conversation; a time for humor; a time for shedding our cares and worries; a time for ambitious contentment; a time to look forward to fragrance and flavor in the kitchen and at the table; a time to anticipate new taste thrills as satisfaction for the flavor buds on our palates. Our anticipation should increase geometrically.

Besides nourishing our bodies, a good meal nourishes the spirit and gives us the courage to meet head on the many problems that are so much a part of modern living. A mundane meal is better than no meal at all, but very little better. To achieve inner satisfaction we must make use of spices and herbs. When used adroitly and with a flourish, spices and herbs can make the simplest food come "alive."

4. Spice chart:

how the spices are used

PEPPER	GROUND: eggs: omelet, boiled, deviled, fried. Meats: beef roast, stew, steaks, chops, ground beef, lamb, veal or beef patties, turkey, duck, pheasant, pork. Sea food. Indispensable for meat sauces, gravies, and most vegetables.
CLOVES	WHOLE: baked ham, pot roast, hot tea, tomato soup, prunes, baked pears, beef tongue, pickles, cucumbers, peaches, tomatoes, and onions. GROUND: pickle relish, fruit pies, a sprinkle on orange slices, chocolate drinks, and puddings, spice cakes, and cookies.
CINNAMON	WHOLE: pickled beets, cucumbers, peaches, pears, and crab apples; for flavoring hot chocolate; as muddler for tea; simmer with fruit for compotes.

GROUND: french toast, fruit pies, sweet potatoes, baked custard, and in chocolate, lemon, butterscotch, banana, and lemon pies.

NUTMEG

Desserts: custards, eggnogs, muffins, cakes, pies, cookies. Vegetables: asparagus, cauliflower, lima beans, spinach. Meats: beef roast, chicken, stews. Lobster Newburg. Fruit: sliced bananas, fruit salad, rhubarb pie, apple pie. Hard sauce for plum pudding, also hot sauces for apple dumplings. Delicious when added to cream cheese on melba toast.

MACE

GROUND: pound cakes, chocolate pudding, most fruit pies. Vegetables: creamed potatoes, creamed turnips. Stuffing for chicken and turkey. Creamed soups, shrimp chowder. Fruits: superb with bing cherries, apricots, peaches, and pears. Good in jellies, salads, and biscuit doughs.

ALLSPICE

WHOLE: versatile for meat, vegetables, and dessert; beef, fish fillet, tongue, pork roast, roast duck, lemon slices for tea.
GROUND: pickle relish; boiled shrimp; pot roast, gravy; beets; vanilla ice cream.

BAY

Dried bay very pungent; use sparingly. Swiss steak, beef, pot roast, stewed chicken and dumplings, lobster bisque, fish chowder, pork, soup, and sauces. Bay is included with spices because it must be bought where imported spices are sold.

GINGER

WHOLE or CANDIED: pear salad, dressing for fruit salad, cakes, and candies.
GROUND: creamed chicken, fish sauces, roasts, shrimp curry, applesauce, brown bettys, squash (baked or creamed), cakes,

and cookies. Sparingly over grilled cheese sandwiches. Wonderful in baked carrots.

CARDAMOM   WHOLE: candied as a confection, shaved on chocolate drinks, in fruits, salads, and sauces.
GROUND: chicken curry, shrimp curry, hard sauces, fruit pies, Danish pastry, and demitasse coffee.

VANILLA   EXTRACT: ice cream, cakes, chocolate pie, sauces, custards, puddings, floating island, candies, hot chocolate, brown bettys, breakfast muffins, coconut pie, and egg-nogs.

TURMERIC   Curry is a blend of spices and herbs,
or   mainly turmeric, cumin, and sage.
CURRY   GROUND: chicken, veal, fish, shrimp, liver, eggs, baked beans, French dressing, buttered cabbage, creamed onions, clam chowder, chicken salad, tuna salad, tomato bouillon, asparagus, fried eggplant, hash, and swiss steak.

SAFFRON   Chicken curries, rice, bean soup, pudding, fish sauces, creole sauce, fish stuffings, lobster bisque, flavoring for cakes and pies, coloring for liqueurs.

CAPERS   Sea food salads, sauce for tomato and lettuce salads, canapés. Especially good with crab meat and lobster. Use this spicy little flower bud sparingly.

CAPSICUM   WHOLE: when pods are used in cookery they are called chilies.
GROUND: RED DEVIL SQUASH CASSEROLE, fish fillets, scrambled or soft-cooked eggs, chicken fricassee, baked beans, corn, lamb or beef stew, vegetable soups, hamburgers, and SAVORY TAMALE PIE.

PAPRIKA

Creole sauce, creamed chipped beef, new potatoes, eggs, salads, veal, fried chicken, broiled fish, potato salad, salad dressings, garnishings. Paprika is a mixture of peppers but must be bought as a spice.

5. Beverages

COFFEE
Coffea arabica

Water is the number one beverage in the world today. In second
place is coffee, the background of which is as intriguing as that
of the far-flung spices and herbs. According to legend, the flavorful
wonders of coffee were discovered in the third century A.D. Monks
fleeing from persecution found refuge in the highland of Abyssinia
across the Red Sea. One night a father tending the flock ran to the
monastery and cried, "The animals are bewitched. They gambol and
play as if it were a spring morn." The prior tried to reassure him.
He would go to the fold. He found that the monk was not seeing
things. Night after night the animals continued to frisk about instead
of sleeping as they should. The prior, after much study of the plants
the animals browsed upon, was convinced that the sleeplessness was
caused by the leaves and fruit of an unfamiliar shrub that grew in
profusion there. He picked some of the ripe cherrylike fruit, chewed
the seeds, felt exhilarated, and was very wakeful that night.

Whether or not legend is correct, Abyssinia and Arabia were
the original homes of the coffee shrub. The Turkish ambassadors
are said to have been responsible for the spread of coffee from Arabia

to Constantinople, Venice, England, France, and other European countries. Coffeehouses sprang up almost immediately and became popular with people of fashion, artists, and men of letters. The first coffeehouses in England were established in 1652 and within twenty years were playing such an important part in the social and political life of the day that Charles II tried to suppress them on the grounds that they were "seminaries of sedition." Garroway's was one of the best-known coffeehouses in England. Many coffeehouses were also set up in Paris and became so important there that our common name for restaurant (café) is the French word for "coffee" or "coffeehouse."

Until the seventeenth century all of the coffee of commerce came from Arabia. It was shipped from Mocha (or Mokha), once the capital of the province of Yemen. The name Mocha is still applied to all Arabian coffee as well as to other coffee resembling the Arabian in color and taste. From Arabia, cultivation spread to Java in the Dutch East Indies and finally throughout the tropics of both hemispheres.

It is said that three fourths of the world's coffee stems from a single tree. A few plants taken from the East Indies were presented to the king of France, who promptly sent them to the West Indies to be planted. This voyage was long and tempestuous and the plants gradually died one by one until only a single plant was left. Water became scarce but the faithful officer to whom the mission had been entrusted divided his tiny allowance with the plant, which lived to become the parent tree for the plantations of the New World.

The coffee plant thrives best in a fresh, dry atmosphere, where the temperature never goes below sixty degrees, and on land from eight hundred to five thousand feet above sea level, where the soil is rich with red iron rust or with gray volcanic rock. The Brazilian state of São Paulo produces more coffee than any other place in the world. The other chief coffee-growing regions are Colombia, Venezuela, Central America, Mexico, Arabia, Africa, India, the East Indies, the West Indies, and the Pacific islands, especially Hawaii and the Philippines.

A fazenda or coffee orchard is a fascinating place to visit. As you approach, the wind sweeps out a great wave of fragrance like that of white honeysuckle, but sweeter by far. The shiny, dark foliage is covered with sparkling jasminelike flowers and it looks as though snow has just fallen. Gorgeous butterflies, bees, and locusts flutter and buzz all around while an endless number of hummingbirds dart about the trumpet-shaped flowers. The wild varieties of coffee grow as high as twenty feet but the cultivated ones are maintained at a level of six to ten feet so that the berries can be picked more easily. The berries are cherrylike and change from green to light yellow, then to scarlet, and last of all to a deep crimson or black. The skin shrivels when the berry is ripe and the pair of seeds found in most berries are covered with sweet yellow pulp. These seeds are the familiar coffee beans. Since the coffee tree often bears blossoms, green berries and ripe red berries at the same time, the berries must be picked by hand. No harvesting machine has ever been devised that could distinguish green from red!

In some berries there is only one seed. These are separated from the others because they bring a higher price in the market. The main blooming season in Brazil comes during the South American springtime months of September, October, and November. It takes the berries six or seven months to mature, so the harvesters are busy from late April to early August. After depulping and many other complicated steps used in getting at the beans, they are packed in bags weighing 132 pounds. Then they go to the seaports for distribution over the world. It is interesting to know that the flavor of coffee is improved if the raw beans are aged from one to four years before roasting. After roasting, however, they should be used as soon as possible since the delicate bouquet of roasted coffee deteriorates with age.

Practically everyone in Brazil drinks coffee, where it is made very thick and served in tiny cups for sipping. It is strong and invigorating. The United States buys approximately half of the world's coffee crop, as American consumption is the highest in the world; in proportion to population, however, consumption in the Scandinavian countries is slightly higher. Americans use the equivalent of 500 cups per person every year.

Coffee has been described as being the most versatile beverage in the world, and quite frankly I was amazed by this versatility as brought out through information very kindly furnished to me by the Pan-American Coffee Bureau. For instance, coffee is a rich source of niacin, an important B-complex vitamin. One well-brewed cup of coffee contains as much niacin as five slices of enriched bread. According to scientists, about half of the average daily requirement of niacin is found in five or six cups of coffee.

Further, if your family uses a pound of roasted coffee a week it is consuming the annual crop of about fifty-two coffee trees each year. About two thousand hand-picked berries are required to provide enough beans for a single pound of roasted coffee. This is slightly more than the annual crop of one average tree.

There are many ways in which to make and serve coffee before, during, and after a meal. But first let's look into the basic things to remember in preparing coffee, no matter what brand or type you use.

First, it is important that you buy the correct grind of coffee for your coffee maker. Try not to buy more than a week's supply at a time. Coffee exposed to the air for longer than that loses much of its flavor. Remember that the coffeepot itself must be very clean. Rinsing alone is not enough to remove the oils that collect on the sides each time it is used.

Once these prebrewing details are taken care of, the actual brewing rules themselves are remarkably simple. Use enough coffee. You can't make good coffee if you skimp on the amount. The Pan-American Coffee Bureau recommends two level measuring tablespoons (or one standard measure) of coffee to each three quarters of a measuring cup of fresh cold water for each serving. These same proportions apply no matter what type of coffee maker is used.

If you use a vacuum-type coffee maker or a percolator, timing is important. Percolator coffee should be "perked" gently for six to eight minutes after it begins to show color, and vacuum coffee must be kept over a low heat for not more than three minutes after the water has risen to the upper bowl. Drip coffee needs no timing, but if you stir the brew after it has dripped through you will get even strength throughout. And remember! Coffee must never, ever be allowed to boil!

Here in America we have relatively simple tastes in our favorite brew. No matter whom you asked how they like their coffee, the same answer would probably come from all of them and that would be, "Make it fresh, make it strong, and make it hot." But let's see how the rest of the world likes coffee.

In Arabia the average Arab drinks twenty-five to thirty cups a day, roasting his coffee beans at home and pounding them in a mortar. He boils water in a long-handled pot called an *ibrik*, tosses in the pulverized beans, and lets the brew foam up three times, removing it from the heat each time. He serves it in tiny, egg-shaped cups called *fin-djans*. In Armenia, Syria, and Turkey we find the same type of coffee, but with powdered sugar added to taste. In all these countries a pinch of saffron or cloves, or a few cardamom seeds, may be added before serving.

In Italy, coffee beans are roasted very dark, ground fine, and brewed, usually, in an espresso machine that uses live-steam pressure. The coffee is served strong and black with lots of sugar. A good Italian demitasse coffee can be made in small *machinettas*, available here, or in any drip or vacuum coffee maker, using two level measuring tablespoons of Italian-roast coffee to every three ounces of water. Sometimes a twist of lemon peel is added or a cinnamon stick is used to stir the coffee, giving it a slightly spicy flavor. This demitasse coffee is also the favored drink in Latin America.

Next we stop in Paris and Vienna. During the day the French people drink demitasse coffee similar to the Italian, but brewed in an ordinary French drip pot. For breakfast, though, our happy lot is café au lait, equal parts of fresh, strong coffee and hot milk, poured simultaneously. In Vienna they top their café au lait with a teaspoon of unsweetened whipped cream.

Here are some proven recipes that will enable you to have fun with coffee:

HOT MOCHA JAVA

There is a happy affinity between coffee and chocolate. Hot Mocha Java blends these two fine flavors. Here is enough for a party.

4½ measuring cups hot coffee
4½ measuring cups hot cocoa

Combine equal quantities coffee and cocoa. Serve hot, but do not boil. Pour into cups or mugs and top with marshmallows. Serves 12.

IRISH COFFEE

Irish coffee traveled from Shannon straight to San Francisco, and from there to the rest of the United States.

strong black coffee
fine granulated sugar
Irish whisky
slightly whipped cream

Into a warmed table wineglass, place 2 teaspoons sugar and fill glass about two-thirds full with hot coffee. Mix. Add about 2 tablespoons Irish whisky and top with softly whipped cream. Serves 1.

COFFEE WITH LIQUEURS

Coffee has a talent for mixing sociably with a variety of liquors and liqueurs. Begin with strong demitasse coffee and fill the demitasse cup about three-quarters full. Then add a dash of any of the following: white crème de menthe, curaçao, kummel, anisette, or cointreau. Cognac in demitasse coffee becomes COFFEE ROYALE, but bourbon or rum may also be used.

CAFÉ BRÛLOT DIABOLIQUE

No New Orleans visit is complete without dinner at Antoine's. And that dinner won't be complete until you have the spectacular *spécialité de la maison*, café brûlot diabolique:

> 6 *pieces lump sugar*
> 8 *whole cloves*
> 1 *1-inch cinnamon stick*
> 1 *cut-up lemon peel*
> 4 *jiggers cognac*
> 4 *cups demitasse coffee*

Place all ingredients, except coffee, in chafing dish. Ignite cognac with match and stir ingredients until well blended. After a minute or two slowly pour in the hot coffee and continue to stir. (In winter, heat brandy before using.) Strain into brûlot or demitasse cups. Serves 4.

COFFEE ALEXANDER

Here is a short, summery, after-dinner drink that tastes as good as it looks.

> *crème de cacao*
> *strong, ice-cold coffee*
> *whipped cream*

Pour 2 tablespoons crème de cacao in bottom of table wineglass. Fill almost to top with strong, ice-cold coffee. Mix. Float softly whipped cream on top. Serves 1.

SPICY ICED COFFEE

For those who like their cool drinks tall, dark, and handsome, there's nothing more flavorful than spicy iced coffee. If you're calorie-conscious, try drinking it as is. Otherwise, it's fine with cream and sugar.

3 cups hot, double-strength coffee
2 cinnamon sticks
4 cloves
4 allspice berries

Pour coffee over spices. Let stand 1 hour. Strain. Pour over ice in tall glasses. Serve with cream and sugar. Serves 4.

COFFEE-GLAZED HAM LOAF

2 pounds lean pork, ground
1 pound smoked ham, ground
1 cup soft bread crumbs
2 eggs
¼ cup ketchup
few drops Tabasco
½ teaspoon salt

Combine all ingredients and shape into loaf. Bake, uncovered, at 325° F. for 2 hours. During last hour baste four times with COFFEE GLAZE. Serves 6 to 8.

COFFEE GLAZE

1 cup firmly packed brown sugar
1 cup brewed coffee
1 teaspoon dry mustard
1 tablespoon mixed pickling spices,
*   tied in cheesecloth*
1 teaspoon vinegar

Combine all ingredients and bring to boil. Simmer until mixture forms a thick syrup. Remove spice bag.

There are hundreds of additional uses for coffee. For example, try it in desserts, in pies, in cakes and breads, candies and cookies, and in sauces and frostings. You will enjoy a new taste thrill when you enhance the bouquet of meats with coffee. Baste a leg of lamb sometime with a cup of coffee. Remember that the famous "red gravy" of the South results from ham basted with black coffee. Also, try adding a little coffee to any meat gravy. There seems to be no end to the things you can do with coffee, a most unusual companion piece to the thread of life that never wears out—CONVERSATION!

TEA
Camellia Thea

An old legend tells us that the wonders of tea were discovered by the emperor of China, Shen-Hung, quite by accident. Shen-Hung has always been thought of as the "father" of Chinese medicine and agriculture. One morning he was boiling a pot of water near the woods (why an emperor should be boiling water this way is unknown) and leaves from an overhanging branch dropped into the pot. At the time his back was turned toward the fire, but he was aware of a fragrant smell under his nose. Turning in all directions and seeing the leaves in the boiling water, he traced the fragrance to it. Shen-Hung felt that any elixir that could do this, the likes of which he had never experienced, should be very flavorful. So he decided to sip the brew. Its bouquet was so appealing that he finally drank the entire contents of the pot. It was not long before he felt a new sensation—one of stimulation and vigor. The emperor immediately deleafed several branches from the overhanging tree, so that he could introduce this new wonder beverage to his court and later to his people. They shared the emperor's attachment to the new fragrance and flavor. This was the first step toward the expanded use of an exciting beverage that was destined to be associated with things pleasing and colorful.

The earliest reliable written record of tea is the *Ch'a Ching,* or *Tea Classic,* published in A.D. 780 by a scholarly circus clown named Lu Yu. He said, "The best quality leaves must have creases like the leather boots of the tartar horseman, curls like the dewlip of a mighty bullock—unfolds like mist rising out of a ravine, gleams like a lake touched by a zephyr, and be wet and soft like fine earth swept by rain."

Tea is indigenous to India and China, where it has been used for more than two thousand years. Some botanists say that it is a native of the entire monsoon area. China cultivates more tea than any other country and about one half goes for its own use. India is second in total cultivation but first in export volume. Japan and Formosa are other major sources for tea, and Ceylon, Sumatra, and Java also cultivate it as a major crop.

Tea plants will grow to a height of thirty feet if left untended, but for greater ease of picking, they are pruned and maintained at a height of three to five feet. The tea plant grows best at moderately high elevations in a warm moist climate. It reaches maturity in three years. During the blooming season there is a profusion of scented white or pinkish blossoms that look like little wild roses with petals circling a cluster of yellow hairlike stamens tipped with pollen. The leaves of the tea plant are leathery and lancet-shaped. They resemble the rose leaf and grow to a length of three inches. However, we never find them so long when we buy them because, during the picking, only the bud and three or four smaller leaves are harvested and none of these is over two inches in length.

When the tea plant reaches maturity it sends out an abundance of young leaf shoots and this is known as the "flush" or the time for picking. As new shoots are grown on the twig, a new crop is picked. In Ceylon, Java, and Sumatra the climate is warm enough to bring about a "flush" every ten days. In the colder parts of China, India, Japan, and Formosa new crops can be picked only three to five times each year.

Tea trade names don't come from the different tea plants but from the position of the leaf on the stem. The nearer the leaf is to the tip of the stem, the better it is in quality. Other determinants of quality are the height of the garden on the slope and care in cultivating and fertilizing plants.

The flavor of tea comes from the method of curing and the essential oils in the leaf. Its stimulating and refreshing qualities come from the small amount of theine, chemically the same as caffeine in coffee. It is an alkaloid and acts as a mild heart and brain stimulant. It could be dangerous if taken in excessive quantities. As a beverage, tea has the best fragrance and flavor when the leaves are steeped, never boiled, in hot water.

The processing of tea leaves is carried out in an exact manner wherever adequate equipment is available. First it is "withered" outside for twenty-four hours. Then comes rolling, which consists of twisting or crushing slightly to bring the juices to the surface of the leaves. From here on the processing is slightly different for black tea and green tea. Black tea is fermented for four to five hours. Oxidation has then changed the leaves to a golden-brown color and they have a pleasant aroma of ripe apples. Green tea is not fermented. (India and China prefer green tea while Britishers must have theirs black.) Between the extremes of black tea and green tea there are several kinds of teas that are submitted to varying degrees of fermentation. Among these is Oolong tea, only slightly fermented. It comes from Formosa and is the favorite of Americans. Next comes firing for half an hour. Hot air at a temperature of 220° F. is passed over and through the leaves.

Before tea is exported it is given a special firing and packed in lead-lined containers to keep out salt air, which would spoil the flavor. Tea absorbs odors most readily and it is sometimes scented in China and Formosa. Layers of jasmine flowers may be laid out on top of the tea for a few hours.

The Japanese, like the Chinese, prefer green tea. In Japan the drinking of tea has been elevated to such a pedestal that it now is taken with religious reverence. The tea ceremony is centuries old and is an institution in the cultural education of every Japanese of good family. Proper appreciation and proficiency take three years of study.

Coarse tea, steamed and pressed into bricks, is sent to Tibet and

Mongolia, where it is used as currency. For the Tibetans and the Mongolians, tea is more than a beverage, it is a food. They add butter, soda, salt, and barley flour. They make this into a paste and call it *tsamba,* and they eat it as often as they can because it is such an unusual combination of fragrance and flavor. It is a staple in Tibet, as rice is in China and bread in Europe.

Turkestan likes fermented tea boiled until it is nearly black. Then cream and bread are added and it is eaten with a spoon. The Persians boil their tea and add spices of all known types. In Switzerland cinnamon is often steeped with tea leaves. The people of North Africa like an infusion of mint and tea.

Australians drink tea so strong that it tans the throat. The teapot is kept simmering on the fire all day. Australia's hobo, the swagman, carries a billy can in which he makes his tea. He carries it on his hip and calls it "Matilda." As the swagman walks, the Matilda seems to waltz around and around on his hip. "Waltzing Matilda" has become a favorite Australian folk song.

The Russians like pressed brick tea. They sip the brew either from a saucer or from a tall glass similar to our ice cream soda glasses. They sweeten it heavily with a large lump of sugar and then add a piece of lemon for extra flavor.

The English drink five times as much tea as the Chinese, an average of about six cups per day per person. They use fresh tap water, which they boil furiously, and let the tea steep for a full five minutes.

The leaves from a number of plants other than tea plants are used in making tealike beverages. The most popular one is Paraguay tea, which is made from leaves taken from a holly-like tree in Brazil and Paraguay. American Indians also made a tea, called *yaupon,* from the leaves of a holly-like tree. It resembled strong black tea and was not unlike Oolong. *Yaupon* was widely used during Revolutionary times because of the very high taxes on regular tea. A tea is also prepared in Peru and Bolivia from dried leaves of the cacao tree. Trinidad tea is made from a decoction of the leaves of the pimento (or allspice) tree. It is used both as a beverage and as a medicine.

Tea played an important role in our fight for freedom during the American Revolution. The Boston Tea Party, which took place

on December 16, 1773, is remembered by everyone, but some of the
reasons for it may have slipped temporarily from our memory. As
the American colonists grew in stature and "thinking" down through
the years following the first settlement, it became apparent that there
was a need for "collective thinking and action" to protect the common interest, so the colonies were formed. Many years passed before
they were able to stand up successfully for the things they believed
in. Prior to the tea party the colonists gained confidence because of
several successes with the British. In one case England was forced to
repeal many objectionable measures. During that period such men as
Patrick Henry and Samuel Adams were just waiting for a chance
to crystallize the "patriotic spirit."

England obliged them by taxing tea and giving the East India
Company a number of concessions, one of which was a monopoly
on American trade. To prevent a consignment of taxed tea from
being accepted in Boston, a group of indignant colonists had the
famous tea party. These and other retaliatory measures were so dras-
tic that they led directly to the rebellion of the American colonies.

American consumption of tea is lower now than at any time in
the past, while coffee has reached an all-time high. Our "taste in
tea" is a simple one. We generally use one type and we like it either
plain or with cream or sugar, with perhaps a hint of lemon. But
there is a broad, exciting field just waiting for us to step into it. Here
are some hints that I hope will get you started on a new enjoyment of
tea:

FINA'S "TALKING LEAVES" TEA

> 2 *lemons*
> 3 *oranges*
> 1 *quart water*
> 12 *cloves*
> 2 *cups sugar*
> 2 *quarts prepared* Oolong *tea*

Extract juice from lemons and oranges and hold. Bring water
to a rolling boil. Add cloves, then add rinds from lemons and oranges.

Add sugar and boil 5 minutes. Remove from heat, add lemon and orange juices. Discard lemon and orange rinds before serving. Add the 2 quarts tea. Serve either piping hot or iced. Wonderful for tea parties. Makes 3 quarts.

TEA FROM ANISE

Use ½ teaspoon anise seeds per cup of water. Bring water to a boil, pour over the anise seeds in teapot. Steep for about 5 minutes. Sweeten to taste and serve hot or iced.

Prepare several cups of plain tea and you can have fun alone or in serving your guests by using a different flavoring in each cup. Here are some flavorings you may want to start with; then use your own imagination.

mint
crystallized ginger or ginger candy
allspice
marjoram
balm (flavor combination of mint and lemon)

Tea is a good base for punch. Treat yourself by trying some of the combinations of tea, spice, and everything nice!

COCOA
Theobroma cacao

Linnaeus, a famous botanist, gave cocoa the botanical name of *Theobroma cacao*, meaning "food of the gods." Not many other things on the earth can claim such an illustrious title. The hand of nature blends to perfection both the fragrance and the flavor that make up cocoa's bouquet right on the tree. Cocoa is the dried and powdered seed kernels of the cacao tree; as a beverage, it is more digestible than chocolate because part of the cocoa butter, or fat, contained in the beans is removed.

Cocoa first reached Europe from Mexico in the sixteenth century. It arrived about the same time as coffee and tea, and by the eighteenth century it had become popular throughout Europe. Cortez, conqueror of Mexico, was responsible for one of the first shipments to Europe. He demanded three hundred loads of cocoa from Montezuma, emperor of the Aztecs, as a part of the tribute to be paid.

Cocoa was looked upon with suspicion and uneasiness when it first entered the European picture. One superstition led to another. Europeans wanted to know just what this stranger from the West Indies was. Was it a food or a drink? Was it a nut or an invention of the devil? As soon as the superstitions were overcome, cocoa houses were established everywhere and with remarkable speed.

The cocoa tree grows to a height of ten to twenty feet, with long, shiny, dark green and reddish leaves. The trunk of the tree is gray and white; the seed pods grow out of the trunk. When Friedrich von Humboldt first saw a cocoa tree, he wrote, "Flowers were growing so low on the trunk as to be bursting through the roots right up out of the earth." His delight was increased by the delicacy of the flower itself. The tree is a prima donna among trees. It either flourishes or dies quickly and it is even necessary to have a nursemaid to provide just the right amount and type of shade. Seeds will not sprout unless they are planted within twenty-four to thirty-six hours after being picked. The tree reaches full development in the sixth year and will produce for as long as sixty years. The only successful large-scale plantations are located in Central America, the West Indies, and the South American and South Pacific areas.

There are many ways to prepare the "food of the gods" but because of its very delicate and elegant flavor the method of preparation must be in the same vein.

THE DRINK OF THE GODS

Hot chocolate à la Mexicano is made from the black buttery squares created just for the drink. The woman of Tehuantepec mixes it in a tall gourd (*jicara*) with a whirling stick that acts like a churn in her deft hands. Into the *jicara* go the chocolate, a cup of hot water, sugar or honey, nutmeg, and an egg. Whirling and whirling, the whole becomes a foamy liquid delight. It is served to you in a carved gourd bowl, dark and rich but not too sweet. Once, for the Aztec and Mayan rulers, it was served in solid gold chalices with tortoise-shell and mother-of-pearl spoons.

English cocoa is very sweet and milky, with a dust of nutmeg on top. The French make a more savory chocolate by using cream, rum, cinnamon, or nutmeg. The Swiss make it with milk and vanilla. Americans like a rich cocoa, or hot chocolate, made with milk and a float of whipped cream on top.

POT DE CRÈME

> 3 *squares unsweetened chocolate*
> 1 *teaspoon water*
> 6 *egg yolks*
> 3 *tablespoons sugar*
> 3 *cups heavy cream*
> 2 *tablespoons crème de cacao*

Melt chocolate in water. Add well-beaten egg yolks and sugar to cream; add crème de cacao to mixture. Blend with melted chocolate slowly. Strain into cups. Place cups in pan of warm water and bake at 300° F. until set. Serves 6.

CHOCOLATE SAUCE

> ½ *pound unsweetened chocolate*
> 2 *cups sugar*
> *pinch of salt*
> 1 *can evaporated milk*
> 1 *teaspoon vanilla*

Put chocolate, sugar, and salt in double boiler and cook 45 minutes, stirring occasionally. Add the milk and cook another half hour. Cool and add vanilla.

QUICKIE COCOA CAKE

> 1 *box spongecake mix*
> 1 *pint heavy cream*
> ⅔ *cup instant cocoa*
> ½ *cup confectioners' sugar*
> ⅓ *cup chocolate shot (cake decorations)*

Make cake according to directions on the box. Bake cake in loaf or funnel cake pan and cool. Whip cream, not too stiff, add cocoa and sugar. Ice cake all over. Sprinkle chocolate shot over top of cake to decorate.

BEVERAGE CHART:
HOW THE BEVERAGES ARE USED

COFFEE

Hot coffee, iced coffee, coffee ice cream, coffee-flavored toppings for desserts, Mocha icing for cakes, English toffee confections, pies, liqueurs, gravies, breads, candies, cookies.

TEA

Hot tea, iced tea, tea as a base for fruit punches. Hot Russian tea is made with whole cloves, cinnamon, allspice, and sugar; Swiss tea is made by steeping leaves with cinnamon. Try tea with any of the spices or flavorings; also try tea with ginger ale in equal portions and add mint and lemon.

COCOA
and
CHOCOLATE

Breakfast cocoa, hot chocolate, chocolate ice cream, chocolate sauces, chocolate syrup, chocolate puddings, chocolate cakes, candies, chocolate sodas, chocolate sundaes, and anywhere else where perfect bouquet is needed. Puts a new taste in coffee.

6. Salt

Salt is a word of only four letters, yet these four letters have had
a profound influence throughout the whole world! It is hard to
imagine where civilization would be today without it. Salt has been
used as a seasoning and preservative for food since time began. Bio-
chemically, it is known as sodium chloride and it is absolutely essential to human beings and animals for healthy living. For this reason
salt has played an important role in the rise and fall of empires down
through the centuries. High taxes on salt were among the causes of
the French Revolution, and the British monopoly on salt brought
unrest in India to the point of mutiny.

It is very plentiful on this earth but it is not evenly distributed.
Where there was no supply near at hand, salt was brought from great
distances. One of the oldest roads in Italy was called Via Salaria
(Salt Road) because it was a salt transportation route. Salt made
up much of the caravan trade in the Sahara Desert. Cursed by lack
of salt, west and central Africa drew supplies from the open mines
of Taoudéni in the desolate heart of the western Sahara, where it
was quarried in tombstonelike blocks and reached Timbuktu and
Goundam, four hundred miles to the south, by caravans of as many
as six thousand camels. It is said that the French Sudanese reject
any other salt, believing it lacks the curative properties of the desert

product. Cakes of salt have been used as money in Tibet and the interior of Africa and it was so valuable in early times that our word for salary came from the Latin word *salarum*, which means "salt money." Roman soldiers were given an allowance to buy salt. This is the same common salt that we have on our tables at every meal and take so much for granted.

The world's most famous salt mines are located at Wieliczka, Poland. These mines were Poland's main source of wealth for centuries, but so much better salt is produced elsewhere that these once priceless mines have lost much of their importance in commerce. They are famous today as a show place and are illuminated by electric lights for visitors, who can ride a railroad down to a depth of a thousand feet. The mines form an underground city with sixty-five miles of "galleries," on the walls of which miners have chiseled an endless array of fantastic figures. The figures depict a religious theme that was very often deliberate, but at other times accidental. There are holy images and two entire life-size chapels cut in salt.

Cardona is another famous name connected with salt. It is a small town in the northernmost part of Spain, close to the French border and not too far inland from the great eastern seaport of Barcelona. A huge dry ocean of extremely pure salt lies just three miles east of Cardona and there is not even the slightest trace of gravel or mold in it. From Cardona, salt goes to nearby small towns and to Barcelona and Tarragona, from whence it is distributed all over northern Europe and England. Numerous other salt beds are found in the surrounding lofty mountains. This mountain salt is the most unusual in the world. It is not white like other salt but is made up of all colors: rose, scarlet, blue, green, violet, yellow, and every shade of brown. When this beautifully colored salt is pounded, however, every last vestige of color disappears and it becomes snow white. Men have tried to preserve specimens but after a few years the colors fade and the salt crumbles.

The United States is the largest salt producer and our thickest beds are found on Avery Island just off the coast of Louisiana. Our very plentiful supply is one reason for our number one position in the industrial chemical field. Salt is the source of chlorine and sodium, two of the most basic building blocks in the world of chemistry. Only three per cent of salt production goes for human consumption. Salt is useful in the herb garden. It is a safe weed killer when used in the hot weather. One pound to one gallon of water will kill the weeds quickly.

The next time we see it we should inspect the small white grains with loving care—it is a part of us, and we should be "worth our salt."

QUAINT PERFUMED SALT BEADS

2 tablespoons cornstarch
¼ cup eau de cologne or toilet water
3 drops food coloring
½ cup table salt

Mix cornstarch, cologne, and food coloring to make a thin paste. Put salt in a heavy skillet, heat to very hot. Add salt to paste, mix and knead it until a thick dough has been formed. Shape small, medium, and large rolls of dough about 3 inches long. Cut off small uniform pieces and shape into balls. Put a toothpick through each ball or bead and stand pick in a block of styrofoam. Let stand overnight until beads are dry. String on elastic thread or dental floss. Experiment with different colors of food coloring for interesting effects.

Fragrant Victorian ROSE PETAL BEADS can be made by putting 2 quarts of fresh rose petals in a bowl. Twist and crush the petals into a pulp. Dye the pulp with food coloring or, to obtain black beads, spread the pulp in an iron skillet and let stand overnight. Turn frequently so every part comes in contact with the iron surface. While the pulp is moist, shape and string as you would the salt beads.

Beads make nice party favors.

7. Sugar

Saccharum
Officinarum
From the
Arabic
Sukkar

Apparently the "sweet tooth" has been with us always. In olden days fruits, which are chock-full of sugar, helped to satisfy mankind's desire for sweetness. The ancient Romans and Greeks had no sugar as such and used honey instead for sweetening. The busy bees were kept even busier to take care of the demand. This went on for centuries until man finally discovered a way to provide endless quantities of sugar by growing cane. Sugar was first produced in India as early as the first century of our era, either from bamboo or from sugar cane, but for many centuries it was used only as a medicine or as a rare delicacy at feasts. The Arabians, who gave Europe so many wonderful things, brought the sugar cane plant from India to the West and gave us its name. They introduced it first into the valley of the Tigris and the Euphrates, then into Egypt, and finally into Spain. It was not until the time of the Crusades, however, that sugar became generally known in Europe. The fourteenth century marks the earliest record of sugar in England and at that time it was used only as a medicine. The value of two pounds of it was equal to that of a pig or to as much as a carpenter could earn in ten days.

By the end of the fourteenth century Europe had developed a

flourishing trade in sugar, spices, and other products from the Orient
by the overland route. Venice was the center of this trade and maintained a monopoly until the fifteenth century, when a water route
was found to India by Vasco da Gama. Gradually sugar cane
reached the West Indies, Cuba, Mexico, and Brazil from Madeira
and Hispaniola and the European nations were impelled to insure
an ample supply by reaching out for tropical and subtropical colonies. We all know the history of that era. Sugar cane was first grown
in the United States in 1751 but it was of no great importance until
seventy-five years later.

As a child, I remember walking with my father through the
sorghum (*Sorghum vulgare*) fields on our farm in Virginia. He
would break the tender stalks and taste the juice to test for flavor
before cutting the cane for making molasses.

SUGAR
BEET
Beta Vulgaris

The sugar beet now accounts for one third of the world's sugar
production. The sugar beet comes from the temperate regions
of Europe and America and first entered the picture at the beginning
of the nineteenth century, at the time of the Napoleonic Wars.
When the allies blockaded continental ports, Napoleon made large
grants of land and money to encourage the sugar beet industry. The
industry grew by leaps and bounds during the middle of the nineteenth century in Europe but did not become commercially important in America until the final decade of the century. Today, both
the cane and the beet are very important crops.

If you should happen to be a visitor in Amritsar, India, today
you would be presented with a tiny cup of sugar and you would be

expected to make a small present in return. The word "candy" was taken from Kandy, India, where a confection was made from sugar or molasses and combined with other substances to flavor, color, or give the desired consistency.

You have very probably heard the saying that the only part of the pig lost by slaughterhouses is the squeal. With sugar cane, not even that much is lost. When the sugar is processed from the cane, a heavy molasses results and from this is obtained rum, alcohol, food for cattle, and fertilizer. The crushed stalks are also used as food for cattle and as fuel to run the mills, or it is made into fiber board for insulation. All that is actually lost is moisture, which returns to the atmosphere for a useful purpose.

It is sometimes said that we eat our weight in sugar every year and sugar consumption in a country is often referred to as an indication of its prosperity. This certainly must be true of America, since our sugar intake has increased right along with the growth in our standard of living. Sugar, over the long pull, is a good business indicator.

MARGARET'S SUGAR TORTE

> *4 eggs*
> *3 cups sugar*
> *8 tablespoons flour*
> *5 teaspoons baking powder*
> *½ teaspoon salt*
> *2 cups chopped tart apples*
> *2 cups chopped pecans or English walnuts*
> *2 cups heavy cream, whipped*

Beat whole eggs until very frothy and lemon-colored. Sift together sugar, flour, baking powder, and salt. Add to eggs, with the apples and nuts. Pour into two well-buttered baking pans about 8 by 12 inches. Bake at 325° F. about 45 minutes or until crusty and brown.

To serve, scoop up with pancake turner (keeping crust side up). Pile on large plate and cover with whipped cream and sprinkling of chopped nuts to garnish. Serves 16.

8. Dedication of Gerard's Herball

"TO THE RIGHT HONORABLE HIS SINGULAR GOOD LORD AND MASTER, Sir William Cecil Knight, BARON OF Burghly, Master of the Courts of Wards and Liveries, Chancel-loer of the Universities of Cambridge, Knight of the most noble Order of the Garter, one of the Lords of her Majesties most honor-able Privy Councill, and Lord high Treasure of England.

"Among the manifold creatures of God (right Honorable, and singular good Lord) that have all in all ages diversly entertained many excellent wits, and drawn them to contemplation of the divine wisdome, none have provoked mans studies more, or satisfied their desires so much as plants have done, and that upon just and worthy causes: for if delight may provoke mens labor, what greater delight is there than to behold the earth apparelled with plants, as with a robe of embroidered worke, set with Orient pearles and garnished with great diversities of rare and costly jewels? If this varietie and perfection of colours may affect the eie, it is such in herbs and floures, that no Apelles, no Zevxis ever could by any art express the like: if odours or if taste may worke satisfaction, they are both so soveraigne in plants, and so comfortable that no confection of the Apothecaries can equall their excellent vertue. But these delights are in the out-ward senses: the principal delight is in the mind, singularly enriched with the knowledge of these visible things, setting forth to us the invisible wisdome and admirable workmanship of Almighty God.

The delight is great, but the use is greater, and joyned often with necessitie. In the first ages of the world they were the ordinary meate of men, and have continued ever since of necessary use both for meates to maintaine life, and for medicine to recover health. The hidden vertue of them is such, that (as Pliny noteth) the very bruit beasts have found it out: and (which is another use that he observes) from thence the Dyars took the beginning of their Art.

"Furthermore, the necessary use of those fruits of the earth doth plainly appeare by the great charge and care of almost all men in planting & maintaining of gardens, not as ornaments onely, but as a necessarie provision also to their houses.

"And here besides the fruit, to speake againe in a word of delight, gardens, especialy such as your Honor hath, furnished with many rare Simples, do singularly delight, when in them a man doth behold a flourishing shew of Summer beauties in the midst of Winter forces, and a goodly Spring of floures, when abroad a leafe is not to be seene. Besides these and other causes, there are many examples of those that have honoured this Science: for to passe by a multitude of the Philosophers, it may please your Honor to call to remembrance that which you know of some noble Princes, that have joyned this study with their most important matters of state: Mithridates the great was famous for his knowledge herein, as Plutarch noteth. Evax also King of Arabia, the happy garden of the world for principall Simples, wrot of this argument, as Pliny sheweth. Dioclesian likewise, might have had this praise, had he not drowned all his honour in the bloud of his persecution. To conclude this point, the example of Solomon is before the rest, and greater, whose wisdom and knowledge was such, that hee was able to set out the nature of all plants from the highest Cedar to the lowest Mosse. But my good Lord, that which sometime was the study of great Phylosophers and mightie Princes, is now neglected, except it be of some few, whose spirit and wisdome hath carried them among other parts of wisdome and counsell, to care and studies of special herbs, both for the furnishing of their gardens, and furtherance of their knowledge: among whom I may justly affirme and publish your Honor to be one, being my self one of your servants, and long time witnesse thereof: for under your Lordship I have served, and that way emploied my principall study and almost all my time, now by the space of twenty yeares. To the large and singular furniture of this noble Island I have added from forreine places all varieties of herbs and flowers that I might any way obtaine, I have laboured with the soile to make it fit for plants, that they might delight in the soile, that so they might live and prosper under our clymat, as in their native and proper countrey: what my sucesse hath beene, and what my furniture is, I leave to the report of they that have seen your Lordships gardens, and the little plot of myne owne especiall care and husbandry. But because gardens are private, and many times finding an ignorant or negligent successor, come soone to ruine, there be that have sollicited me, first by my pen, and after by the press to make my labors common, and to free them from the danger wherunto a garden is subject: wherein when I was overcome, and brought this History or report of nature of Plants to a just volume, and made it (as the Reader may by comparison see) richer than former Herbals, I found it no question unto whom I might dedicate my labors; for considering your good Lordship, I found none of whose favour and goodness I might sooner presume, seeing I have found you ever my very good Lord and Master. Againe, considering my duty and your Honors merits, to whom may I better recommend my Labors, than to him unto whom I owe my selfe, and all that I am able in your service or devotion to performe? Therefore under hope of your Honorable and acustomed favor I present this Herball to your Lordships protection; and not as an exquisite Worke (for I know my Meannesse) but as the greatest gift and chiefest argument of duty that my labour and service can affoord: wherof if there be no other fruit, yet this is of some use, that I have ministred Matter for men of riper wits and deeper judgements to polish, and to adde to my large additions where anything is defective, that in time the Worke may be perfect. Thus I humbly take my leave, beseeching God to grant to you many daies to live to his glory, to support of this State under her Majestie our dread Soveraigne, and that with great increase of honor in this world, and all fulness of glory in the world to come.

"Your Lordships most humble
and obedient Servant,
"JOHN GERARD."

9. *Assembly of the herbs*

Gerard's great, awe-inspiring book on herbs and plants has had
    such a profound influence upon my thinking that I should like
to describe it here so that you will know something about the way
its information is presented. The *Herball* is of such magnificent
scope and nature that nothing for the reader has yet appeared to
equal it. To make this tremendous volume complete and readable,
Gerard used wonderful illustrations showing the complete plant (the
root, the stem, the flowers, and the seeds). Each plant was thus
given a true identity about which there could be no question. To
each plant he gave a botanical name and a common name. He told
about the best time for planting and the type of soil that each plant
would feel best in. He gave the origin of each plant and told how
each one expanded through use all over the world. His next sections
on each plant were "Temperature," "Virtues," and "Use."

The unsurpassed eloquence of his book starts this way:

"Courteous Reader,

"Here are many things which I think needful to impart unto
thee, both concerning the knowledge of PLANTS in generall, also
for better explaining of some things pertinent to the Histories, which
I have set forth much amended and inlarged. For the great difference, affections, and etc. of Plants, I hold it not fitting nor neces-

sary for me to insist upon them; neither do I intend in any large discourse to set forth their many and great uses and virtues: Give me leave only to tell you, That: God of his infinite goodness and bounty hath by the medium of Plants, best bestowed almost all food, clothing, and medicine on MAN."

Gerard must have been an inspiration to everyone with whom he came in contact, either in person or through his *Herball*.

Brothers of the Spade, which contains the correspondence of Peter Collinson of London and John Custis of Williamsburg, Virginia, should also be explained at this point, at least in brief, because it shows us that plant exchange on a large scale was possible on an international basis even before the days of modern transportation. It also impresses upon us the absolute necessity of plant exchange to make for a fuller life. The correspondence, covering the period from 1734 to 1746, was collected and edited by E. G. Swem in 1948. Very simply, it is the story of how Mr. Collinson sent herbs and other plants from England to Mr. Custis in America and how Mr. Custis reciprocated by sending to Mr. Collinson varieties of herbs and plants indigenous to America. Here is one of the letters, quoted verbatim as it appears on page 103:

London January 31: 1743/4

My Dear Sir
Colonel Custis
        I have only time to tell you that I have sent you a Box of sundry seed, for your Kitchen Garden & Beg the Box may be return'd Filled with Cones of your Common Flowering poplar or Tulip Tree—and some Cassena Seed and any other sort you please, Pellitory in particular umbrella, papa, sweet flowering Bay. I shall in a particular manner thank You for the Box of seeds & all Came safe by Captain Friend and in good Order.

My Dear friend My best Wishes
Attends you from your affectionate
friend
P. Collinson
The box Comes by Captain Robinson
in the York

This one letter expresses the purpose of this section of my book: "kitchen garden" is the key phrase because a part of every kitchen garden should be an herb garden. By growing herbs in the garden we can enjoy the beautiful blossoming flowers with their innate fragrance, and we can be assured of garden freshness in the kitchen when we want to use these palate-caressing flavors.

In Genesis we are told: "God said, Let the earth bring forth . . . the herb yielding seed" and that in the earth there was "every herb of the field."

Meditating on the perfect union of fragrance and flavor in these herbs of the field brings to mind a beautiful little poem:

WE THANK THEE

For flowers that bloom about our feet,
For tender grass, so fresh, so sweet;
For song of bird and hum of bee,
For all things fair we hear or see,
Father in heaven, we thank Thee.

For blue of stream and blue of sky,
For pleasant shade of branches high,
For fragrant air and cooling breeze,
For beauty in the blooming trees,
Father in heaven, we thank Thee.

RALPH WALDO EMERSON

Rosemary is the traditional symbol of remembrance. Thousands of years ago, when the Mediterranean was the center of the world, rosemary, one of the small blessings of the herb family, grew along the northern shores and on the many islands. I like to think of it adding its fragrance to the winds blowing out over the bright blue sea. I can almost see the simple herb gatherers going from place to place along the shores and around the islands in their primitive boats propelled by paddles, their rush baskets filling with sweet-smelling herbs such as anise, rosemary, savory, and many others to sell or trade with the adventurous Phoenician traders. Also in the picture are the Greeks and Sicilians who sailed the waters of the rippling Mediterranean in luxurious barges laden with products from their homeland to barter for treasures of this exotic region. With all of these priceless things afloat it was quite natural for piracy to thrive around Marseille, the principal port of the time. Those ships fortunate enough to avoid pirates sent their precious cargoes inland from Marseille.

I have been told that monks at the mountain monastery of La Grande Chartreuse in France planted the sweet-smelling herbs in borders around the flower beds as well as in the herb garden. As they walked softly among the tender blessings of the gardens, they decided to plant small low-growing herbs between the stepping-stones. When lightly trod upon, they would give of themselves completely, yielding from their innermost depths a lovely scent to make the evening stroll a fragrant and agreeable pleasure after the dew fell. Everyone is well aware of the fact that monks make the most delectable cordials in the world, flavored with anise, mint, and many other herbs.

The art of cooking is almost as old as man himself, and even the earliest man soon learned that the pungent and aromatic little herb plants added a tantalizing bouquet to things eaten. As civilization progressed, these same age-old bouquets were achieved with sauces, stews, and desserts. In this section I include some of my special recipes that call for herbs.

A recent survey made by one of the world's largest spice houses says, "Few women know how to use spices and herbs, therefore fear them. Yet it can be the difference between good and bad cooking. The standard spices of most women are pepper, nutmeg, mustard, cinnamon, cloves, garlic and celery salt, yet there are more than one hundred in use today."

A FEW FACTS ABOUT HERB COOKING

A half teaspoon of dried herbs is equivalent to two scant teaspoons fresh. To bring out the aromatic oils lurking in the leaves, buds, and seeds, crush or chop fresh herbs before using; soak dried herbs in oil, wine, or broth, then crush.

Fine chopped herbs are called *fines herbes*.

A fagot of herbs is a bunch tied together, usually thyme, bay, and parsley.

A bouquet garni, frequently mentioned in French cooking, is a mixture of herbs and seasonings, usually parsley, thyme, bay leaves, celery, and leeks, tied in a cheesecloth bag and added to the cooking pot.

> *We may live without friends, we may live without books,*
> *But civilized man cannot live without cooks.*

ARISTIPPUS

10. Herbs tell their stories

AMBROSIA
Oke of Cappadocia

This fragrant herb from Asia Minor moved the poets in ancient times to suppose that it was meat and food for the gods and that it conferred immortality on mortals who ate it. This is an indication of the tremendously interesting and varied background of ambrosia.

Pliny, the Roman, said that ambrosia is a wandering name, often given to other herbs—a prime example being botrys, otherwise known as the oke of Paradise or the oke of Jerusalem; it has also been given to the Mexican tea (*Chenopodium ambrosioides*), which is made into a nectar delicious in both taste and aroma.

Ambrosia has many virtues. It has been used as a medicine for coughs and colds. The leaves can be candied or made into a conserve. The leaves give a divine flavor to the famous ambrosia dessert made with fresh grated coconut and fresh orange sections for the traditional Christmas feast. The leaves, dried and laid among garments, not only smell sweet but protect them from moths and silverfish. No herb garden is complete without the romantic and heavenly fragrance of the oke of Cappadocia . . . and its misty lace-like foliage will enhance the beauty of all the other plants in the garden. Once you have it growing it needs very little attention as too much cultivation will kill it.

Here is the beautiful description of ambrosia by Dioscorides, the Greek physician: "It groweth to the height of two cubits, yealding many weak, crooked and streaked branches, dividing themselves into sundry other small branches, having from the middle to the top thereof many mossie yellowish floures, standing one before the other in good order. And the whole plant is as if it were covered with a bran or mealy dust: the floures doe change into small cornered buttons, much like unto Tribulus Terrestris; wherein is contained black and round seeds, pleasant in taste and smell: the leaves are shaped like the leaves of mugwort, but thinner and more tender: all the whole plant is hoary, and yealdeth a pleasant savor: the whole plant perished with me at the first approach of winter."

I shall add—more than all of this has been proved of ambrosia!

ANISETTE AMBROSIA

> 1 *pint orange sherbet*
> 6 *Temple oranges, peeled and sectioned*
> 1 *fresh coconut*
> 3 *tablespoons anisette*
> 1 *cup fresh orange juice*
> 1 *bunch ambrosia leaves*

Put scoops of orange sherbet in sherbet glasses and arrange orange sections around the sherbet. Grate fresh coconut over orange sections and sherbet. Mix anisette with orange juice and serve as a sauce over ambrosia. Garnish with ambrosia leaves. Serves 6.

ANGELICA
Archangelica
officinalis
of the carrot family

Angelica was probably the first "wonder" drug. Of all the herbs I have looked into, particularly from the standpoint of medicinal use, none have been described as having even one half of the medicinal uses attributed to the roots of angelica. Here are just a few of these uses: angelica root is a singular remedy against poison and the plague; just holding a piece of the root in the mouth will chase away anything that could be bothering one; the root also opens the liver and spleen; a decoction of the root made in wine is good for the cold agues; it is good for the heart and will also cleanse the system thoroughly; the root is reported to be powerful against witchcraft; it cures the bites of mad dogs and all other venomous beasts—the list goes on and on.

There are several varieties of angelica, and to simplify matters we shall describe the one called garden angelica from here on. It seems to grow best in the northern temperate regions and New Zealand. The angelica plant is most unusual in its architecture. From the roots, very great thick and hollow stalks spring up, sometimes as high as six or seven feet. They are jointed or kneed in appearance and other arms and branches develop from these joints. Tufts of whitish flowers grow at the top of the branches shooting out from the joints; the flowers bloom during the months of July and August.

The garden angelica is used primarily in California sweet white wines and tonics—and the roots are generally powdered and used in rose jars and sachets. The primary use of the stalks is in making angelica candy.

Another variety of angelica, called wild angelica, is grown in Great Britain. The British use the roots for medicinal purposes and in the preparation of gin.

Although there is very little use for angelica in the home, many things we bring into our homes contain it, so we should learn to appreciate it more and more. Knowledge often makes for warmth of heart.

ANGELICA CANDY

4 cups angelica stalks cut about
2 inches long
4 cups water
1 tablespoon salt
2 cups sugar

Soak stalks overnight in 2 cups cold water and 1 tablespoon salt. Drain off salt water and add stalks to a thick syrup made with 2 cups sugar and 2 cups water. Let stand overnight. Drain off syrup and boil to a thick consistency, add stalks, and let stand overnight. Drain candied stalks and serve. Syrup can be used for cool drinks, or rhubarb can be cooked in the syrup.

ANISE
Pimpinella anisum
of the carrot family

This is one herb that almost everyone has come in contact with at one time or another, probably without knowing it, since the taste of licorice and the word "anise" have been associated very infrequently by most people. It is a must for the kitchen herb garden because of its many uses. The oil from the seeds of anise is in great demand by drug houses because it is an excellent flavoring for all kinds of medical preparations and children seem to like it particularly.

Foxhounds are familiar with anise to a certain degree . . . especially those that are used in a drag hunt. The trend in drag hunting is to lay an artificial scent by saturating a sack in anise oil and having a horse and rider make a lay trail by dragging the artificial scent a mile or two across the countryside. Two leader hounds are taught the fox scent as well as the artificial scent. The leaders are used to train the pack for the drag and the real hunt. Drag hunts help to maintain enthusiasm on the part of the hounds, the horses, and the hunting men for the sport of the challenge cup race, the steeplechase, and riding to the hounds in pursuit of a fox.

Anise is native to southwestern Asia, northern Africa, and southeastern Europe but it has been introduced into the temperate regions of both hemispheres. It is an unusual plant in that it never seems to stray from its garden; so far as can be ascertained, it has never been found growing wild. It is mentioned frequently in the

Scriptures and we know it has been cultivated for more than two thousand years. In the ninth century Charlemagne commanded that it be planted and grown upon the imperial farms. Many Greek and Roman authors, such as Dioscorides, Theophrastus, Pliny, and Palladius, wrote extensively about its use and cultivation.

Anise is a magnificent specimen of nature and will beautify any garden. It generally grows to a height of about eighteen inches and bears small yellowish-white flowers. The stems are slender and cylindrical, very erect and branchy, and the stem leaves are more and more finely cut toward the upper part. The fruits or "seeds" of anise are greenish gray in color and their shape is ovoid or oblong. For growing purposes, the seeds should never be more than two years old and should be planted as soon as the weather becomes settled in early spring.

The various parts of the anise plant have many uses. The leaves are frequently used for garnishing and flavoring salads. To a smaller extent, they are used as potherbs. The seeds are used on a far larger scale. Their flavoring power is so strong that they must be used sparingly to avoid overpowering other flavors present. The seeds are used as a flavor in various condiments, especially curry powders, many kinds of cake, pastry, and confectionery, and in some kinds of cheeses and breads. The oil extracted from the seeds is in great demand and is generally obtained by distillation with water. About one pound of oil is obtained from fifty pounds of seeds. This oil is also widely used in making perfumes, and various combinations of anise with other materials are used for sachets, perfumed soaps, and many toilet articles. Anisette is a cordial prepared from or flavored with the anise seed.

Look at one of the "Suggested Patterns for Growing" in Chapter 12 to see where anise will fit into your plans. Remember that with anise, as with most of the herbs, you will have wonderful balmy beauty outside as well as an aromatic flavor in the kitchen.

APPLE-ANISETTE

> *6 firm apples*
> *1 cup sugar*
> *3 tablespoons butter, melted*
> *½ cup chopped pecans*
> *1½ teaspoons anisette*
> *½ cup water in baking dish*
> *6 marshmallows*

Core unpeeled apples, place in glass baking dish. Mix sugar, melted butter, pecans, and anisette. Stuff apples with the mixture. Bake at 350° F. for 45 minutes; add marshmallows the last few minutes of cooking. Sprinkle each marshmallow-covered apple with anisette to lend licorice flavor. Serve in glass baking dish. Serves 6.

BALM
(Lemon Balm)
Melissa
officinalis
of the mint family

What could be more delightful than to have little Melissa flavoring our finger bowls or giving to our iced tea her green beauty, her very lemonlike flavor, and her fragrance that is pure freshness? This lovely aroma has been used in medicines, liqueurs, potpourri, cooking, and beverages. The bees, who are known for being particular, greatly appreciate the abundant nectar of the flowers as much as we like the sweet aromatic leaf. The flowers are a beautiful purplish white and they appear on the plant in well-formed clusters.

This beloved perennial is a native of southern Europe but it is now found growing in nearly all temperate climates throughout the world. The plant grows to a height of about two feet and the bright green crinkled leaves possess a scent that makes the ardent gardener and the flower arranger alike want to give it a choice spot in the herb garden. It is truly another one of the "little blessings" of the kitchen garden, and for the apartment house dweller it is ideal to grow in a pot or will do very nicely in a window box.

An old Arabian proverb conveyed this promise: "It makes the heart merry and joyful." For a delightful, sweet-and-spicy drink to dispel melancholy, the leaves may be heavily steeped in water. For a more delicate drink with the same flavor (but less of it), the leaves should be allowed to remain in the water for a very short time. This one should be served with thin lemon slices and sugar. Lemon balm will also make either hot or iced tea develop a more pleasing bouquet. One of the first things you should do with the lemon balm plant is to try some of the tender sprigs or leaves in fruit cups or salads.

BERGAMOT
(Bee Balm)
Monarda didyma
of the mint family

A long, long time ago a ruby-throated hummingbird was flying from his home in the North to visit in the South. When he had completed about half of the journey he decided it was time to look for something to eat. He saw a field of flowers in the distance and soared toward them as fast as his wings could carry him. As he drew nearer and nearer he was almost overwhelmed by the brilliant color of the flowers. They had seemed pale pink from above, but now they were literally bursting their petals with vibrant red. The humming-bird felt certain that anything so beautiful would have a refreshing nectar to match. His first sip was so delectable and satisfying that he sipped and sipped to the bursting point. He was so pleasantly satis-fied that he hurried to tell the butterflies and the bees. He described the flower heads as resembling the honeycomb. Later the mischie-vous bees told the wasps how to pierce holes in the bottom of the tubes of the honeycomb flower heads to steal the nectar from the hummingbirds and the butterflies.

Bergamot is a showy plant that grows from Maine to Florida in dry soil or thickets. It is colorful in flower arrangements or herb borders. It is a perennial and generally grows to a height of two to three feet. The plant exudes a rich mint essence.

A delicious tea can be made from the pungent tender leaves of bergamot; it was used on a large scale for tea when early colonists boycotted English imports. The colonists had learned of this tea from the Oswego Indians and named it Oswego tea after this tribe.

Bergamot has many uses: as garnish for wine cups and fruit punch bowls; as a flavorful ingredient in salads (delicious when used lightly); as a potpourri; and the French are said to use it sometimes as a flavoring.

BETONY
Betonica officinalis
of the mint family

Many years ago while perusing one of the old and famous herbals, I saw the name "betony" and was struck at once by its poetical sound and spelling. The name was so intriguing that I felt an urge to know personally the plant that carried this beautiful name. It has had a prominent spot in the wild-flower section of my herb garden ever since and, happily, the plant and the name formed the perfect synonym. The stem of this particular Betonica grows to a height of approximately twelve inches; its leaves are long and broad with a deep dark green hue. Snow-white flowers appear in June and remain throughout July. There is another type of Betonica that is similar to the one just described except that it has purple and red flowers.

Betony is a native of Europe and found most of its usefulness in the field of medicine. The monks of old distilled simples from herbs, and the "vertues" of betony rated very high. A few of them are:

Makes for a good stomach and appetite for meat. Brings on good humor. Good against the pain of sciatica or ache of knuckle bone. Cures bitings of mad dogs, good for ruptures, cramps, and convulsions. Most singular against poison, supposed to break stones in kidneys. Good against falling sickness and singular against all pains of the head.

WOOD
BETONY

Two other betonys are important. Wood betony (*Pedicularis canadensis*) is widely grown in America, as far west as Colorado. It grows slightly taller than the Betonica and flowers from April to June. The greenish-yellow and purplish-red flowers are a picture of sheer beauty on their short dense spikes. They prefer dry, open woods and thickets. This is also a wonderfully eye-pleasing sight and it fulfills its mission by beautifying our roadside banks, dry open woods, and copses. The wood betony is loved dearly by the bumblebees, probably as much as bergamot. In the Middle Ages it was said to have been used as a charm against evil spirits.

PAUL'S
BETONY
Veronica officinalis

Paul's betony grows lower than either of the other two. Its stems range from three inches to ten inches in length. The flowers, which stay on the plant from May to August, are very small, beautiful pale blue, and crowded on long spikes. It prefers dry fields, uplands, and open woods.

An ancient legend of the medieval flower lovers is that a maiden saw Jesus on his way to Calvary and, observing the suffering on his face, thought she would wipe away some of the anguish with her handkerchief, which was scented with betony. It has been declared that ever afterward the handkerchief bore the imprint of Jesus' sacred features. Of course special healing virtues were attributed to the handkerchief, and it became one of the most precious relics at St. Peter's in Rome. Since very few people could go to Rome to be cured by the handkerchief, the roadside plant was named for St. Paul the apostle.

All of the betonys have a tremendous background of history and this makes for interesting reading. After you have planted your betony or betonys, visit the library and browse through this history. You will like it.

BORAGE
Borago officinalis
of the Boraginaceae
family

Borage is a "cool" herb, imparting that touch to salads, lemonade, and other cooling drinks. The fresh foliage has a flavor very much like that of the cucumber. It is native to the Mediterranean, like so many of its brothers and sisters. It has been naturalized throughout the civilized world by Europeans who cultivated it originally more for medicinal than culinary purposes. Like angelica and lovage, borage was at one time considered what we would call a "wonder drug" today but, like the others, it has managed to throw off the superstitions and unfounded medicinal uses attributed to it.

It was listed by Peter Martyr, according to the Scottish poet Hew Ainslie, as having been planted on Isabella Island by Columbus' companions. It is very probable that borage was brought to America by the colonists during Queen Elizabeth's time. It first appeared in American seedsmen's catalogues in 1806.

The case of borage, and others like it, is one of the primary reasons this book was written. Borage is a wonderfully versatile plant that gives fragrance and beauty in the garden *and* fragrance and flavor in the kitchen. Yet the demand for it has always been small, and it is quite possible that most people have not become aware of its culinary uses, having always thought of it in terms of medicine if they thought of it at all.

No other plant is more easily grown than borage and it flowers so freely that is is ideal for a bee forage. This is just one of the bonus uses offered by borage. It is a somewhat branchy, hairy plant that generally grows to a height of one and a half feet. The oval leaves and other green parts are covered with whitish, rather sharp hairs. The flowers are in clusters and are sky blue, a truly beautiful shade that will enhance any garden and particularly any herb garden. The seed will grow in any soil, but borage seems to have a preference for light, dry soils, waste places, and steep banks, where it develops more flavor.

The tender upper leaves and flowers are used to a large extent in salads, to which they impart an always enjoyable but seldom recognizable flavor. It is because of borage's ability to blend so subtly that few people are aware of what they are enjoying. The lower, mature leaves are cooked like spinach and it is just as full of vitamins and energy, with a cool, cucumber taste.

BURNET
Poterium
sanguisorba
of the rose family

Little burnet came originally from Europe and Asia, bringing with it a fragrance of fresh greens and a flavor resembling fresh cucumbers. It is not very well known in the United States. It is a perennial with large low-spreading leaves that present a dark green underneath and a lighter green above. These will generally cover an area measuring about two feet across the top. The flowers come in June and are of a reddish copper color, with stems that reach upward to a height of twelve to fifteen inches. The little flowers have been called weather prophets because before a storm, on a cloudy day, they fold their petals and hide.

The young leaves make a beautifully compatible mixture with tarragon and rosemary. This would make a good starting point for those meeting burnet for the first time. Burnet is included in recipes for spiced vinegars, cooked greens, green salads, cream and cottage cheese, and it makes a zestful cup of tea.

CALAMUS
Acorus calamus
marsh herb
of the arum family

This perennial plant with its fragrant leaves and roots came to
us from Syria and Egypt and the history, adventure, and romance connected with it are quite without parallel. It has been called
the true aromatic reed of the ancients, who used these reeds as writing pens. It has been referred to as being a viceroy but could well
be called a king among plants. It grows best in marshland or very
wet places but will do very well in ordinary garden soil.

Calamus, often known as sweet flag, has been in high esteem
since the very earliest days of our civilization. It was written about in
the Song of Solomon. John Gerard, whose fame dates back to the
sixteenth and seventeenth century, wrote at great length about calamus. Here is one quaint remark he made about it:

> *It is boiled also in baths for women, and decoctions for Clisters,
> and it enters into plaisters and perfumes for the smells sake.*

Ladies of colonial times grew calamus in their herb gardens
especially for its leaves, which were used in creams, puddings, and
custards. The roots were used during that period to keep moths and
insects out of closets where clothing and furs were stored. Today the
roots are widely used in perfumes and medicines, which necessi-
tates our importing many, many tons per year. In the field of medi-

cine, the calamus root is still in wide demand the world over, especially in the United States, for use in a home remedy for colic.

Enjoyment of its fragrance is more than sufficient reason for growing this plant, and it is easily propagated from division of the roots. In the case of older plants, the roots are often several feet long and two inches thick—and this makes calamus ideal for plant exchange with neighbors and other friends.

CAMOMILE
Anthemis nobilis
of the aster family

This is one of three different plants bearing the name "camomile," and the one most widely grown because it is more adaptable to changing soil and climate. *Anthemis nobilis* (and perhaps the other two camomiles as well) has been cultivated for more than two thousand years as a combination ground cover and beautifying ornament.

Camomile is quite different from most of the other herbs, both in appearance and in internal make-up. Its stems like to stay close to mother earth and they weave their way along, rooting as they go. The stems of the flowers reach upward about one foot above the ground and are topped with daisylike blossoms, with white florets surrounding a yellow center disc. The leaves are many and fernlike, much divided, so that they tend to form mats at each rooting spot of the creeping plant stem. They are gray-green and make an ideal ground cover for pathways. In fact it is said that many of our very old gardens had raised mounds of earth covered with the mossy-looking camomile, which made a soft and comfortable place to sit.

Camomile can be used in most areas that will not support the growth of grass. It is a very hardy perennial, native to the northern shores of the Mediterranean, and both the foliage and the flower heads are very aromatic. The dried flower heads are the only parts of the plant utilized commercially. An oil is extracted from them that is an important ingredient of many hair preparations and shampoos. The dried flower heads are also used in making camomile tea, a wonderfully tasty beverage, said to be good for the complexion.

Camomile flowers practically all summer. It is suggested that it be used in your herb garden (or flower garden, for that matter) as an edging or ground cover. And remember that camomile fills the surrounding air with a pleasing, pungent fragrance.

Another of the three camomiles is one called the German camomile (*Matricaria chamomilla*) and is of no interest to the herb gardener. It is mentioned here because an oil is extracted from the dried flower heads and used in medicine as an emetic. The third one differs from the plain camomile (*Anthemis nobilis*), sometimes referred to as the Roman camomile, only in that it has a double row of white ray florets in its blossoms.

Anthemis nobilis has been called the "apple of the earth." My English grandmother served camomile tea by steeping the fresh or dried leaves as you would any tea leaf (three teaspoons fresh or one dried in her cup). She would serve the children at the party one half cup camomile tea and one half cup hot milk with sugar. We knew this as cambric tea.

CARAWAY
Carum carvi
of the carrot family

Caraway is almost unique, at least from the standpoint of history, in that it is one of the very, very few herbs that created a friendly rivalry between cooks and doctors, each vying to give it more prominence than the other. Now the cooks seem to be in the lead, since there are many culinary uses for caraway while only one primary usage remains in the field of medicine: to disguise the flavor of repulsive drugs.

At one time it was believed that caraway was a native of Asia Minor, but it seems well established now that actually it first came from Europe. Twelfth-century writings describe its growth in Morocco and they also point out that the Arabs grew it in the thirteenth century. Apparently the use of caraway spread first with the Phoenician commerce to western Europe and from there throughout the rest of the civilized world. It has been so very widely distributed that it is possible to find it almost any place on the globe.

Caraway is one of the "herby" herbs, with everything to offer from the standpoint of fragrance, flavor, and beauty. It is biennial or annual but it self-sows itself year after year by dropping or exploding seeds. It can be very easily grown from seed and it germinates readily. The following description of the plant itself will tend to make you aware of its beauty in the garden, its utility in the kitchen, and its usefulness in making flower arrangements. The plant has a fleshy root that is yellowish on the outside and whitish on the inside, with a slight taste of carrots. From this root a rosette of finely divided leaves is developed and at a later date the sparsely leafed, hollow, branching flower stems bear umbels of small white flowers. The stems will reach a height of between eighteen and thirty inches and this is the main reason for using the caraway plant in flower arrangements. After the flowers come the oblong, light brown, aromatic fruits that are the caraway "seeds" of commerce.

The caraway seed is one of the most widely used seeds in the world and can be found in rye bread, cake, cheese, German sauerkraut, apple pie, baked apples, and cabbage soups. Caraway can be sugar-coated for confectionery to be munched after meals as a preventive of indigestion. It also goes into perfumes, various toilet preparations, liqueurs, soaps, and, as mentioned earlier, is used to disguise the flavor of medicine that is difficult to take. The young roots of the caraway plant are sometimes boiled as vegetables. A pale yellow essential oil is distilled with water from the seeds, which normally contain between five per cent and seven and one half per cent of the oil.

Complete and simple growing instructions may be found in Chapter 12.

CATNIP
Nepeta cataria
of the mint family

This is one herb that has shown remarkable popularity down through the ages although it does not possess the blending, flavor-imparting fragrance of thyme or sage or any of the most widely used herbs of today. It is mentioned here because it is definitely a part of the herb picture and is also a well-known "weed." The Greeks and Romans grew it to make their cats happy, but there is much more reason for growing it today. It is a stately, ornamental plant that will add beautiful white clusters of flowers to an herb garden from June to August. In earlier days catnip was used in making tea for infants and beverages for adults. It was also used as a tranquilizer for babies.

It was native to Europe and western Asia but has been naturalized over most of the civilized countries. It will grow with practically no care in any fairly dry soil. Seed can be sown either in the fall or spring and all that is needed is to keep the weeds down. The stems grow to a height of eighteen to thirty-six inches.

Actually, a fairly large number of cooks still use catnip as a seasoning. The foliage has a faint aromatic scent not unlike that of lemons. It is an herb that requires special "know-how" of use and this know-how comes only with experience. First, plant it in your herb garden (or any garden) for its ornamental value and the great pleasure it brings to cats. Then, when time permits, start working it into some of your established seasoning mixtures and sauces. A pleasant surprise will be yours.

CHERVIL
Anthriscus
cerefolium
of the carrot family

This is a distinguished name, and one that will always draw
the respect of the discriminating people who use chervil so
wisely and delectably. It is a native of southern Europe and is a
milder form of parsley, which some think has been overused. The
gastronomically wise French have always been the largest users of
chervil. They think so much of it that it is now in their world-famous
combination of *fines herbes*. Some of the other European countries
are becoming more chervil-conscious and the English are only
slightly behind the French in appreciation of its wonderful attributes. It is not widely grown in the United States as yet, but it is the
type of herb that could "catch on" quickly, once more is generally
known about it.

The chervil plant is easily grown from seed and, unlike other
members of the parsley family, the seed germinates readily. It will
grow to a height of twelve to twenty-four inches in most sections of
the country. The stems shoot out many, many branches that bear
very finely cut, much-divided, almost lacelike leaves. The flowers
are white and tiny, with the white florets arranged in small umbels.
The seeds that follow are long and black. The plant resembles parsley
in growth and appearance and looks well in any herb garden.

Only the leaves are used today but in ages past Pliny thought
that hiccoughs could be stopped by drinking vinegar containing the
seed of chervil. Parkinson, some of whose writings appear in
Brothers of the Spade, said that "some recommend the green seeds
sliced and put in a sallet of herbs and eaten with vinegar and oil, to
comfort a cold stomach of the aged."

The whole chervil plant has a delightful aniselike fragrance; its
flavor resembles that of anise with a very light sprinkling of pepper.
Chervil leaves and salad are synonymous in France. The effect of the

leaves in potato salad is matchless. They are also used as a condiment in soups, egg dishes, and on fish. They are found in many sauces, particularly in béarnaise and ravigote, and they greatly enhance butter sauces for chicken and wine and butter sauce for cutlets.

You will be pleased with chervil in your herb garden and in your kitchen.

CHICORY
Cichorium intybus
of the composite
chicory family

On a dewy morning or through a cloudy day
These blue and starlike flowers brighten up our way.

These clear, bright blue flowers are found in unexpected places such as fields, waste places, and along roadsides. Chicory has grown wild in these places since it was naturalized in the United States. It is a native of Europe, but it is said that the name "chicory" comes from the Arabic *chicourey*.

Chicory has an unusual background in that it seems to have gone through cycles down through the centuries of use and cultivation. In fact, during the late 1800s and early 1900s, chicory was launched as a huge farm crop in America. This development came about through a prejudice on the part of the principal users, who at that time happened to be European immigrants. They felt that the American-grown chicory was inferior to that obtainable from Europe on a duty-free basis. In 1898 or '99 advantage was taken of a protective duty and several factories were constructed in the United States. Farmers were alerted in advance and had large crops (roots) available when the first factories were finished. The entire project was abandoned after a few years because there was not enough profit in the operation, despite government help.

Today, chicory is grown as a farm crop for the roots, which are dried and ground for use with coffee. In the beginning, ground chicory was used to "adulterate" coffee and quite possibly there may still exist coffee "adulteration" on a fairly large scale. Certain sections of the country, however, such as New Orleans and its environs, prefer a mixture of chicory and coffee to the pure product, and sizable companies have been marketing a chicory-coffee blend on the retail level for several years.

There is scarcely a part of the chicory plant that has not been used at one time or another. The young roots have been cooked as carrots and served with butter, salt, and pepper. The stalks have been blanched by heaping soil around the base of the plant and eaten like celery. The young leaves of the chicory plant have been eaten in salads and as greens. A special strain of chicory called Brussels witloof is available today as a plant or seed. It is a perennial and the roots can be dried and used as a substitute for coffee; the leaves are used when young and tender as greens or those of the older plants are blanched in much the same way as celery. The best-known foliage of chicory used for salads or greens is called witloof. To get the crown of uncolored leaves now known as witloof, the roots are trimmed on the lower end to a length of eight or nine inches, then placed upright in soil or sand in a box. The crown is covered with about eight inches of sand and the temperature is kept at 60° F. In two or three weeks the white salad witloof should be ready, a good "head" being six inches long.

Chicory is a very handsome plant, rangy by nature, and has clean green leaves that seem to be content in their supporting role. The star, of course, deserves the role she is playing. She is that beautiful, bright, clear blue dainty flower that started this story, although types with white, pink, or purple flowers appear now and then. The flowers are in bloom from July to September or October and they open their petals for the world to see the intricate workmanship inside only when the sun is shining, and then only until noon, or on a dark day.

CHIVES
*Allium
schoenoprasum*
of the lily family

"Chives bring forth many leaves about a hand-full high, long,
slender, round like to little rushes; amongst which grow up
small and tender stalkes, sending forth certaine Knops with floures
like those of the onion, but much lesser. They have many little bulbes
or headed roots fastened together: out of which grow down into the
earth a great number of little strings, and it hath both the smell and
taste of the onion and leeke, as if it were participating of both."
That is Gerard's quaint and accurate description of chives.

In all probability, salads were eaten before chives knocked on
the door of the "Green Rooms" asking to be let in. The fact that
they were let in and became reigning king of the salad bowl is well
known to all.

Chives were first grown in European gardens during the sixteenth century and entered our gardens sometime before the year
1806. It is seen in well-kept records that chives began colonizing the
American salad during the latter part of the eighteenth century and,
of course, they have maintained rigid control of it during the country's growth. In the early gardens of Virginia this small ornamental
perennial plant was used for borders. The delicate violet-pink cloverlike blooms were used in bouquets and the tender blades were cut
for making butter sauces and salads. In the fall, clumps would be
lifted and potted for the window garden since the dried leaves of
chives are useless.

Chives are very closely related to the onion, having just about
the same aroma and taste, though far milder, and in physical appearance the only real difference is in the size of the bulbous base.
Practically everyone is familiar with the various sizes of onions avail-

able and, in comparison to even the smallest onion, the base of a chive is much smaller and looks like the slightly swollen base of the stem. In my garden chives grow to a height of about six inches and the leaves, or hollow tubes, have a yellow-green color.

Chives have a magic name among chefs, and it is difficult to find one who would be without them, because they seem to work miracles in any dish that needs a light touch of onion flavor. They are particularly delectable in salads and omelets and give the taste buds a change without making them do somersaults. There are so many culinary uses for chives that only a few of these are mentioned but they are representative: cheeses, soups, potato salad, fish, spaghetti, and various vegetables. I hope this will spur you to experiment in your kitchen, after having grown them, keeping the tops cut for fresh new growth.

They should be permanent fixtures in your herb garden. A fresh, continuous supply can be purchased in the stores in the spring or fall.

ICEBERG SALAD

> 1 *head lettuce*
> ¼ *cup red wine vinegar*
> ¼ *cup olive oil*
> ¼ *teaspoon salt*
> ⅛ *teaspoon white pepper*
> ¼ *cup chopped chives*

Tear lettuce in chunks. Put vinegar in jar, add olive oil, and shake well. Put lettuce in salad bowl, pour the wine dressing over it, and toss lightly until lettuce is well coated. Add chopped chives, salt, and pepper and toss lightly. Serve in individual wooden salad bowls. Serves 4 to 6.

CLARY
Salvia sclarea
of the mint family

A native of the Mediterranean, clary is definitely a part of any
herb picture, though it has now settled into a less prominent
spot than it occupied during the old days of herb use. The herb
gardener of today will be interested primarily in clary as an ornamental source of pleasantly different fragrance, a spicy fragrance that is
similar to that found in sage, to which it is closely related.

It is a biennial and will not flower until the second season, but
the leaves can be harvested at any time. The leaves are not so much
used today in culinary practice because much of the flavor is lost in
cooking. They are still used sometimes in omelets and the flowers
find their way into aromatic teas. Rhenish wines in Germany at one
time owed their muscatel raisin flavor to a combination of clary
leaves and elder flowers. *Muscateller sallier* is the German name for
clary and means muscatel sage.

Commercially, clary is a most important herb. Very widely used
in perfumery and in making sachets is clary sage oil, which is extracted from the leaves, of which the smaller and uppermost are
richest in the essential oil.

During the seventeenth and eighteenth centuries the fragrance
and flavor were so highly prized that many noted tavern keepers in
London gave their patrons all manner of food and drink containing
clary. There is no record of the reaction of the patrons to this clary
treatment but, since it continued for so long and with the same
patrons, it must have been one of complete satisfaction. As with

most of the older herbs, many unusual traits were at various times attributed to clary. Among these was the thought that clary was good for "weak backs and to straighten the reins being made into tansies and eaten otherwise." It has been listed in seedsmen's catalogues since 1806.

Picture the ornamental effect, perhaps as a flower border, from the following description of the plant. The stems are square and covered with hairs that look like shiny wires; they reach a height of two to three feet. The leaves present a singular spectacle, being large and very broad on the lower part of the stems and becoming smaller as they ascend the stem. They are grayish green, oblong in shape, obtuse, opposite, and woolly-haired. The flowers arrive in June of the second season and remain in bloom almost all summer. They are lilac or greenish white, very showy, and have a perfume that is almost overpowering. They are borne in numerous conspicuous spikes twelve inches or more in length over the upper half of the plant. Here are beauty and fragrance of an unusual nature, just waiting to grace your garden.

CORIANDER
Coriandrum
sativum
of the carrot family

This herb, which has been of such great importance to mankind, has been cultivated so long that it is now doubtful that its origin can be ascertained with even a measure of accuracy. The seeds of coriander are probably the most unusual of all the herbs. When the seeds have ripened and are dried, they develop a scent and flavor resembling orange, anise, and cumin. Their bouquet is so very desirable and savory that it has been described in the following ways by different professional people in the cooking field: "sweet and tart

. . . extremely pleasant . . . lemon peel with sage odor," and as we mentioned just above, "resembles strongly the effect of mixing orange, anise, and cumin." The seeds are so good that we import over three million pounds annually.

Coriander seeds have been found in Egyptian tombs of the Twenty-first Dynasty. They were well known in Pliny's time and he wrote that the best seeds came to Italy from Egypt. At one time in the dim past it was thought that the use of coriander caused people to become avaricious, but this was undoubtedly tied in with the superstitions that so often were associated with herbs used medicinally. Eventually it was decided that coriander has practically no medical value, but at one time it was sprinkled over meat to keep it from spoiling. Just for the record, coriander was planted in America by the earliest colonists and was actually planted within our shores before the year 1670.

The plant resembles anise in some respects. Slightly divided leaves at the base form the foundation for branching stems that grow to a height of about two and one half feet. Near the top the leaves are much divided and in these are found linear segments of small rosy-white or plain white flowers. Next comes a pair of brownish-yellow seeds that are about the size of a pea seed. Always remember that the seeds are to be ripened and dried before use. Coriander likes warm, friable soil best although it will do a good job of plant production in most any good soil. Seed has been planted in the fall with success but it is recognized that springtime is better for planting. The seeds appear about ninety days after sowing and should not be picked until it is distinctly brown. It is at this time that the fruiting clusters should be cut and dried. Many seeds will be lost if left too long on the plant. They should be stored in very tightly stoppered containers.

One of the primary uses for the seed is as one of the innumerable ingredients of curry powder. It is used in flavoring pickles, in the manufacture of liquors, and in meats, sausages, sauces, bread, cookies, and confectionery. It also makes pea soup delectable. Biscuits and poultry stuffing are greatly enhanced by the seed. Apple pie is more delicious with it; and try rubbing it on pork before roasting. It makes tossed chef's salad truly delightful and it does the same for some Mexican dishes also.

COSTMARY
Chrysanthemum
balsamita
of the Compositae
family

We can give our thanks to western Asia for producing this tall, beautiful, stately-looking plant. When you consider the over-all architectural structure of costmary, there is no handsomer plant for the herb garden. It grows to a height of three feet or more but is rather woody and sprawling unless cut back frequently. Most people who are fortunate enough to have costmary in their herb gardens cut the young leaves very often and this has a twofold effect: number one, it keeps the plant within the range of garden beauty; and number two, the younger leaves are far more succulent than the older ones.

From the standpoint of pure fragrance there is no herb that can equal costmary in the garden. Even without bruising the leaves between the fingers, there is always evident a lovely scent of a combination of lemon, chrysanthemum, and mint. It is thought of as one of the most fragrant of all herbs.

Costmary is a hardy perennial that dies to the ground every winter but at the first signs of spring it is up again; it seems to like a dry, sunny situation. The leaves are rather large at the lower part of the plant and become smaller as the top is approached. These leaves are a beautiful green with a tinge of gray and a slight downy appearance. Incidentally, the dried leaves make a good tea. Costmary blooms in August and the flowers are beautiful, with a yellow center and a white outer floret or series of florets.

Costmary has been known to man almost since the beginning of recorded history and has been grown for many, many centuries in Europe. It is not very well known in the United States; however, indications are that it will become better known as time goes on. It is a very highly aromatic plant throughout and in cookery it should be used sparingly; for example, one recipe that has come to light calls for but one costmary leaf for an entire meat or vegetable stew.

The history of the common and botanical names of this plant is interesting. *Balsamita* comes from the balsamic odor of the plant and "costmary" comes from costus, a violet-scented plant from the Himalayas. The roots of this plant are used to prepare a very expensive perfume. The "mary" part of the name comes from the Virgin Mary, to whom the plant seems to have been dedicated in most European countries. Various writings from the fifteenth century tell us that costmary was a very popular plant at that time and was exported from Spain to all parts of the world.

Costmary in the herb garden is a valuable and stately herb, its fragrance unequaled. In cookery, when used sparingly, it can make a great contribution to our eating habits. It is suggested that you grow costmary in your herb garden, first to look at and then, after a time has passed, take part of the leaf structure into the kitchen and experiment with it. You will find that there are many untold treasures lying there just for the asking.

CRESSES of the mustard family

> Upland Cress (*Barbarea verna*)
> Water Cress (*Nasturtium officinalis*)
> Garden Cress (*Lepidium sativum*)

We know that spring is really here when we see the crisp jade green of the upland cress shining forth, followed shortly thereafter by the water and garden types.

UPLAND CRESS

This is the true American upland or winter cress, as it is some-times called. It should not be confused with water cress, which it resembles. Nor should it be confused with fine curled cress, which is also called peppergrass. Upland cress has also been called dry-land or land cress. The names "creasy salad" and "highland creasy" have also crept into the naming picture in certain areas of Virginia where upland and a similar botanical variety grow as weeds. If the seeds of the upland are sown in early spring in rich soil, the leaves are ready for use in late summer. It is a hardy perennial and will have another crop of leaves for you in the spring. Gerard says this about it: "It groweth in gardens among pot herbs, and very common in the fields neere unto paths and highwaies almost every where." Make the most of the succulent freshness of the earliest of spring salad greens!

WATER CRESS

True water cress trailing in wet ground and springs makes a picture that is mouth-watering. It is the aristocrat of the cresses and is easily grown from seed. Water cress is best for greens when cut for use in early spring or fall. Gerard mentioned this about it: "Water cress is evidently hot and dry; and should be eaten in March when it's at its best, says M. Gooyer." Sharpen your appetite with this delightful concept of a dainty tidbit—the WATER CRESS SAND-WICH—prepared as follows: Use very thin sliced bread (white or brown) and sweet butter. Cream the butter and spread it generously on the bread. Chill and wash cress carefully and spread on bread nicely. Fascinating!

Gerard also says: "Water-Cress hath many fat and weake hollow branches trailing upon the gravell & earth where it groweth, taking hold in sundry places as it creepeth; by means whereof the plant spreads over the great compasse of ground. The leaves are likewise compact and winged with many small leaves set upon a middle rib one against another, except the point leafe, which stands by its selfe, as doth the ash, if it grow in his natural place, which is in a gravelly Spring. The upper face of the whole plant is of a browne colour, and greene under leaves, which is a perfect marke to know the physicall kinde from the others. The white floures grow alongst the stalkes, and are succeeded by cods wherein the seed is contained. The root is nothing else but as it were a thrum or bundle of threds."

GARDEN CRESS

You are always assured of that new, fresh crispness in the leaf of the cress if you plant an annual, and garden cress is an annual. It grows quickly and makes wonderful greens for salads, cooking, or garnish for meats and salads. Then eat the garnish for zestful energy! And remember, the richer the soil, the better the plant.

All of the cresses are full of vitamins.

CUMIN
Cuminum cyminum
of the carrot family

It is difficult to find another herb of such ancient vintage or of so varied a historical background as cumin. It is mentioned in Matthew 23:23 that cumin, along with dill and mint, were used in tithing. Many of its earliest uses back in the days of Isaiah were more fancied than real, such as its powers to keep lovers from being fickle and to keep poultry from straying. As time passed, however, cumin came into its own . . . to such a point that Pliny is said to have considered it the best appetizer of all condiments. It was extremely popular during the Middle Ages and it is written about extensively and glowingly by all of the writers of the older herbals of the sixteenth and seventeenth centuries.

Cumin makes an ideal border plant, since it is diminutive and seldom exceeds a height of six inches. It is multi-stemmed, has linear-leaved foliage and small lilac flowers, in little umbels of ten to twenty blossoms each. The seeds resemble those of caraway and coriander, and have long hairs that fold up when the seed is dry.

The records show that cumin is native to the Nile Valley, but it has been cultivated in the Mediterranean region, Africa, Egypt, Morocco, India, China, and Palestine from very early times. Today it is extensively cultivated in Malta and Sicily. It is also grown to some extent in the United States. The greatest single use of cumin today is as an ingredient of curry powder. The ground seeds go into many things, such as chili sauce and cheeses; they also find their way into the flavoring of pickles and soups.

The cumin plant has a strong aromatic fragrance and its taste is hot. When used correctly—and by this is meant proper blending and sparing use—cumin is a wonderfully versatile herb to have around. You will find that a little experimentation will give you a knowledge of its proper use. It is heartening to learn that some of our most modern cooks are beginning to use it again in rice, meat and fish dishes, and soup.

Please do not forget that cumin can be used as a small dwarf facer in your herb garden, as well as to impart demure beauty and fragrance to your borders. Cumin is an all-purpose herb. Look at one of the suggested herb garden plantings in Chapter 12 to see where cumin might best fit your plans. It is easy to grow and the only thing you will have to watch out for is to make sure the plants are not overrun by weeds.

CUMIN SAUCE FOR ENCHILADAS . . . PRIMARILY

1 onion, chopped
2 cloves garlic, chopped fine
2 pounds lean ground beef
3 tablespoons olive oil
¼ teaspoon salt
¼ teaspoon cayenne pepper
¼ teaspoon black pepper
2 tablespoons chili powder
½ teaspoon cumin seed
2 cups beef stock
1 can pinto or garbanzo beans
½ can tomato paste

In a large iron skillet sauté the onion, garlic, and meat in the olive oil. Add salt, pepper, chili powder, and cumin seed. Simmer 15 minutes, stir often. Pour in stock, beans, and tomato paste and stir. Simmer on low heat for 1 hour, stirring often. Serves 4.

DANDELION
Taraxacum officinale
of the Compositae family

The dandelion is a courageous little plant that has almost no peer for hardiness. Whether or not mankind agrees, it feels it has an important place among us and tries hard to please. It is one of the first to join us in the spring when many of its brothers and sisters stay covered and cozy until all signs of frost have disappeared. Its golden-yellow starlike blooms gleam forth like a reflection in the sea-green grass and its petals seem to say, "Be of good cheer—spring is almost here."

The dandelion plant will grow year after year from a deep, fleshy root and the deeply scalloped leaves grow in a low crown near the ground. They have admirable adaptability and can grow to a height of two or three feet to reach the sunlight, but will hug the ground if the lawn mower keeps them cut low. They say the only way to get rid of them is to poison them or to cut their roots. Many people do this. They still must have their place, however, because I have recently seen (with surprise and amusement) packets of dandelion seed displayed in the seed store near the grass seeds.

The dandelion is a native in Europe and Asia but is now common to temperate climates all over the world. It is a master at seed scattering, because each flower has a hundred and fifty or more little florets set in a cup and each floret is really a little flower. It has parts for growing and catching pollen, and the lower end produces a seed. When ripe, the seed "builds" a feathery network, a pappus, on a stalk thinner than #60 thread. All of the pappi in the pappus make up what we know as a "blowball," and the wind does the rest.

The Italians have always had a soft spot in their hearts for the dandelion, remembering that it is a first cousin to chicory, endive, and lettuce. They learned centuries ago that the secret of using dandelion to the palate's best advantage lay in the time of harvesting. The young leaves have a milky juice containing a pleasing bitterness that imparts that unusual something to a salad. If the leaves are young enough they can be used alone for salad greens. Even the roasted roots can be used as coffee.

DANDELION WINE

> 1 *gallon dandelion blossoms*
> 1 *gallon boiling water*
> 3 *lemons*
> 1 *orange*
> 3 *tablespoons sugar*
> 3 *tablespoons dry yeast*

Put blossoms into the boiling water and let stand 24 hours. Cut lemons and orange in thin slices and add to blossom liquid. Add sugar and yeast, then let stand ten days. Strain and put in jugs, but not airtight.

DILL
Anethum
graveolens
of the carrot family

With an oil so fragrant that some consider it to be the true anise of the Bible, dill is one of our oldest and most important herbs. It is native to the Mediterranean and Black Sea regions, although it was cultivated in Palestine in ancient times. Dill was very well known in Pliny's time and many writers of the Middle Ages extolled its virtues. It has been grown in the United States for about a hundred and fifty years and today most of our cultivation of the plant is done in California.

Dill makes a beautiful addition to any garden and is to be considered a "must" for the herb gardener. It has smooth, hollow, branching stems that generally grow to a height of two to three feet and hold almost threadlike leaves. Numerous small yellow flowers appear in clusters around midsummer. Seeds are produced very freely and are flat in appearance. While the entire plant is extremely fragrant, the fragrant oil is in the seeds and they should be cleaned and dried with great care.

The dill seeds that are grown commercially do a creditable job but the fresh, home-cured seeds are even better. Another reason why the herb gardener should have dill high on his list is that the fragrant foliage loses much of its savor when dried. The fresh foliage can be harvested at any time.

Dill is famous the world over as a pickle ingredient, the largest single use for dill. It has been used for this purpose since the seventeenth century. In colonial days dill cakes were made for babies to chew on when they were teething because it purportedly had some soothing effect on the gums. It has been reported, too, that at one time dill was known as dilling or dulling because of its ability to soothe pain. This was probably just one facet of the medicinal stage that all of the better-known herbs went through.

Today there seems to be a growing interest in the use of the seeds, young leaves, and young stems for flavoring and seasoning a host of foods. The French have been the most ardent users of dill in cookery and they, of course, took the slight trouble to learn the specific "know-how" of its use. Dill, with its wondrous bouquet (when used sparingly), would very probably have been used on a vastly larger scale in cookery had not most people overused it in their first experience with it. The fresh, chopped foliage is excellent with most meat and fish dishes. Another use that should be mentioned here is that of flavoring soaps. For this, the oil is extracted from the seeds.

It is suggested that you plant dill in your herb garden at least for its ornamental value and fragrance until time permits a little experimenting in the kitchen. Try the young, fresh leaves in soups, sauces, and salads, first with other established herb combinations known to you. Later it should be possible to get the most out of this very aromatic plant in your own way.

Seed should be sown early in the spring, preferably in warm sandy soil and in a place that will allow full sunshine. The plant does not seem to care particularly for transplanting. For other data on this subject, see Chapter 12.

DILL SAUCE DE LUXE

1 cup mayonnaise
2 tablespoons vinegar
¼ teaspoon salt
1 tablespoon minced sweet pickles
½ teaspoon Worcestershire sauce
4 drops Tabasco sauce
½ teaspoon tarragon
1 teaspoon parsley
¼ teaspoon powdered mustard
1 tablespoon chopped fresh dill

Mix all ingredients thoroughly and serve from your prettiest sauce bowl with french fried shrimp or broiled fish.

DILL POTATO AND EGG SALAD

2 hard-boiled eggs
3 medium potatoes
1 medium dill pickle
1 medium onion
½ cup mild white vinegar
½ teaspoon salt
1 teaspoon sugar
¼ teaspoon pepper
1 teaspoon chopped fresh dill
½ cup mayonnaise
⅛ teaspoon paprika

Cook potatoes until tender. Cool. Cube potatoes. Chop eggs, pickle, and onion, add to cubed potatoes. Add vinegar, salt, sugar, pepper, and dill to mayonnaise. Blend well, pour over potatoes. Put into your favorite salad bowl. Sprinkle paprika over salad. Chill. Serves 4.

FENNELS
Foeniculum
of the carrot family

This great land of ours was blessed with three of the fennels.

While there are some minor differences among them, the most important attributes of each are common to all. As this is being written, a large plot of fennel is growing just outside the window. It is truly an inspiration to see its many divided leaflike structures, which give it an exquisite fernlike appearance. Here is a species native to southern Europe, although it was early found growing along all of the Mediterranean shores.

The fennels are really in the elegant class, since they possess all of the features required and desired by the herb gardener. These include fragrance and beauty in the garden, and by beauty we mean contrasting beauty that sets it apart from most of the other herbs but enables it to blend harmoniously with the over-all picture. The other features include the widespread uses for various parts of the fennel plant in cookery.

Since there are really three plants known generally as fennel, these are listed by their common names and botanical names as follows:

ORDINARY FENNEL (*Foeniculum vulgare*)—this is the common fennel of commerce that uses both the foliage and seeds for flavor. Common fennel will grow to a height of four to six feet.

SWEET FENNEL (*Foeniculum dulce*)—this is the one that is often called Florence fennel and even more often finochio. Sweet fennel, while in various characteristics very like ordinary fennel, grows only to about half the size of ordinary fennel. The fresh stalks of it are eaten to a large extent by the culinarily minded Italians just as we eat fresh celery.

ITALIAN FENNEL (*Foeniculum vulgare piperitum*)—this is the one that is not too well known in the United States but apparently it is readily available in any Italian market. It is used primarily for its fresh stalks. This particular variety has also been called Sicilian fennel or carosella.

The fennels go so far back into history that we have no record of the beginning of their use. Certainly they were among the first herbs to be used. Along with some of the other well-known and widely used herbs, they deserve to be called classics because actually it took something of a classical nature to survive the many misuses that were tied in with the herbs of old. Practically every well-known herb went through a long period of medicinal testing and it is quite remarkable to consider that even though in most cases they were found to be of minor medical value, they have maintained their place in the culinary arts.

For the herb gardener, the fennels are of the utmost importance. It has fragrance, flavor, beauty, and grace. They are delightfully and faintly anise-scented. Flower arrangers will find them very attractive, especially for church decorations.

There are some odd legends concerning fennel. Pliny said that before serpents cast off their old skins they ate fennel; he is also reported as saying that the juice of the fennel plant made the eyesight better; cures for cataracts on the eyes have been attributed to the roots of the fennel plant.

All of the fennels are easy to grow as annuals but they require a long growing season. For this reason most of the growth in the United States is in California. The foliage of sweet fennel and the young stalks of carosella are extremely popular in salads and in the preparation of hors d'oeuvres.

In addition to the medicinal value of the various fennel seeds, discriminating cooks use the seeds in breads, cakes, and pastries of all sorts. They are also used in sauces, in many soups, as a flavor for teas and for more ardent drinks like wines and anisette. The fennels are truly remarkable herbs that everyone should take advantage of.

OLD-FASHIONED APPLE PIE

6 tart apples
1 cup sugar
2 tablespoons flour
½ teaspoon chopped fresh sweet fennel
2 tablespoons butter

Peel apples and slice very thin. Combine sugar (brown sugar may be substituted for white sugar with wonderful results), flour, and fennel. Mix with the apples. Fill 9-inch pastry-lined pie pan. Dot with butter. Bake at 450° F. about 40 minutes. Serves 6.

FENNEL
FLOWER
Nigella sativa
of the buttercup
family

The fennel flower is one of the loveliest of all flowers, yet it is so versatile that it is not commonly associated with beauty. Nature has done a tremendous job in handling all connected parts properly, in bringing out and maintaining its exotic beauty, which has been spoken of as "youthful"! The chances are that it will remain, even unto its dried stage, exotic and beautiful.

The fennel flower is an Asiatic annual, welcomed by the horticulturist who is looking for the added touch of "true blue" streaming blossoms for the garden and flower arrangements. To further enhance this effect, imagine how the featherlike foliage on the fennel flower would look with this blue stream. Flower arrangers cannot help being inspired by this combination. The plant grows to a height of ten or twelve inches, which contributes to its versatility. The feathery foliage is made of very finely chiseled leaves that are fragile, greatly resembling ferns, the basis for many church arrangements.

The fennel flower is among the oldest known herbs. Among the ancient Romans it was very highly esteemed in cookery and this accounts for one of its common names, Roman coriander. The fennel flower is said to be the "Gith of Charlemagne" and the word comes from the Hebrew, *gesah*, which is mentioned in the Bible. Pliny makes frequent reference to it.

FEVERFEW
*Chrysanthemum
parthenium*
of the chrysanthe-
mum family

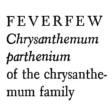

Fedderfew . . . feferfew . . . feberfew . . . and it was once supposed to be a valuable febrifuge, or abater of fever. Hence the name, which means to drive away. With its tender, torn, and jagged leaves and its double, white, miniature flowers full of pleasant pungence, feverfew is loved dearly by herb growers and is a "must" for flower arrangers. The fact that it flowers all summer long is a great bonus to both groups. It makes an excellent background plant and will grow in almost any kind of soil.

Gerard says, "It groweth in hedges, gardens, on old walls, it joyeth to grow among other odd places." He also says, "Feverfew is hot in the third degree and dry in the second, it clenseth, purgeth, and scoureth, and fully performeth all that bitter things can do. The fedderfew growing in my garden has a most pleasant flavour in respect of any of the rest."

Feverfew is a native of Europe and today there are three well-known types: golden ball, lemon ball, and snow ball. The snow ball is especially lovely when used with roses for artistic arrangements. All three of these perennials dry beautifully for winter bouquets.

GARLIC
Allium sativum
of the lily family

There is nothing subtle about garlic. Even the most cursory
thought of it evokes an almost overpowering flavor, a flavor that
is not fleeting. That's garlic. It is well to remember to chew a sprig
of parsley after eating foods seasoned with it. Like the guest who
stays on and on, well after bedtime, garlic has to be diplomatically
reminded that it is time to go; and parsley is the diplomat to handle
garlic.

It is a hardy plant with broad leaves, a sister or brother of the
onion and leek, all of the lily family. Garlic is a native of the south of
Europe where it is used at mealtime just as freely as we use salt.
Seasoning prepared from this herb comes from its pungent bulb,
which is made up of many smaller bulbs called cloves. Many varieties are found, some with white buds and some with red cloves.
There is one variety that is frequently called ramsons, the leaves of
which are used by Europeans as we use spinach or as the French
use sorrel. It is generally cooked in salted water containing butter
and a generous sprinkling of pepper. Although garlic's greatest contribution to mankind has been in putting the sparkle into food, it
has also been used as a medicine.

Garlic can be an attractive addition to the kitchen herb garden
with its showy dark green foliage and pink flowers. Bulbs can be
set in November and December or can be planted in the spring after

all signs of frost have passed. Plant as you would plant onion sets. By late summer, when the tops are dry, take up the entire plant from the ground and dry thoroughly. Then separate cloves and remove the outer skin and all roots. It is best to store in a dry place. Garlic seems to have been put on earth for a purpose that is tied to our purse strings, because it can put zest into the dullest, ghostlike particle of food.

GARLIC CLAM CRISPS DE BLANCHE

> 1 tablespoon butter
> 2 tablespoons finely chopped onion
> 1½ tablespoons flour
> ½ teaspoon Worcestershire sauce
> ¼ teaspoon minced garlic or
>   dash garlic salt
> 1 7½-ounce can minced clams
> 12 slices bread

Melt butter in small frying pan over low heat. Sauté onion 2 or 3 minutes, add flour, and blend. Stir in Worcestershire sauce and blend. Stir in garlic and clam juice. Cook until thick. Cool. Cut crusts from thin sandwich bread. Roll each slice flat with rolling pin and spread with garlic clam mixture. Roll like a jelly roll, cut in slices. Put on well-buttered cooky sheet. Brush with melted butter and bake at 450° F. until brown. Serve hot with cocktails. These may be frozen and baked as needed.

CHARCOAL-BROILED STEAK À LA ED AND BETTY

> 1 clove garlic
> 1 tablespoon salad oil
> 2 pounds flank steak
> ¼ teaspoon pepper
> 1 teaspoon salt

(over)

Prepare charcoal burner for cooking. Cut garlic clove in half and soak in salad oil. Using ½ clove garlic for each side of steak, rub steak with garlic. Sprinkle with pepper. Place steak on broiler for 5 minutes on one side, turn, pepper, and broil 5 minutes on this side. Carve crosswise in very thin slices. Salt to taste. *Do not salt before cooking,* or you will loose valuable juices. Five minutes' cooking time on each side is for medium-rare steak. Cook from 8 to 10 minutes on each side for well-done steaks. Serves 4 to 6.

GERANIUM-SCENTED LEAVES of the geranium family

Rose Geranium (*Pelargonium graveolens*)
Lemon Geranium (*Pelargonium limonseum*)

These are widely different-looking plants. The apple, citron, lemon, nutmeg, peppermint, rose, and many others make up this highly select group of scented geranium leaves. The rose- and lemon-scented geraniums are the ones most used for making fragrant bouquets, flower arrangements, and potpourris. The leaves are also used to flavor jellies and puddings.

ROSE
GERANIUM

From the Cape of Good Hope came this one and it will grow as high as four feet in warm climates. Stems are literally stabbed to death with the many branches on it. The leaves, yellow-green in color, are darker on top and lighter underneath. They are much divided, subdivided, and have soft short hairs rough to the touch. The flowers really steal the show with their lavender and pink hues that cannot be described.

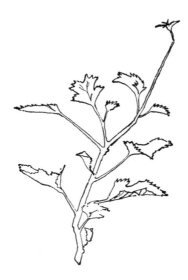

LEMON GERANIUM

The lemon geranium differs from the rose geranium in foliage pattern and flavor. Both reach upward about equally, and both are beautiful. The flowers are equally eye-pleasing and both bloom in June and July.

The rose- and lemon-scented geraniums are extremely ornamental when used as border plantings. For the cheerful and gay window box, these two will not fail you. For a fresh, clean scent and gay flowers, put a small arrangement on the breakfast table.

GERMANDER
Teucrium
chamaedrys
of the mint family

When growing this lovely perennial, you get the feeling that it
is growing especially for you because it is the flower of our
dreams and fills the gardens of our desires. I had the recent pleasure
of visiting a lovely paved terrace and fenced-in herb garden. Completely surrounding the terrace was a border of germander. In the
background bed were the taller herbs to complement the blue leather
on the wrought-iron chairs. In planting boxes on each side of the
kitchen door were chives, leeks, rocambole, and parsley for seasoning. On the wrought-iron-gate side were the sweet and fragrant rose
and lemon geraniums. This quaint garden was truly an herb garden
as it should be, but its focal point was the lush green border of
germander. Gerard says, "They floure and flourish from the end of
May to the later end of August." These flowers are reddish purple.
The plant has many curved stems and grows to eighteen inches in
height. Germander grows well in light sunny places in reasonably
good soil and is used for ornamental borders. It has many uses in the
field of medicine also.

Fragrance has been saved until the end here. It is magnificent,
with undertones and overtones of other members of the mint family.

HOP
Humulus lupulus
of the cannabinaceae
family

This fascinating plant never fails to bring back memories of my
childhood in Virginia; one in particular is of a hop vine near the
outdoor kitchen of one of the old homes. Every time my parents took
me to this place for a visit, my first stop was to say hello to my climbing friend with its pineapple-like cream-colored flowers. Without fail,
it would seem to be returning the greeting and at the same time trying
to pretty itself up. At the dinner table it would always come to me—
or at least part of it would—first as a flower bud in the salad; next
in fragrant, crusty loaves of bread.

Gerard gives this interesting description of the hop: "The Hop
doth live and flourish by embracing and taking hold of poles,
pearches, and other things upon which it climbeth. It bringeth forth
very long stalkes, rough, and hairie; also rugged leaves like those of
the Vine, or rather of Bryony, yet blackur and with fewer dented defi-
nitions; the floures hang downe by clusters from the tops of the
branches, puffed up, set as it were with seales like little canes or
sealed Pineapples of a whitish colour, tending to yellowness, strong
of smell: the roots are slender and diversely folded one within the
other." He also made the remark: "The hop joyeth in a fat and fruitful ground." Pliny mentioned hops among the prickle plants. He
said, "They are more toothsome than nourishing, for they yield but
very small nourishment."

The hop vine is a native of northern temperate zones and today the lupulus species is widely grown commercially for brewing. Only the female flowers are useful for this purpose and they form, in pairs, the conelike body that contains the lupulin so valuable in brewing. In the United States, New York and Oregon are the chief growing centers. Tasmania, the Australian island state, contributes largely to the world supply and eighty-seven per cent of its production comes from one place, the Derwent Valley. Here harvesting begins around the first of March and continues for six weeks or more. Family units make a gala occasion out of stripping the cones from vines up to eighteen feet in height, laughing and joking and making the work seem like play. Lunchtime is like a picnic. After stripping, the cones are stuffed into burlap bags and taken to oasthouses or kilns for drying.

The hop vine would make an interesting conversation piece in any herb garden.

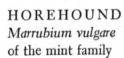

HOREHOUND
Marrubium vulgare
of the mint family

Horehound is a rare beauty in the herb garden—that is, for those who appreciate simple and uncomplicated lines and patterns. It should be a favorite with flower arrangers. When you look at the composite picture, the reasons become obvious.

The horehound plant pushes its way up to a height of about eighteen inches. It has very erect stems that are branchy and on these appear the toothed, grayish-green leaves, which are covered with a grayish-white down, smoother than velvet. The leaves are almost square and this should also excite the flower arranger's imagination. The plant bears beautiful white flowers in clusters that form whorls and spikes. The seeds are brown and have an oblong shape. It is a perennial, but a fresh sowing should be made after a few years, if at all possible, since the oil starts to lose quality as the plant becomes older. Seed should be sown in the early spring as soon as the soil can be worked. It does best in a poor soil and likes the sun. After it gets started, very little care is needed and no protection from cold weather need be given the horehound plant, as it is hardy. If the soil is too rich and moist, there will be less of the essential oil and it will be of poorer quality.

Horehound is one of the most unusual of the herbs still being used today in quantity in one way or another. It is unusual because it has touched historic, romantic, and adventurous chords down through the years; it dates back to the earliest times. It is also unusual in that it was widely used in cooking, though its use today in this field is limited to candies, used primarily for coughs and other mild respiratory ailments. Horehound, like practically all of our well-known herbs, has run the gantlet in the field of medicine.

It has been with us for a long time, and there appears to be no letup in the demand for its end-products, though it is not popular as it once was. Some of its past uses should be mentioned to demonstrate how popular it was years ago. A horehound drink was once made in Norfolk, England. Pliny said that it was a highly esteemed medicinal plant. Ancients believed that if it were put in milk and placed near flies it would kill them in one fell swoop. Long ago a snufflike material was made from the leaves. It was listed in Prince's catalogues in 1790, in Bartram's catalogue in 1814, and in the *American Herbal*, written by Stearns and published in 1801.

A popular author of many years ago listed the following recipe for horehound candy: "To one pint of a strong decoction of the leaves and stems or the roots, add eight or ten pounds of sugar. Boil to candy 'height' and pour into molds or small paper cases previously well dusted with finely powdered lump sugar, or pour on dusted marble slabs and cut into squares."

Bees are very partial to horehound nectar and a pleasant, top-quality honey is made from the flowers where they are abundant.

Undoubtedly, horehound is like many of our other formerly popular herbs and its successful use depends almost entirely upon the knowledge of how to use it. It should be used in minute quantities at first in conjunction with something sweet to buffer its bitterness. It is strange indeed that, with all the feeling against it, we still import sizable amounts each year.

HORSE-
RADISH
*Armoracia
rusticana*
of the mustard
family

Gerard says, "Horse Radish brings forth great leaves, long, broad, sharpe pointed, and snipt about the edges, of a deepe greene colour like those of the great garden Dock, (called of some, Monks Rubard, of others Patience) but longer and rougher. The stalk is slender and brittle, bearing at the top small white flowers; which being past, there follow small cods, wherein is the seed. The root is long and thick, white of colour, tast sharp, and very much biting the tongue like Mustard." Gerard also has an interesting statement that refers to the tendency of horse-radish to spread: "Divers thinke that this Horse Radish is an enemy to Vines and that the hatred between them is so great, that if the roots thereof be planted neere to the Vine, it bendeth backward from it, as not willing to have fellowship with it."

Horse-radish is a native of the ancient oriental world and of southeastern Europe, and while it is grown today for the large root only, it has been said that long before the roots were first used the leaves were cooked just as we cook collard greens.

For the discriminating gardener, Burpee says that horse-radish is easily grown in any good garden soil. One that is moist, fertile, deep, and medium heavy produces the largest and smoothest roots to grate for tender, pungent, stimulating flavor.

HORSE-RADISH AND CHEESE SANDWICHES

8 slices whole wheat bread
½ cup butter
½ cup mild spreading cheese
4 teaspoons fresh grated or bottled
    horse-radish

Spread bread with butter, top with cheese and top cheese with horse-radish. Butter each side and toast. Serve with baked beans. Makes 8 sandwiches.

HYSSOP
Hyssopus
officinalis
of the mint family

Glamor and enchantment are built into the name "hyssop."
There is still a tendency to hold the name almost in awe, for a number of reasons, one of which is frequent reference to it in biblical writings, even though scholars are convinced that the hyssop we know today is not the same. Enough confusion still surrounds the matter to add to the intrigue.

Hyssop is one of our oldest herbs from the standpoint of wide-spread use. Many famous ancient authors wrote about it romantically, medicinally, and culinarily. It is a beautiful evergreen native to the Mediterranean regions and was grown by the ancients and by medieval populations primarily for its use in medicine and to a lesser extent for its ornamental effect and use in cookery. Hyssop in most regions will grow to a height of eighteen to twenty-four inches. It has smooth stems; the terminal spikes contain the entire leaves and hold small clusters of blue flowers. There are also pink (or red) and white forms but it might be advisable for the herb gardener to stick to the blue-flowered variety as it is supposed to be hardier. Here is one of the few herbs that seems to thrive best in partial shade; if the soil is too rich the plant will have a lush growth but the aromatic qualities drop off sharply. The seeds retain their viability for about three years. It is best to sow the seeds in early spring and transplant in early summer. If planting very much, sow the seed about six inches apart and in rows eighteen inches between.

Hyssop today is not used as extensively as in the past in cookery but this is due primarily to the vagaries of human nature and taste. The stems, foliage, and flowers are all highly aromatic and have a hot, bitter taste, but it is this very bitterness of the oil that can enhance foods so much when used sparingly and adroitly. Almost everyone tends to use an overdose of herb seasonings, and this seems to be the case particularly with hyssop. The monks in Europe use the oil in flavoring sauces and soups. In some sections of Europe the oil is extracted commercially (one pound of oil from five hundred pounds plant) and used in toilet article preparations.

You will enjoy hyssop in your herb garden and chances are great that, in addition to the fragrance and beauty you will enjoy outside, you will learn the artistry of using various parts of the plant in cookery, if you remember that a little bit goes a long, long way.

LAVENDER
Lavandula spica
of the mint family

> At arms, each spikèd shrub doth stand
> In couple-colored gallantry,
> Taught to submit before commands,
> Yields now a soft perfumery.

> JON BRADSHAW

Here are fragrance and beauty galore that are a part of almost
every landscape design, whether it be around the house, in the
flower garden, or in the herb garden. Lavender is one of the most
wondrous products of nature. It has enjoyed a tremendous popularity
down through the ages just for its fragrance and beauty, although at
one time in the dim past it was put to the test in cookery, but to no
avail. It is a fairly hardy perennial that is native to the dry upland
regions of southern Europe.

As to its appearance in the garden, compact clumps up to two
and one half feet are formed and there are numerous erect stems
with small gray leaves above which slender square flower stems arise.
There is a multitude of violet-blue spiky flowers. Lavender does best
in light, limy or chalky soil and it is well to remember that, if grown

in rich soil, the plant grows larger but the flowers lack the very fragrance for which lavender is so famous.

There has been some confusion in the past in naming lavender. There are some who call *Lavandula vera* the true lavender. This same lavender has also been called *Lavandula officinalis, Lavandula augustifolia,* and *Lavandula spica.* All of the lavenders grow wild in the southern part of France, Spain, Italy, Corsica, and Sicily. There are, of course, many other varieties of lavender, which will not be mentioned here since it would only tend to add to the confusion that already exists.

Lavender with its fantastic history and background is a natural plant for legend. In this connection, it is said that in Tuscany lavender is used to protect little children from the evil eye, and in North Africa it is said that the Kabyle women believe lavender protects them from mistreatment by their husbands.

The name is derived from the Latin word *lavo,* which means to wash; a distillation of the flowers was used in ancient times to perfume water for washing the body. Today the United States alone imports over a quarter of a million pounds of oil of lavender each year, practically all of which goes into the preparation of toilet waters. The oil is distilled from fresh flowers, the most aromatic part of the plant. Since the entire plant contains the oil, the scent of lavender grown in the garden can be preserved simply by drying the young foliage and flowering tops. The best of all lavender perfumes are made in England, where the oil is extracted from cultivated plants. In France the oil is distilled from wild plants. It is thought that *Lavandula vera* produces the best oil for perfumery. An interesting aspect of the use of lavender in perfumery is the fact that, the deeper the color of the calyx, the stronger the fragrance. It is said that the yield of oil from sixty flowering spikes of lavender amounts to only one ounce and in England, where the best oil is produced, it is said that twenty-five pounds of oil can be expected from one acre of cultivated plants.

The word "lavender" seems to me to encompass all of the things we know about the plant: lavender means fresh, lovely, lasting, fragrant scent for the herb garden, beauty that is almost awe-inspiring, and flower-fresh linens, sachets, potpourris, and nosegays.

LEEK
Allium porrum
of the lily family

To tender palates and taste buds, leek is more pleasing than onion. It is one of the milder members of the lily family and it is for this very mildness that leek is growing more and more toward king-size stature in the field of cookery.

It originated in central Asia, followed by cultivation in western Asia and Mediterranean lands. It is mentioned frequently in the Bible, which states how, during the wanderings of the Israelites in the wilderness, they longed for the onion, leek, and garlic they had had in Egypt. It has been in common use all over Europe for as long as there is a record of plants, and by 1775 leek was in cultivation by the native Indians and early colonists of America.

The name comes from the Anglo-Saxon word *leac;* the Romans called it *porrum,* and they considered that the best leeks came from Egypt. Nero had a tremendous appetite for leek and it is said that he was named *porrophagus* because of it. Strangely enough, Nero was of the opinion that leek improved his voice. Leek is so famous that it is the national emblem of Wales. There was a time in the Middle Ages when leek and garlic both were more popular than the onion, but now, of course, the reverse is true.

The stems of the leek generally grow to a height of two to two and one half feet. They are flat and solid as compared to those of the onion, which are round and hollow. Like the onion, too, leek forms a true bulb and in one reliable reference book it is described as having a bulbous, cylindrical root and long, broad succulent leaves. It likes a rich soil containing plenty of humus, and while it can be grown from a seed bed with later transplanting, it is more easily grown from young bulbs or "sets."

The bulb and the base, which is usually blanched by having soil heaped about it continually, are the parts of leek used in salads and to give a wonderful flavor to stews. It can be used to great advantage in anything for which onion flavor is a bit too strong. In fact many people have become so accustomed to the milder flavor of leek that they do not think in terms of onion any more. Now it is leek and more leek.

For those who may be interested, there is a wild leek, an American plant known as *Allium tricoccum.*

LEMON VERBENA
Lippia citriodora
of the verbena
family

Lemon verbena, unlike most of the other herbs, is not a hardy plant and cannot stand cold winters. It has so much to offer, however, that it is still worth while to have even in the colder areas of the country where it will be necessary to transplant it from the ground to a pot or a small tub during the months of frost and snow. From Virginia south, there seems to be no need for such protection.

Lemon verbena is a native of the Argentine, Chili, and Peru. It first reached Europe in 1784 and has become naturalized there, especially in the southern portions. It is also grown in many other sections of the world, such as India and South Africa.

The plant is unusual in its over-all appearance. The stems are woody and branching with a slight downy effect and in places one will find marks of red. The leaves are pointed, light yellow-green in color, with an oblong shape, very shiny above and dull below. The underside is rough to the touch. It is such a fragrant plant that, when brushed against even slightly, an odor of lemon emanates from it. It has a very long blooming season and you will find flowers in both summer and autumn. They are small and arranged in spikes with colors of white and purple intermixed. Some have said that they are not especially decorative but they are pleasant to look at. The plant is one of the tallest herbs, at times growing to a height of as much as ten feet, although in most cases it averages from four to six feet in height.

Because of the nature of the plant, lemon verbena is commonly thought of as a pot plant and is grown primarily for its fine and delicate lemon fragrance. However, it does have some culinary value in teas and fruit drinks. Oils extracted from the leaves are also used in perfumery.

LOVAGE
Levisticum
officinale
of the carrot family

Like angelica, lovage was one of the first "wonder drugs," according to the quaint expostulations in John Gerard's *Herball.* Its use today, however, is primarily in the confectionery field, where the young stems are handled like those of angelica; these candied stems are delightful.

Lovage is an unusual-looking plant that could be the conversation piece of your herb garden. It is a hardy perennial and native to the Mediterranean region. It has dark green shining leaves with a

"different" look about them, usually divided into two or three segments. Close to the top, the hollow, erect stems divide to form
whorled branches on which appear bundles of beautiful yellow
flowers during the blooming season. The fruits (or seeds) are hollow and highly aromatic.

Seeds can be planted in either fall or spring and preferably in
rich moist soil. You can look at one of the suggested landscape patterns in Chapter 12 to see how and where lovage will fit into your
plans for the future. There are still many culinary delights locked
in the "safe for exciting tastes," waiting for someone to discover the
right combination. You may be that person.

POT
MARIGOLD
Calendula officinalis
of the Compositae
family

This gem of the garden is considered by some the showiest and
most decorative plant in the herb garden. Its beauty is so outstanding that it is in a class by itself. Growing to a height of twelve
to eighteen inches, the plant has graceful lines, sweetness, and
spiciness.

The pot marigold is native to Asia and southern Europe but
has grown in this country since the time of the earliest settlers. Its
stems are furry, deep dark green, and many-leaved. The leaves are
soft and long, sometimes reaching six inches in length. The flowers
put on a dazzling show, with blossoms opening all summer long and
most abundant in the fall, long after the first frosts. The blossoms
are yellow and orange, with round flat tops, and they are velvety to
the touch. Many rows of ray florets, some yellow and some deep
orange, surround the ones making up the center disc, and—most
unusual—they have no scent. This tender annual grows readily from
seed if you wait until warm weather has definitely arrived before

sowing. Two sowings can be made in most sections, one in the spring and one about July first, so that two harvests can be made.

Uses for the pot marigold include seasoning, coloring for butter, and a replacement for saffron. There are some who claim that it has no flavor, since it has no scent, while others claim that it has flavor if you know how to use it and even go so far as to claim that the tastiest marigolds are those with the deepest orange color.

MARJORAMS of the mint family

Sweet Marjoram (*Marjorana hortensis*)
Pot Marjoram (*Origanum vulgaris*)

SWEET
MARJORAM

Of all herbs that have been known to date, sweet marjoram is near the top of the popularity list. It is probably the most popular of all savories and there are innumerable recipes that call for its use. In addition, it is certainly one of the most fragrant herbs to have in the garden. The plant is extremely attractive, being of dainty texture, as smooth as velvet, and having tiny green balls hanging from the stems like ornaments on a Christmas tree. The flowers come from these tiny balls.

Sweet marjoram is native to the Mediterranean region and has been known and used for many centuries. In the warmer climates it grows as a perennial, but because of its inability to cope with frost and snow, it has to be grown as an annual in the colder climates. At various times through the ages sweet marjoram has been acclaimed for almost every imaginable use in the fields of beauty, fragrance, flavor, and medicine. At one time it was thought that it had the power to keep fresh milk sweet, which accounts for the first part of the name "sweet marjoram." Many legends are connected with sweet marjoram. On the isle of Crete it was the symbol of honor, and it has been reported that at one time in Sicily it was thought to possess the gift of banishing sadness. In India it is said to be sacred to Siva and Vishnu. Having survived many centuries of medicinal testing, sweet marjoram has found its widest acceptance as an important cooking aid.

When one is close to nature and its complex "simplicity," it seems natural to think of it as being made up of billions of manufacturing plants. In the case of the herbs, each one is a tiny manufacturing plant specializing in the production of oils that we call essential oils. These oils determine the use and acceptability of the herbs, and the essential oil in sweet marjoram is one of nature's finest. Large quantities of it are imported into the United States every year. It has a host of uses, including some in medicine and others in perfumery, toilet preparations, and soaps.

As far as the herb gardener is concerned, it is the leaf of the sweet marjoram plant that is of the greatest importance. When the leaves are fresh, their fragrance and flavor are an unusual combination of sharpness and pleasant aromatic bitterness, with perhaps an overtone of camphor. Dried leaves are more subdued and the fragrance and flavor are more reminiscent of perfume.

There is scarcely a more colorful herb to add beauty to any garden. The main stem of the plant is a brownish purple in most areas, while the side branches have a reddish tint. These stems will normally grow to a height of twelve inches. The leaves are really the most beautiful part of the plant, since they are soft-textured, greenish gray in color, rather small, and covered with a beautiful down. The flowers are rather inconspicuous but also present a most unusual appearance. They are white or cream in color and seem to creep out a leaf one at a time from a container that might be likened to a sea shell or a cocoon.

The culinary uses of sweet marjoram are so numerous that they cannot be listed here singly but it is the perfect seasoning for chicken and turkey stuffings, and mushrooms taste very different when cooked with the right amount of sweet marjoram. Many people who find sage, our most widely used herb today, a little too flavorful for them turn to sweet marjoram for poultry stuffing. Recently I learned about its use in sweet fritters made with spinach in Italy. It is also an excellent garnish for salads and is very good when used as a salad green.

Sweet marjoram, either alone or with other herbs and spices, is widely utilized by food producers.

No herb garden should be without sweet marjoram. You will find that it is ideal as a facer plant for any semiformal or informal garden. It is also ideal as a border plant or edging. Once you are accustomed to the wondrous delights of sweet marjoram, you will find that a larger space than anticipated will be needed to grow it.

There seems to have been some confusion in the botanical naming of sweet marjoram. According to one author in the field of herbs, some dealers offer seeds under the old but incorrect name of *Origanum marjorana*. It has been pointed out that the Latin name, *Origanum*, belongs to the perennial pot marjoram and only confusion results when it is applied to the sweet marjoram.

POT MARJORAM

This plant is often referred to as wild marjoram. It is a true perennial and a native of Europe. Although sweet marjoram seems to have been in the spotlight for centuries, pot marjoram was probably known and used for quite some time before sweet marjoram came on the scene.

It has gone through all of the trials and tribulations suffered by other widely used, well-known herbs and seems to have survived in good fashion. At one time it was used or at least tried for just about every imaginable dish and ailment. Pliny wrote at great length on its medicinal uses. Today, pot marjoram finds its widest use in

Latin American soups, vegetables, and meats. One important feature of pot marjoram should be remembered at all times by the cook: the fragrant oil in the leaves of pot marjoram is very strong-tasting and therefore must be used sparingly and with discrimination. Gradually you will develop a feel for its use.

The plant is a pleasing one that grows to a height of two to two and one half feet, has an abundance of aromatic leaves, and in July bears flowers in flat-topped clusters that have a pink to purplish tint. Pot marjoram lends itself to indoor growing, and is especially pretty in the kitchen window box or as a potted herb.

MAY
APPLE
Podophyllum
peltatum
of the barberry
family

Here is an herb that really calls for attention, because it is one of the very few that is native to America. It is an unusual plant in many respects and has stood in high esteem since ancient times. It should fill a shady corner in your herb garden or an especially cool moist place in the wild-flower garden.

The shield-shaped leaves and single white cuplike flower make it an interesting plant to watch. The umbrellalike leaves are said to unfurl only during April showers, as if to protect its lovely white blossoms. In July it bears a sweet, many-sided fruit resembling a lemon. It has been known as the mandrake and wild lemon, but without a doubt the name "May apple" fits it best. May apple grows to a height of about one to one and one half feet and its leaves sometimes measure twelve inches across. The leaves are on flowerless stems, coming from separate rootstock, and are a dark green above and a light green below. The fruit generally measures about two inches in length. This is the only edible part of the plant.

The sweet fruit has been used for making preserves, just as we use the ground cherry. An old formula for the mild May apple was to boil slowly with peppers and other hot spices.

Pioneers and woodsmen found the fruit refreshing but were warned against eating any other part of the plant. They were asked to mark well the locations where the plants grew for the qualified herbalist, as their virtues were many in the field of medicine.

Strange effects are supposed to be inherent in the May apple, or mandragora, later to be called mandrake. In biblical times Rachel desired philters made from the ground dried roots of this loved plant, which resembled the male and female form. It was said to cause women to be fruitful and bear children. We are told that young Reuben, son of Leah, brought home the plants for their beauty and the fruits for the sake of their sweet smell. There is a legend that says May apple is to be found only in the shadow of the gallows, or where a life has been lost. It was supposed to spring up in profusion to restore vigor, or help to maintain life. This must have been one of the reasons why John Bartram called Virginia a "Garden of Eden," on his trek through the virgin territory, which was filled with the wonderful bounties of nature.

The ancients knew the plant well from the Mediterranean region. It is found more generally in the Blue Ridge and Appalachian Mountains. The May apple is said to be found as far south as the Gulf of Mexico and west into Minnesota and Texas in the United States of America.

MINTS of the mint family

   Peppermint (*Mentha piperita*)
   Spearmint (*Mentha spicata*)
   Apple Mint (*Mentha rotundifolia*)

The mint bed was a "must" for the landed gentry and plantation owners. Mints made a cool, refreshing contribution to the way of life at that time as they do to our modern way of living. Peppermint, spearmint, and apple mint are grouped together here because they make up a compatible mint bed. They are grown this way in my herb garden; they are also among the most widely used members of the important mint family.

PEPPER-
MINT

Peppermint is native to Europe but has been naturalized in the United States to such an extent that it will grow well in almost any moist garden. This plant should be included in a mint bed because it possesses fragrance, flavor, and beauty. Its fragrance is more delicate than that of spearmint because the menthol present in the peppermint plant, the main constituent found in oil of peppermint, is responsible for the more cooling and stimulating flavor. The plant is a handsome one, with branching stems up to three feet in length which do not stand erect but curve outward. The stems are on the reddish side and the tips are often entirely red. The leaves are a deep green, numerous, spear-shaped, and have toothed edges. Cylindrical spikes of beautiful rosy lavender flowers appear toward the end of July and remain through August.

With its great importance since the earliest days of recorded history, it is natural that ancient scholars should have described mint. Many unusual claims were made for it. Pliny said that mint stimulates the brain and therefore students should wear a crown of mint while studying. He also advised sprinkling the room with vervain water, to make guests merry at a dinner party, because in the language of flowers the vervain signifies "enchantment."

Peppermint is important commercially as the source of oil of peppermint, which is distilled from the plants. Plucked from the mint bed, the leaves will give you an almost endless source of pleasant coolness in most any beverage, including plain water. In flavor and fragrance, it dominates all other herbs used as teas. Peppermint tea is good either hot or iced; it should not be made too strong. A hot cup of tea in the middle of the afternoon, together with a few crisp gingersnaps, is very refreshing.

SPEAR-
MINT

If there is to be a mint bed, then there must be spearmint. This is the mint that makes the kitchen more fragrant and full of flavor. A native of Europe, it has often been referred to as curly-leaf mint. It is a little lower growing than peppermint and is a more compact plant. The stems, like those of peppermint, curve outward and do not stand erect. The leaves are smaller than *Mentha piperita*, more crinkly, and tend to fold up within themselves. They are in opposite pairs and the edges are indented to give a pointed effect. The flowers are off-white and generally arrive late in July.

The spearmint plant is also important commercially. The extracted oil is used to flavor chewing gums, soaps, and dental preparations. It is best known in the kitchen, where it is used in a host of ways. No cook needs to be reminded of its value in UNIVERSAL MINT SAUCE for the traditional leg of lamb, in drinks, and in salads. It is also very popular for fruit cups, various confections, and french dressing for a macedoine of fruit. Many prefer it in iced beverages. It goes well with dainty sandwiches.

Another pleasing feature of the spearmint plant is that when it is dried it has tints and tones of red and bronze and can be used nicely for winter arrangements in copper containers.

APPLE
MINT

There are many other well-known members of the mint family, but apple mint has been selected because it illustrates a different portion of the over-all mint picture. Apple mint blends, in a most unusual way, fragrance and flavor reminiscent of all that is good in fruit, with the mellowness of the apple and overtones of pleasant mintiness. It is a beautiful plant that will generally grow to a height of eighteen inches. It is a soft plant, with more down on the stems than on the leaves, which are greenly cool in appearance. It has lovely creamy flower spikes. One of the most attractive features of apple mint is that the erect stems are not crowded with leaves. For the flower arranger it could be a real gem in the soft luster of pewter containers.

APPLE ALE

½ *cup sugar*
1 *cup water*
18 *sprigs apple mint*
4 *lemons*
1 *quart ginger ale*

Boil sugar and water until sugar is dissolved. Remove from heat and add 10 sprigs apple mint. Chill. Add the juice of 4 lemons and strain. After filling mint julep glasses with crushed ice, add ½ cup apple ale and fill to top with ginger ale. Add sprig of apple mint and serve. Serves 4.

MINTED CUCUMBER CONSERVE

> 1 cup peeled, diced cucumbers
> ¾ cup crushed canned pineapple
> ¾ cup lemon juice
> ¾ cup apple juice
> 5 cups sugar
> 4 drops green food coloring
> 1½ teaspoons mint flavoring
> 1 bottle fruit pectin
> ½ cup chopped walnuts

Combine cucumbers, pineapple, lemon juice, apple juice, and sugar in large kettle. Stir well and bring to full rolling boil for 1 minute, stirring constantly. Add coloring and mint flavoring. Remove from heat. Stir in pectin, skim, and stir for 5 minutes. Add walnuts. Put in scalded jars or glasses and cover with ⅛ inch hot paraffin. Makes 8 8-ounce glasses. Serve with lamb.

UNIVERSAL MINT SAUCE

> ½ cup chopped mint
> ⅔ cup mild white vinegar
> 3 tablespoons sugar

Wash mint before stripping leaves from the stalks. Dry thoroughly, chop finely, and add vinegar and sugar. Put in a crockery jar and let stand overnight. Be sure sugar is dissolved. Serve with roast leg of lamb.

MUSTARDS of the mustard family

Black or Brown Mustard (*Brassica nigra*)
White or Yellow Mustard (*Brassica alba*)

Mustard has been known to man since prehistoric times, long before anyone discovered that the addition of either turmeric or saffron to prepared mustard gives it that very eye-appealing yellow color and delightful flavor. So people then must have eaten mustards that we probably would not look at a second time.

Jesus mentioned mustard at least twice: "If ye have faith as a grain of mustard seed, ye shall say unto this mountain, remove hence unto yonder place and it shall remove." He also said, "The kingdom of God . . . is like a grain of mustard seed."

BLACK OR
BROWN
MUSTARD

The black or brown mustard with its tall-growing stalks (sometimes up to four feet high) and small yellow flowers was used in medieval times in concocting love potions, but long before that Pliny had recommended it "to overcome lassitude in females."

WHITE OR YELLOW MUSTARD

The white mustard is the one so much used in the herb garden for its young foliage, which has always been a favorite for salads.

Mustard originally came from Europe and southwestern Asia. Today we grow large quantities of it in this country and import the rest of our supply from Canada, Denmark, the United Kingdom, and the Netherlands.

Prepared mustard, as we know it now, is a comparatively recent thing, according to one writer. It was first mixed a few hundred years ago by a woman in Durham, England, from the ground seeds of wild mustard.

NASTURTIUM
Tropaeolum minus
of the Tropaeolum
family

Think for a while about those herbs that are most precious to you. Wouldn't you be apt to put the generous nasturtium at the top of the list? It offers much in ways that have seldom been equaled.

If there is to be a garden at all, whether it be a flower garden or an herb garden, there must be nasturtium. It can be called one of the classic herbs, for it fulfills the requirements of any gardener: it has fragrance and beauty in the garden and fragrance and flavor in the kitchen. These are the true measuring sticks that determine whether or not an herb belongs in the select classical group.

Coming originally from the Andes of Peru where only pure, clean, soft air prevailed, this annual fills the surrounding atmosphere with a fragrance so magnificently elegant and penetrating that its name, "nasturtium," describes its ability to make the nostril quiver and twist: from the words *nasus* (nose) and *torquere* (to twist) came nasturtium, the "nose twister."

Wherever you find a temperate climate you will find the nasturtium. There are two types: *Tropaeolum majus*, which grows very tall, and *Tropaeolum minus*, the low-growing, less space-taking, more abundantly flowering type. It is the latter one that is described here. It grows to a height of twelve inches normally, with leaves that tend to be round, smooth, and lighter green underneath than on top. It has very conspicuous flowers that range in color from yellow through orange to dark red. The entire plant is covered lightly with down and gives off a spicy fragrance.

The nasturtium is so easily grown that nothing special need be said here, except that if you use soil that is too rich you will have mostly foliage and very few buds and blossoms! You will find very simple growing instructions on the Growing Charts in Chapter 12.

The flowers are so eye-pleasing that one tends to lose sight of the many culinary uses for the foliage, seeds, flowers, buds, and pods. Everything but the root is used in the culinary field. The young tender stems and leaves are extremely succulent in salads, the chopped young leaves are very tasty in sandwiches, the blossoms enhance fruit salads, and minced blossoms can be blended into creamed butter or cheese for use as a spread. The unripe and still green seeds with their peppery taste are the zestful part of the plant and are used as substitutes for the exotically flavored capers. The unopened flower buds are peppery like the seeds and find wide use in many dishes. Try a single seed in a cup of tea for a real taste thrill!

PICKLED NASTURTIUM PODS

> 1 *pint nasturtium pods*
> 1 *clove bud*
> 1 *allspice bud*
> ¼ *teaspoon mace*
> 1 *tablespoon olive oil*
> ½ *teaspoon freshly grated horse-radish*
> 2 *cups mild white vinegar*
> ¼ *teaspoon salt*

Pick only plump, green, well-filled nasturtium pods. Wash and set aside. Place clove, allspice, mace, olive oil, and horse-radish in pottery container; heat vinegar and salt. Then add pods to spices. Pour vinegar over all ingredients and let marinate for 24 hours. Use as you would use capers over stuffed tomatoes or sea-food salads.

ORÉGANO
Origanum vulgare
virens
of the mint family

This is the merry herb of old Spain that has a hot, biting taste but a sweet smell. It is a native of the Mediterranean area and has been naturalized in North America. Orégano is the Spanish name for marjoram—though the flavor is stronger and has a pleasantly bitter undertone.

Gerard said this about organy (as he spelled it): "These plants grow wild in Spaine, Italy, and other hot countries. The first of these I found growing in divers and Chalky fields and high-waies neere unto Sittingburne and Rochester in Kent, and also neere unto Cobham House and Southfleet in the same country." It has been said that in Pliny's time orégano was known as the "joy of the mountain" or "goates marjoram."

It has lavender clustered flower heads that bloom in August and deep green leaves that dry to a lovely light green color. This perennial generally will grow to a height of eighteen to twenty-four inches. Italy, France, Greece, Chile, and Mexico supply us the dried leaves. It is also available in crushed and ground forms.

Orégano should be numbered among the many other wonderful spices on our shelves and used in tomato dishes, mushroom dishes, with beef, lamb, pork, and chicken. It is also used in soups, sauces, and French dressing. You will find additional uses for orégano in the Herb Chart in Chapter 11.

ORÉGANO PORK MEXICANA

> *2 pounds fresh pork tenderloin*
> *1 clove garlic*
> *½ teaspoon orégano*
> *½ cup salad oil*
> *½ cup ripe olives*
> *½ cup seedless raisins*
> *½ cup green peppers*
> *1 cup tomato purée*
> *2 teaspoons salt*
> *1 teaspoon chili powder*
> *¼ teaspoon cayenne pepper*
> *2 tablespoons flour*
> *2 cups water*
> *½ teaspoon cumin seed*

Rub pork tenderloin with crushed garlic and orégano. Brown pork on each side in salad oil. Slice ripe olives, then add to the pork with raisins, green peppers, tomato purée, salt, chili powder, and cayenne pepper. Mix flour in ¾ cup water, stir into pork pan gently. Add remaining water and stir until smooth. Put into oven and bake until pork is tender. Before serving sprinkle generously with cumin seed. Serves 4 to 6.

PARSLEY
*Petroselinum
crispum*
of the carrot family

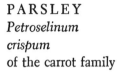

This is one of the oldest known herbs and records indicate that it has been under cultivation for at least two thousand years. It is native to the Mediterranean; Bartram, in his *American Herbal*, stated that it came to the Americas in the seventeenth century. Theophrastus described both the crowded, dense, curly-leaf type and the open-growing type as early as the fourth century. During the first century the Romans were familiar with the plain and curled types. They wore parsley in chaplets around their necks to ward off intoxication. Both Greeks and Romans knew it well for its fresh fragrant beauty as a garnish and for its wonderful flavor. It is probably the best known of all the herbs. This is borne out by the fact that it has long received endorsement from the gardening world and history and legend are full of stories about this ancient plant.

Parsley is easily grown and no kitchen garden should be without it. The flat-leaved varieties are known to contain more vitamins and iron than the curly-leaved types, but for beautiful garnishing and exotic edging for herb borders, I recommend the Emerald, sometimes called the curled dwarf, because it is a frilly queen in the garden. Since the seeds are very slow to germinate, I have successfully mixed parsley and radish seeds and sown them in the radish bed. As the radishes grow, they will shade the soil and help the little parsley plants get started. After the radishes have been harvested, the parsley will not have to be thinned out.

Parsley has many uses, not only for garnishes, but for soups, stews, sauces, salads, and on and on. Don't forget to chew a sprig of parsley after eating food seasoned with garlic so you will be more acceptable to your friends! Please remember to take every possible advantage of the many uses of health-giving parsley.

PARSLEY BROILED FILLETS

> 12 *fish fillets*
> 2 *cups milk*
> 12 *tiny white onions*
> 12 *fresh mushrooms*
> 1 *green pepper*
> 8 *tablespoons butter*
> 2 *tablespoons flour*
> 1 *pint heavy cream*
> ¼ *teaspoon white pepper*
> ½ *teaspoon paprika*
> ½ *cup chopped fresh parsley*

Poach fillets in 1 cup milk until tender and set aside. Cook onions, mushrooms, and green pepper in 2 teaspoons butter until tender. Make white sauce with 4 tablespoons butter, 2 tablespoons flour, 1 cup milk, and 1 pint cream. Flake fillets. Put onions, mushrooms, and green pepper in a well-greased casserole, then add flaked fillets and white sauce. Dot with remaining butter, sprinkle with pepper, paprika, and parsley. Place under the broiler until the top is a golden brown. A delightful dish with a velvet touch!

PARSLEY PARTY PÂTÉ

> 1 *envelope plain gelatin*
> 1 *can beef consommé (undiluted)*
> 2 *cans liver pâté*
> ½ *teaspoon Tabasco sauce*
> ¼ *teaspoon minced garlic*
> ½ *teaspoon Worcestershire sauce*
> 2 *teaspoons chopped parsley*

Dissolve gelatin in warm consommé by placing saucepan over low heat and stirring until gelatin is completely dissolved. Pour into small mold or bowl and chill in the refrigerator until set—about 2 hours. Combine pâté, Tabasco sauce, garlic, Worcestershire, and parsley. Remove bowl of gelatin from refrigerator and scoop out center of gelatin, leaving about ¼ inch gelatin around sides and on bottom. Put gelatin in saucepan. Pack pâté mixture carefully into mold. Melt gelatin removed from the mold over low heat; cool and pour over top of pâté; chill until completely firm. To unmold, set bowl in warm water briefly to loosen, invert plate over top, then turn. Serve with crackers. Garnish with ripe olives, radish roses, carrot sticks, and water cress. Scrumptious!

PENNYROYAL
Mentha pulegium
of the mint family

Whether it's pennie royall, pudding grass, or pennyroyal, here is royalty . . . although one does not generally associate a penny with royalty. Here is royalty that loves the hillsides, and the sunny roadsides, and the meadows. Pennyroyal also loves moist creek banks —hardly the natural habitats of a prince, but certainly those of a roaming vagabond prince. And what a merry prince he is! He is actually a native of Europe and portions of Asia but now has become a good-will ambassador with the world for his domain. He roams about, generally acting himself, but at other times disguised as a dusty beggar or a country urchin . . . and in fact he has been called an urchin by some unknowing people. He seems to prefer anonymity, seldom calling attention to himself . . . yet he is most certainly a part of the herb picture.

Pennyroyal has square prostrate stems that will readily take root at the nodes; these stems bear grayish-green, almost round leaves. The slightly hairy or fuzzy leaves hold whorled clusters of little lilac-blue flowers, which rise in tiers, one above the other, at the nodes. They bloom from June to August.

As I mentioned earlier, my father was a timber surveyor and contractor, and itinerant timbermen and lumberjacks of many nationalities were always coming from and going to places all over the globe. One of my earliest memories is of how they gathered the merry little pennyroyal to put into their straw ticks (mattresses for their beds), which had been made from new-harvested straw. I remember that they also scattered it all over the floors of their bunkhouses to keep fleas away. We have used it in recent years in straw beds for our collie dogs and found that it does repel fleas.

Pennyroyal is yours for many uses. When horseback riding with our father, he would have us put bunches of pennyroyal in the bridles of our horses to keep flies from annoying them, he also had us crush the leaves in our hands and then rub our faces to keep the gnats from biting when we went fishing with him. Remember that it is the small mint in the garden, is a fairly hardy perennial, and has been cultivated commercially in Europe for the high-quality aromatic oil that it yields. At one time twelve pounds of oil per acre of pennyroyal was considered a good yield. Although peppermint and spearmint seem to have a pleasanter flavor, pennyroyal can also contribute to foods and beverages when used sparingly. The leaves, green or dried, have gone into many tasty puddings and sauces prepared by our ancestors in days long past. They could still if only the gardeners, especially the junior gardeners, would cultivate the acquaintance of this aromatic prince of the mint family. Prince or urchin, it matters not, pennyroyal has been with us a long, long time . . . and we hope that he will be around for a much longer time.

PEPPER
TABASCO
*Capsicum
frutescens*
of the potato family

Here is the hottest of all peppers! It is so hot that it seems as though the seed and plant cannot get the hotness out of their systems quickly enough . . . because they bear fruit prolifically, and the fruit does not grow on the stem of the plant but nearly erect on the branches so that it can be easily gathered. Once off the plant, this pepper tabasco holds its own against the world with no trouble whatsoever. Practically all of these peppers go into the making of Tabasco brand pepper sauce. "Tabasco" is a Mexican word meaning "land where the soil is humid." Cortez stopped at Tabasco on his way to Mexico for the first time. It was there that he saw the Mayans using the small, red, hot peppers with such apparent delight. Woe to the unfortunate person who does not know that these peppers must be partaken of sparingly!

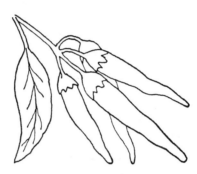

SMALL RED
CHILI
PEPPER

There is one more pepper that must be included here—the small red chili pepper. This plant is very erect and quite bushy, and the bright red fruit is about one and one half inches long, in the form of a cone. This pepper plant with its bright red would add highlights to any herb garden. It is used in pepper sauce and in pickling. Pepper tabasco and the small red chili can be grown in temperate climates. We have them growing in our herb garden.

ENCHILADAS KELSAZ

> *4 fresh eggs*
> *3 tablespoons oil*
> *1 cup milk*
> *1 cup flour*
> *1 teaspoon baking powder*

(over)

Put all ingredients into blender and buzz until blended. Pour on well-greased hot griddle. Cook one large enchilada at a time until golden brown.

FILLING FOR ENCHILADAS KELSAZ

> ½ cup olive oil
> 2 cups ground lean pork
> ½ cup minced onions
> ¼ teaspoon pepper
> 1 cup tomatoes
> ½ teaspoon cayenne pepper
> ½ teaspoon marjoram
> ½ teaspoon salt
> 1 tablespoon paprika
> 1 teaspoon chili powder
> 1 cup grated cheese

Put oil in large heavy skillet and heat. Add lean pork; cook to a light brown. Remove from skillet and drain on paper towel. Reheat oil in skillet, put in onions, pepper, tomatoes, cayenne pepper, marjoram, salt, paprika, and chili powder. Cook until thick. Put a spoonful of pork, a spoonful of cheese, and a spoonful of chili mixture on enchiladas. Roll up as you would a jelly roll. Serve hot.

RED PEPPER POT SOUP

> 1 beef bone
> 3 quarts water
> ½ pound ground beef
> 2½ onions, chopped
> ¾ cup carrots, shredded
> 2 large white potatoes, cut in cubes
> ½ cup finely chopped celery
> ⅓ box spaghetti

½ *cup green peas*
½ *can tomatoes* (*No. 2*)
1 *teaspoon thyme*
1 *tablespoon salt*
¼ *teaspoon red peppers, chopped*
½ *teaspoon black pepper*
¾ *teaspoon paprika*

Cook beef bone 1 hour in 3 quarts water. Add ground beef, onions, carrots, potatoes, and celery, and let simmer 2½ hours. Add spaghetti, peas, and tomatoes. Add remaining ingredients and simmer ½ hour. Serves 6.

RED DEVIL SQUASH CREOLE

6 *medium crookneck summer squash*
3 *tablespoons butter*
2 *medium onions, sliced*
1 *large green pepper, cut in strips*
3 *tablespoons brown sugar*
3 *tablespoons flour*
1 *quart fresh tomatoes, quartered*
Salt to taste
Red pepper (*some like it hot,*
     others hotter)
¼ *pound sharp cheese*

Cook squash until tender, drain off excess liquid. Put butter into a large skillet, add onion rings and pepper strips, and cook over low heat until tender. Sprinkle brown sugar over onion and peppers, add flour, turn gently. Arrange tomato quarters over all and simmer a few minutes. In well-buttered casserole or baking dish, put a layer of squash, a layer of tomato mixture, another layer of squash, and so on. Salt and red pepper to taste. Top with grated sharp cheese. Bake at 350° F. until cheese is well browned, about 30 minutes. Serves 6 to 8.

ACCENT ON CHILI

> 5 onions, chopped
> 2 green peppers, chopped
> 2 pounds lean ground beef
> 2 tablespoons bacon fat
> 2 pint cans tomatoes
> ¼ teaspoon pepper
> 1 teaspoon salt
> ⅛ teaspoon cayenne pepper
> 2 whole cloves
> 1 bay leaf
> 1 tablespoon chili powder
> 1 large can kidney beans

Cook onions, green peppers, and beef on low heat in bacon fat for 30 minutes. Stir often. Cook until onions and peppers are tender. Add tomatoes and all seasonings. Simmer very slowly for 30 minutes, add beans, and serve hot! Serves 6.

PARTY PIC-A-UNES

> 1 package Triskets
> 1 package Rice Chex
> 1 package Wheat Chex
> 1 small box pretzels
> 1 tablespoon seasoning salt
> 1 teaspoon marjoram
> 1 teaspoon savory
> ½ teaspoon garlic powder
> ½ teaspoon onion powder
> ¼ teaspoon cayenne pepper
> ½ stick butter

Place all ingredients except butter in a large baking dish. Cut butter in pieces and dot entire top surface. Place in preheated oven, 250° F., mix gently. Serve hot. Serves 12.

POPPY
*Papaver
somniferum*
of the poppy family

The opium poppy is our subject here, and though it does not
quite measure up to the ultimate in beauty found in the oriental
poppy, it is a showy plant with a rather quiet beauty all its own. It
is a native of the Mediterranean area but has been naturalized in
the United States.

The plant must be described from two separate and distinct
points of view or, rather, two architectural and social planes. One
view shows a beautiful gray-green plant that has been known to rise
to a height of four feet, although it will be found mostly in the two-
to three-foot range. It reaches upward on stems that are bluish green
and stand proudly erect. It is not a many-leaved plant, which fact
contributes greatly to the effect of simplicity, but there are enough
leaves to add a long whorl of grayish-green color at regular intervals,
and these become shorter and shorter as they ascend the stem. The
opium poppy unfolds its delicate white flowers with a ballet-like
grace—at times they are tinted with pinkish-purple flowing lines. The
blooming period is in July and lasts for only a few short days. The
pods are about two inches long and one inch wide and they seem to
be trying to explode with their valuable cargo of tiny brownish-black
seeds. The other view is quite opposite in effect. In brief, the opium
poppy is the source of opium, morphine, codeine, and heroin, and
though these have been used correctly as valuable medicines, they
have also been greatly misused—to such an extent that they have
probably caused more degradation and misery than the products of
any other plant.

Much lore surrounds the opium poppy. Pliny said that a decoction of poppy seeds, honey, and wine was served as a second course

on the tables of the ancients. It appears to have been used as a narcotic since the earliest days.

The seeds from the opium poppy are free of any drug and are widely used as a topping for rolls, breads, cakes, cookies, and pastries, or as a filling for cakes, coffeecakes, and pastries. Try the seeds in noodles and salads: a new taste thrill is yours for the asking. The seeds themselves have a pleasant, crunchy, nutlike flavor. In southern Europe, olive oil is often adulterated with an oil found in the seeds from a dark variety of the opium poppy.

The plant is easily grown and you will find simple instructions for growing on a chart in Chapter 12. However, before you grow the opium poppy, it is necessary to obtain a permit from the Bureau of Narcotics, Treasury Department, Washington, D.C. This comes under the Poppy Control Act of 1942, which provides that a permit must be obtained for the growing of the opium poppy or any species or variety of poppy from which opium can be extracted. The narcotic is derived from the scrapings from the seed pod. The poppy petals are used for wrapping the opium. The fact that you must have a permit should not discourage you from including this very attractive plant in your herb garden.

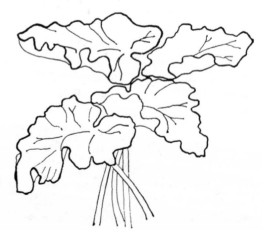

RHUBARB
Rheum rhaponticum
of the Polygonaceae
family

This true rhubarb of the ancients has literally traveled around the world from the Mediterranean and Asia Minor. It is an aristocrat of nature's wonderful herbs.

Gerard devotes three full pages to the description and illustration of the various rhubarbs. He also describes many virtues of this plant. One of these reads: "Mesues saith that Rhubarb is a harmless medicine, and good at all times, and for all ages, and likewise for little children and women with child."

For a variety of color and form in the herb garden, the new Canadian brilliant red rhubarb, which grows only from divisions, should be cultivated. When one stalk is cut, another fills in to take its place. It has an unusual loveliness in flower arrangements and its very colorful stalks and emerald-green leaves create a matchless and sparkling contrast in the arrangement. It is also the sweetest rhubarb you have ever tasted and does not lose its color in cooking. You will find it to be excellent in sauces, pies, and parfaits. Use only the stalk, as the leaves are toxic. Three plants are enough for the average family to grow. It is eye-catching and ornamental for its mass forms in the herb garden.

RED RHUBARB PARFAIT PIE

> 1 baked pie shell
> ½ cup sugar
> 4 cups rhubarb, cut in 1-inch sections
> 2 cups water
> 1 package strawberry gelatin
> 1 pint vanilla ice cream
> ½ pint heavy cream
> 1 cup strawberries

For filling, combine sugar, rhubarb, and ½ cup water; cook over very low heat to a saucelike consistency. Heat 1½ cups water to boiling, add gelatin, which has been dissolved in ¼ cup cold water, and stir until gelatin is completely dissolved. Chill, then add ice cream. Fold cooled rhubarb into ice cream-gelatin mixture. Pour into a baked pie shell. Chill in refrigerator until time to serve. Top with whipped cream. Decorate with whole strawberries. Lovely, luscious, and unforgettable.

RUBY-RED RHUBARB PUNCH

> 2 *pounds rhubarb*
> 3 *cups water*
> 2 *lemons, sliced thin*
> 1¾ *cups sugar*
> 1 *cup orange juice*
> 1 *large square ice*
> 2 *quarts carbonated water*

Wash and cut rhubarb in inch-long pieces, cook with the water and lemon slices about 20 minutes. Strain and add sugar; stir until dissolved. When chilled, add orange juice. Place ice in punch bowl. Combine punch and carbonated water and pour over ice. Serve. Colorful and sparkling. Serves 8.

ROCAMBOLE
Allium
scorodoprasum
of the lily family

Rocambole sounds like the name of a new Latin-American dance step. Most of the Latin-American rhythms subconsciously remind us of most everything we have ever associated with the good things in life. Rocambole, though not a dance step, certainly fascinates and exhilarates the taste buds. It is sometimes known as the giant garlic, and was first grown in Asia Minor and southeastern Europe. It is very closely related to garlic and should be to garlic what leek is to onion. It is milder and more delectable than garlic. Hence, it finds favor with those people who prefer a subtler and more subdued fragrance and flavor than garlic.

The plant's appearance seems to reflect both humorous clownishness and architectural greatness on the move. The stems look like huge shock-absorber springs and they go through peculiar gyrations before starting to stand erect. On top are hidden flowers that eventually become bulbils. These are the rocambole cloves, which are used just as garlic cloves are.

Rocambole has more bonuses to offer than most of its relatives of the lily family. During the summer its brightest of bright green leaves slip into quiet slumber for a short period of time, after which new leaf growth starts. These young leaves are tender and mild and will certainly help to make your salads tastier if you use them lightly!

LESSER-
LEAVED GARLIC

Rocambole scorodoprasum minus is sometimes called rockenbollen because it grows among rye (*rocken* for rye and *bolle* for a bulb). It is much smaller than the giant mentioned above. Its long slender bulbs are wrapped in brownish skins, the flowers and stems have daintier proportions. It is sometimes called a European leek, but it is best known as a lesser-leaved garlic.

ROSEMARY
Rosemarinus
officinalis
of the mint family

No other herb fills such a large part of our hearts as rosemary.
The rocky coasts of France and Spain were its home originally.
Pliny gave it the name of *rosmarinus,* which means sea dew. Rosemary with its lacy foliage is a magnificent gem in the garden for its
haunting yet ever present spiky sweetness. The extraordinarily beautiful fragrance comes from an oil that is extracted on a tremendous
scale in Europe by manufacturers of eau de cologne. This world-
renowned fragrance comes not only from the flowers but from the
foliage as well. In most rosemary areas many women store the leaves
throughout the long winter months because they seem to keep the
surrounding air fragrantly alive, carrying a breath of spring on every
dreary day.

Rosemary is a favorite of the flower arranger and also of discriminating people who can appreciate its use with culinary delights
that are nearly bouquet complete but need that special little blessing
to raise them above the ordinary.

This is an invaluable addition to any herb garden. Besides the
uses mentioned for the kitchen, it is a very ornamental plant. After
the plant has started to mature, it develops tiny leaves that are as
gray as a tropical Spanish moss. There is a lovely legend about rosemary: the Virgin Mary spread her linen over a white-flowered bush
of rosemary and ever after the flowers were as blue as her own robe.

ROSEMARY MEDITERRANEAN SOUP

5-pound hen
2 quarts water
2 carrots
1 onion
3 celery tops
6 sprigs parsley
1 bay leaf
3 whole cloves
1 tablespoon salt
¼ teaspoon pepper
½ teaspoon rosemary
2 tablespoons tapioca

Cook hen in 2 quarts water until meat falls off the bones (save the meat for chicken salad). Strain chicken broth, add diced carrots, sliced onion, celery tops, parsley, bay leaf, cloves, salt, pepper, and rosemary. Simmer until carrots and onions are tender. Strain, cool, skim off fat. Add 2 tablespoons quick-cooking tapioca. Heat thoroughly, serve with shredded hard-boiled eggs, strips of pimiento, or whipped cream passed separately for garnishes. Serves 6 to 8.

R O S E S of the rose family

Damask rose (*Rosa damascena*)
Provence rose (*Rosa gallica*)
Eglantine (*Rosa eglanteria*)

Shakespeare said: "The summer's flower is to the summer sweet." Very probably William Shakespeare had in mind two and possibly all three of these when those lines were written; and he must have been a real prophet and lover of fragrance and beauty. These are the three oldest roses in cultivation. They are considered to be the most fragrant roses in the world and have long been the basis for many perfumes.

DAMASK
ROSE

The damask rose is a native of southeastern Europe, where it
has been used for centuries in making attar of roses. It is second
only to the cabbage rose in the strength of its perfume. It is a hardy
shrub and, once planted, is very easily maintained. The flower is a
pale pink, thin-textured and semi-double. The blooming period
comes generally sometime between the middle of June and the middle of July and lasts only ten days. The greatest fragrance comes
from dried flowers and stems. In obtaining the damask rose for your
herb garden, it is very important that you specify the botanical name
Rosa damascena, since there are some other forms that are similar
and some are even misnamed in old catalogues.

PROVENCE
ROSE

The Provence rose is often called the French rose and, like the
damask rose, has long been one of the sources of attar of roses.
It can be grown in your herb garden just as you grow the damask. It
is a hardy plant and requires very little maintenance, once planted.
The flower is a deep reddish-rose color, semi-double with approxi-

mately fifteen petals. Again, the fragrance increases after the stems and petals have been dried. And again, when ordering the Provence rose for your garden, it is very important that you specify the botanical name *Rosa gallica*, to avoid the possibility of obtaining one of many other forms developed from the true Provence rose.

EGLANTINE

The eglantine is often called sweetbrier in America. It, like the damask and Provence roses, is and has been for ages a source of attar of roses, so widely used in perfumes. It is also easily grown and requires very little maintenance, once started. The eglantine or sweetbrier has a color that is very similar to mauve. The flowers are double and so fragrant that they seem to be straight out of the heavens. In *Cymbelline*, Shakespeare mentioned a low hedge of apple-scented eglantine. It, of course, is a shrub like the damask and Provence and is treelike in growth. It has an unusual type of fruit that is long like an olive, and stone red when ripe, downy within. This part is rich in vitamins. Gerard said, "The fruit when it is ripe maketh most pleasant meats and banqueting dishes, as tarts and such like; the making whereof I commit to cunning cooke, and teeth to eate them in the rich mans mouth." When ordering the eglantine for your garden, be certain to specify *Rosa eglanteria* to make certain you get the true one.

These three roses are simply "musts" for the herb garden. They are the old-fashioned species of roses that have not been hybridized and are grown for their wonderful, matchless fragrance and their food value. The petals of the damask and the Provence rose are used, both fresh and dried, for flavoring dishes and candies of all types. The eglantine contributes its primary "hips," the fleshy swollen bases that ultimately enclose the fruit. These roses are also grown widely for use in potpourri. For this they must be planted on a much larger scale, since the number of petals needed in potpourri is far greater than the number needed for cooking.

All of these roses are so highly steeped in history and romance that no attempt will be made to cover this phase. It is hoped that what has been said here will provide the incentive for you to grow them in your herb garden and arouse within you the curiosity to find out more about their historical background by reading Shakespeare's *Henry VI*.

RUE
Ruta graveolens
of the Rutaceae
family

Among the ancient Greeks and Romans rue was highly esteemed as a seasoning for food and for use in medicine. It was especially noted for the latter, and even in Pliny's time it was considered to be beneficial for eighty-four maladies. Although rue is certainly a bitter and active plant, so are many of the other materials we use every day to make wonderful concoctions.

Rue is a handsome plant for any herb garden. It does very well as a hedge in small gardens and as a border for pathways. Once you have seen the plant in full and mature growth, it will find its way into your heart, and the next thing you know—it will be in your herb garden.

It grows to a height of two feet and this fact will be of interest to flower arrangers. They will also be attracted by its umbels of yellow flowers that cover the lacy blue-green leaves; the flowers bloom all summer long and are borne in corymbs or short terminal clusters on the plant. Rue can be grown from seed, from cuttings, from layers, or by division of the tufts. No special directions are needed except to point out that it prefers a rather poor clay soil. In fact, some people suggest that it be planted in the most barren part of the garden. There is a widespread use of rue in connection with the many ailments common to poultry.

Rue also needs sunshine most of the time. Remember that if the soil is too rich and fertile the plant will sometimes be killed by the frost, but in hardy and poor soil it seems to challenge the elements to the utmost of its being. For further growing information, please refer to the "Herb Growing Charts" in Chapter 12.

Shakespeare was well aware of the virtues of rue and mentioned it along with rosemary as a beauty aid and disinfectant. Other references can be found in *Richard II*.

SAGE
Salvia officinalis
of the Boraginaceae
family

Certainly the most colorful, historically speaking, of all the herbs, sage is also the most widely used herb in the United States. This statement probably applies to the entire world. It can safely be said that it is universally employed as a seasoning or flavoring.

Sage has been cultivated since the earliest days of recorded history. It stemmed originally from the northern shores of the Mediterranean. So wide has been its acceptance that there is scarcely an ancient scholar or naturalist who has not described it profusely in his writings. Theophrastus, Dioscorides, and Pliny all mentioned sage at great length. There is much legendry spun in with the plant's history. No attempt has been made here even to touch upon it. After you have grown sage in your own herb garden and used the freshly picked leaves, your curiosity will provide the incentive to learn more of this phase of the story.

This hardy perennial reaches upward about two feet but it rarely blooms until the second season of growth. Its stems are covered with a soft, velvety down and from them spring the leaf stems. The leaves are most unusual in that they change from sage green to gray back to sage green, et cetera, at different seasons. They tend to be round and are darker on top than on the underside. They are covered with soft white hairs. The leaves are usually bursting, literally, with the oil that *is* sage and the fragrance of the entire plant is similar to that of a mixture of thyme, turpentine, and a pleasant pungent material with a hint of camphor trying to find its place in the crowded theater. The plant produces flowers in June that are just about the loveliest blue spikes I have ever seen. Besides the many culinary uses for sage, it has much fragrance and beauty to offer in the garden.

When the leaves are picked, only the perfect green ones are selected; on drying they turn grayish in color. The leaves are used to flavor pork, veal, sausages, goose and other poultry stuffings among many other things. Commercial meat-packing houses are the largest users. In the industrial field, an oil is extracted from the entire plant for use primarily in soaps and perfumes. We import more than two million pounds per year.

SANTOLINAS
of the
Compositae
family

Lavender Cotton (*Santolina chamaecyparissus*)
Emerald Green (*Santolina virens*)

Just the name seems to express most of the well-known attributes of santolina. The name seems to mean something good, unusual, and even slightly exotic. There are five or more santolina variations in the mint family, and all of them have a magnificent, intriguing beauty. Since they are grown in the herb garden primarily for their ornamental effect (but not entirely—they still are used somewhat in the kitchen), the lavender cotton and the emerald green santolinas have been selected for this space. Their beauty is elegant, classical, and overflowing with fragrance.

LAVENDER COTTON is a hardy perennial with silver-gray foliage. The foliage stems are so branching that compactness seems to be built into the plant; the over-all effect remains one of a tiny gray coral. The leaves are tiny and inconspicuous, yet interwoven into the plant as a whole with a fine architectural touch. This santolina is a native of southern Europe and particularly southern France. It resembles lemon or chartreuse co-ordinated button designs. It contains a pungent essential oil, but the pungency in this one is probably the most pleasing you have ever experienced. The flowers have some medicinal use against ringworm, while the leafy stems are used mainly in perfumes and bouquets for linen closets. Lavender cotton likes a very sunny spot and it should not be pruned too often inasmuch as this tends to retard growth. It is not a really hardy plant and therefore should be protected against the winter snows.

THE EMERALD GREEN SANTOLINA is just as wondrous as the lavender cotton, but in a different way. Its foliage is so dense that it resembles an evergreen cypress. The tinsel-like foliage contains an oil with a racy fragrance made up of a pleasing combination of menthol and peppermint. The flowers resemble those of lavender cotton. The emerald green is a rapid grower and, since it finds wide usage as a hedging, it must be kept cropped and compact.

Lavender cotton grows to a height of eighteen inches, while the emerald green reaches up to twenty-four inches. Once you have seen, touched, and known the experience of santolina, your herb garden will never be without it.

For a delightful fragrance in your clothes closets, try this: in small cheesecloth bags or plastic boxes with holes in the lid put 2 tablespoons crushed cloves, 2 tablespoons cinnamon, ¼ cup dried and crumbled mint, tansy, lemon balm, and santolina.

SAVORY of the mint family

Summer Savory (*Satureia hortensis*)
Winter Savory (*Satureia montana*)

SUMMER
SAVORY

Another of the true herb classics is before us, beckoning with pale, pinkish-lavender fingers that look like short spikes made of whorls in the axils of the green. They are beckoning for us to come to the land of fragrance, flavor, and beauty. The fingers are on arms that will reach a height of about eighteen inches; the entire body or complete plant of summer savory has been said to be the most satisfactory and useful of all the annual herbs.

Summer savory is one of the dainty, delicate herbs that contributes everything desirable to the herb garden—fragrance and beauty outside, fragrance and flavor in the kitchen. It is native to southern Europe and is used in that section of the world by all chefs as a culinary vegetable that puts a delightful, appetizing aroma into their food dishes. Summer savory is used with loving tenderness by all cooks who know anything at all about herbs, for the reason that was recently given by an expert in the field of cooking with herbs and spices. He said that every cook should remember at all times that the function of an herb is to bring out, and not black out, the flavor of a food. Summer savory brings out the flavor in many different types of foods, either singly or in combination. There are more than one hundred recipes available for its use and these cover a world of different bouquets.

Summer savory is a favorite with all "pleasure gardeners," who like to show its beautiful blossoms in edging for borders. They are particularly fond of its piquant, sweet fragrance. The tender leaves may be used any time during the season, and in some seasons it is possible to cut several crops. When used fresh, the leaves should not have been cut for any appreciable length of time. The leaves can be dried for winter use by tying small bunches together and keeping them in a proper storage place during the drying. When the leaves are thoroughly dry they should be stripped from the stems and stored in tightly covered jars. These can be of great help in making *fines herbes* mixtures.

WINTER SAVORY

This is the more hardy member of the savories. The perennial evergreen is a native of the Mediterranean region and normally grows to a height of about one foot but across the top it will generally measure up to two feet. With its touch-of-pink white flowers and its rich green leaves, winter savory adds a real touch of beauty to the herb garden. It has all the virtues of summer savory except that it is slightly more pungent.

SAVORY TAMALE PIE

1½ *pounds ground beef chuck*
½ *pound lean pork*
2 *large cans pitted ripe olives (black)*
1 *quart or 1 pound mushrooms*
3 *small cans tomato purée*
6 *or less dried red peppers, or red pepper*
    (some like it HOT!)
1 *teaspoon dried savory*
3 *cups corn meal*
lots and lots of butter

Combine beef and pork and sauté in large skillet. Stir to keep large chunks from forming. Slice ripe olives and cut mushrooms in small slices. Now get a large kettle. Open the tomato purée and dilute with water to a semi-thick paste. Break up red peppers into this, add meat, olives, mushrooms, and savory, and simmer for 15 minutes. It should be thick but *not dry.*

Now butter sides and bottom of a larger pan—a turkey roaster or a large baking pan. Into 5 cups boiling water, put the corn meal and cook to a fairly thick paste. Pour about 1 inch of the corn meal mush in bottom of pan. Pour the ground beef mixture over the mush. Top with the remaining mush and put lots of butter all over the top.

Cook at 375° F. for 15 minutes. Serve very hot with bread sticks, a salad bowl of all the green salad mixings you have, fresh fruit, and scads of good coffee. Savory tamale pie is a complete dinner, especially good after cocktails. So good and so easy to serve. Serves 6 to 8.

NOTE: The corn meal mush may be made from 1 box of prepared corn meal muffin mix.

SAVORY POTATOES

4 large potatoes
2 large onions
½ teaspoon salt
¼ teaspoon pepper
2 tablespoons butter
1 teaspoon savory
2 cups milk

Peel and slice potatoes and onions very thin. Prepare a well-buttered casserole. Put in a layer of potatoes, a layer of onions, salt, pepper, butter, and a sprinkling of savory. Add another layer of potatoes, onions, and seasonings. Pour milk over all, cover, and bake at 350° F. until tender. Add more milk if needed. Serves 6.

SESAME
Sesamum
orientale
of the Pedaliaceae
family

"Open sesame!" is a phrase familiar to practically every civilized
person in the world and immediately brings to mind the tales
of the Arabian Nights. Far older than the tales of the Arabian Nights
is the plant itself. Sesame has been grown for uncounted centuries,
especially in the Far East, where it is still used on a large scale.
Sesame is often referred to as benne, and this apparently comes from
benne (or Benny) oil, which is made from sesame seeds and is used
almost exclusively in Africa and the Orient for cooking and in
medicines.

To the herb gardener in the United States, the oil for cooking
would be of no interest since other cooking oils are plentiful and
inexpensive here. The plant itself, however, is a beauteous thing in
the garden. The stems are round, rather heavy but glistening, and
grow to a height of three feet (they have been known to shoot up to
a height of five or six feet). On the stems will be found leaves of a
different nature and size from top to bottom. At the lower end the
leaves are opposite and rather fleshy, while the upper leaves are not
toothed but are rather slender and placed along the stem alternately.
The blooming season for sesame is one of the longest of all the herbs
and continues from July to September in most sections of the country. The flowers are the essence of beauty: lavender-tinted whites,
resembling foxglove.

The historical background of sesame is intriguing. According to some, sesame was created by Yama, God of Death, who, after a long penitence, gave his blessing to its various uses, which included funerals and expiatory ceremonies in which it was used as a purifier and symbol of immortality. Both Theophrastus and Dioscorides mentioned sesame in various writings.

Sesame was introduced into the United States by the African Negroes who were brought here. They first cultivated it in Florida. From there it has spread throughout the rest of the United States and Canada. One of the highest compliments ever paid to this herb was that of Ibn of Baithar, who is reported to have said that sesame oil "from the seed" is a good cure for dandruff when used with other oils such as olive oil and myrtle oil!

Sesame is one of the few herbs that has a very definite place in the field of medicine; it is listed in all pharmacopoeias. The oil from the seeds can be used as a soothing external rubbing medium or can be used internally as a mild laxative. In the south of France the oil is extracted from the seed for use in the manufacture of soap.

The primary cooking oil in China, Egypt, and India is that extracted from sesame seed; it is used like olive oil in cooking. Some Southerners make a hearty meal constructed around sesame seeds that are parched over a fire, then mixed with water, and finally stewed with other ingredients. In some parts of the South there are people who make broths from the seeds and at times they candy them with sugar or molasses.

In the United States, the herb gardener will be interested in the sesame plant primarily from three points of view, and these are: beauty and fragrance in the garden; stalks for exotic flower arrangements; the widespread use of sesame seeds on the outside of buns, rolls, and cookies. When the seeds are slightly crunched, a very pleasing fragrance and flavor are emitted.

The sesame plant is easy to grow. It is an annual and, though it is classified as a tropical annual, it can be grown here in America like an ordinary annual.

"OPEN SESAME" COOKIES

> ¾ cups shortening
> 1 cup sugar
> 2 fresh eggs
> ¼ teaspoon almond extract
> ¼ teaspoon lemon extract
> 2 tablespoons sweet cream
> 2½ cups flour
> ½ teaspoon baking soda
> ¼ teaspoon salt
> ¼ cup finely chopped almonds
> ¼ cup sesame seeds

Cream shortening and sugar. Beat until fluffy. Add the unbeaten eggs, one at a time, beat thoroughly. Combine flavoring and cream and add. Sift flour, soda, and salt together. Add to first mixture and blend well. Add chopped almonds and sesame seeds, then chill in refrigerator overnight. When ready to bake, roll out thin on lightly floured board and cut with large cooky cutter. Place on ungreased cooky sheet. Garnish with whole almond in center, sprinkle tops with sesame seeds. Bake at 375° F. about 10 minutes. Yields 2½ dozen.

NOTE: I often use a large doughnut cutter and sprinkle all over with sesame seeds. The small cooky from the center may be garnished with a whole almond.

SHALLOT
Allium
ascalonicum
of the lily family

The lily family seems to cover a wider range of flavors than any
other family, with the onion, garlic, chives, leek, rocambole,
and now shallot, one of the very mild members of the family. It is
classified as an onionlike herb that is grown the same way onions
are. Besides being much milder than the onion, shallot has one major physical difference. Instead of growing one large bulb, with off-
sets, the mature bulb of shallot looks very much like that of garlic:
a series of sections (cloves) that will come apart rather easily.

It is sometimes called eschallot. Shallot is a native of western
Asia and was named for a town called Ascalon in Palestine. When
allowed to flower in cultivation, small head clusters of flowers appear, sometimes white and sometimes violet. Just as in the case of
leek, the shallot can be used in almost any culinary delight if the
flavor of the onion and other members of the lily family seem to be
too flavorful to "fit." The foliage resembles that of the onion. The
young mild leaves are frequently harvested for greens as bunch
onions.

Which member of the lily family you prefer depends upon what
you are eating, the strength of flavor desired, and the condition of
your palate. In many cases, shallot is just right. Try it sometime with
ordinary brown beans or white navy beans. It's a different taste,
milder and, to some, more satisfying.

SORREL

French Sorrel (*Rumex scutatus*)
Garden Sorrel (*Rumex acetosa*)
Wood Sorrel (*Oxalis viclacea*)

FRENCH
SORREL

Three sorrels should be covered here, since each is a very definite part of the "big herb picture." The first is the French sorrel (*Rumex scutatus*), which has always been very dear to the hearts of all French people. The French have known of sorrel and its many wonders almost since the beginning of their recorded history. Their love for the plant is connected particularly with its bright green beauty in the herb garden and its very long succulent leaves in salads, one of their favorite dishes. There is scarcely a particle of the sorrel plant that the French do not utilize. It is cooked just as we cook spinach in America. The French sorrel is of the low-growing variety and has beautiful bittersweet, lush, crisp green leaves. Another great feature to the French is the fact that sorrel takes only sixty days to grow and be ready for cutting and using. It is also a very hardy perennial and the plants will continue to produce leaves for their fine beauty and exquisite flavor for up to five years. After this time some horticulturists suggest that the plants be resowed.

The French sorrel has an almost unbelievable lemonlike tang that can be enjoyed in many dishes such as consommé, soups, fish, omelets, and scrambled eggs. It has also been found to be excellent with lamb, beef, and many vegetables.

GARDEN
SORREL

The second sorrel is the garden sorrel (*Rumex acetosa*), which grows to a much larger over-all size than French sorrel. It has oblong leaves and arrow-shaped bases. This particular sorrel will grow to a height of three feet. In early spring it is almost tasteless but as the season progresses the acid taste in the plant becomes more pronounced. Garden sorrel thrives particularly well in moist soil. The plants should be dug up, divided, and replanted every four or five years. The garden sorrel is as delectable to some as the French sorrel; it is particularly savory in soups and salads. There is one feature about garden sorrel that really sets it apart from all of the other herbs: it is used in diets designed to overcome a deficiency of vitamin C in the body.

WOOD SORREL

The third sorrel is the little wood sorrel (*Oxalis*), which is a native of Europe. It came to America with the earliest settlers. Since its arrival in America it has been found growing all the way from Nova Scotia to North Carolina. The little wood sorrel below the base is made up of tiny bulblets and prefers moist, shady places to find complete contentment. It has been called sourgrass by people who have made it a practice to transplant these tiny bulblets to their herb garden.

One of the most outstanding attractions of wood sorrel is the great contribution it makes to any shady border with its clover-shaped leaves and dainty flowers, which are often pink, lavender, or yellow. Darwin has described at great length the power and movement in plants and in particular the wood sorrel plant. This is what he has to say about wood sorrel: "This little plant goes to sleep at night—it trembles and folds into its shy little self at the least change of temperature."

Wood sorrel is acclaimed for other famous characteristics, among which is the fact that it is called the true shamrock of ancient Ireland; it is also claimed to be the alleluia plant because it blooms at Eastertime. The herb gardener who puts wood sorrel in his garden will certainly find the greatest pleasure in using the tiny cloverlike leaves as a garnish for fruit salads. In colonial times the children used to nibble the leaves as they gathered them for use in early spring puddings.

These are the three sorrels and each has its own set of attractions. One or more of the sorrels should be in every herb garden.

SWEET
BASIL
Ocimum
basilicum
of the mint family

Sweet basil is one of the most popular seasoning herbs known to the world today, and one of the reasons for this is the fact that it has within it the ability to make savory the most inexpensive food dishes. It will be recalled that in olden days one of the primary reasons for using spices and herbs was either to make unpalatable food taste better or inexpensive food taste delightful. The basils, of which from fifty to sixty species are grown in the warmer parts of the world, are extremely fragrant and flavorful to the palate.

An old saying goes: "Good things come in small packages," and this certainly must be true of the basils, particularly sweet basil. It is a bushy plant that grows in some warmer climates to a height of eighteen inches. It is not a many-stemmed plant, but the leaves are particularly unusual in that each pair of opposite leaves is covered with a bloom, yet they glisten on both sides with specks of oil from the reservoirs present. The undersurface is slightly downy. The greatest feature of these unusual leaves, however, is the licorice-and-spice taste when fresh, and when dried a fragrance suggesting a combination of lemon, anise, resin, and spice. No other herb seems to possess this complete versatility of bouquet patterns from the fresh to the dry stage.

The flowers of sweet basil are very beautiful and come at the end of July and August. Although they are small, in pairs and almost inconspicuous, their greenish whiteness seems to add a flair to the plant that is not found in other herbal plants.

Sweet basil is another of the most widely used seasoning herbs and it is often combined with other herbs in mixtures for various preparations. By itself it seems to give its best performance in imparting an almost matchless taste to dishes made with tomatoes, cheese, and eggs. It is also a fine addition to vinegars, various types of soups, many vegetables, most of the meats, some butter sauces, and any other dish in which you can imagine the faint yet distinct bouquet of something resembling "pepperish clove."

One unusual use for sweet basil is as a kind of snuff. Apparently there are still some quaint old ladies who use the powdered leaves for this purpose.

Although sweet basil is being utilized on a large scale, much experimentation remains to be done. A little time spent in the kitchen trying it in new ways should bring taste thrills beyond imagination.

There is another prominent type of basil called bush basil, which is also a neat, bushy, small plant. It is more compact and branched than sweet basil. The outstanding feature of bush basil is that it is extremely fragrant of lemon and spice and its flavor can only be described as being slightly bitter, resinous but stimulating. It is suggested that you familiarize yourself completely with sweet basil before attempting to use bush basil in the kitchen.

SWEET
CICELY
Myrrhis odorata
of the parsley
family

The people from a town high in the mountains of Savoy are responsible for our having received in ancient times one of the most esteemed plants known to mankind. Sweet cicely is this plant and it goes back far in history, even to biblical times. Gerard and Pliny mentioned it, as did Parkinson, who said, "It gives a better taste to any other herb put with it." Seeds were crushed in olden days for their pleasantly fragrant oil, which was used to scent and polish floors and furniture made from oak.

The plant grows two to three feet high and it has very narrow stems. The leaves are much divided, and it is this quality that builds into the foliage architecture the plant's fernlike effect. The polygamous flowers are small and white, reminding one of well-drilled soldiers in the umbel that holds them. The seeds are the most aromatic part of the plant.

As to modern-day uses of sweet cicely, the seeds are used widely in flavoring beverages, especially chartreuse, one of the finest cordials in the world, which is made by Carthusian monks. Sweet cicely is also used to flavor foods, primarily in France. The seeds represent the largest potential use of the plant. They have one remarkable quality that sets them apart from other herbs: the ability to act as a synergist when blended with anything, so long as there is another herb in it. As a synergist, sweet cicely makes the flavor of the final blend so much more palate pleasing than any of the ingredients tasted alone.

SWEET
WOODRUFF
Asperula odorata
of the madder
family

This sweet-smelling, low-growing plant comes to us from Europe and the Orient. It is a naturalized citizen now and loved by all who have had the pleasure of making its acquaintance. This herb is aptly described by Gerard: "The Woodrooffe hath many square stalks full of joints, and every knot or joynt seven or eight long narrow leaves, set round about like a star, or the rowell of a spurr, the flowers grow at the top of the stems, of a white color and of a very sweet smell, which being made up into garlands, or bundles, and hanging up in the heat of summer, doth very well attemper the aire, coole and make fresh the place, to the delight and comfort of such as are therein."

Fragrant sweet woodruff, with the scent of new-mown hay, has made this low-growing herb a favorite for ground covers in the shady and moist places in the pleasure garden. It can also be used as the grace notes in a flower arrangement. The deep green starlike whorls of leaves and the small white star flowers would be especially interesting to children in arranging flowers. It flowers in June and July.

It is ornamental and fragrant and has much to give in flavor (fascinating in fruit cups). Refreshing bouquet is yours with sweet woodruff in beverages, and it puts exquisite aroma into sachets.

There is another woodruff that should be mentioned here. Its botanical name is *Asperula oriental azurea*. A splendid airy effect is obtained with its azure-blue flowers, which tend to relieve the heaviness of the more abundant flowers in the herb garden.

TANSY
Tanacetum vulgare
of the Compositae
family

The definition of a flower garden should, in addition to describing the garden, include a list of flowers to guide the uninitiated in planning a garden. Tansy should be on this list. Too, any book on flower arrangements should include tansy on the list of plants most used by arrangers who need a fernlike background.

The roots are perennial and they easily develop themselves again at the first signs of spring. From the roots grow a great number of stems, up to three feet above the ground, erect, serene, and covered with fernlike leaves. The leaves are much divided, with oval, oblong outlines, rich green, slightly downy on the underside and smooth above. These bear an abundance of small yellow flower heads in unusually crowded corymbs. Grayish-looking seeds follow the flowers. A caution should be added here: tansy is a robust weedy plant that soon grows into thick clumps.

According to folklore, it must be taken internally in the spring to avoid the summer sickness. We are also told that it has been rubbed over raw meat to keep flies away and prevent decay. "Winter posies" are supposedly kept fresh-looking and smiling by the flowers that retain their yellow color all winter. Tansy has been grown in our country so long that it appeared in Prince's great catalogue, printed in 1790, and in the one published by Bartram in 1814.

Although tansy was put through most of the same medicinal trials as other well-known herbs, the *National Standard Dispensary* says today that it has no medicinal value and is really quite poisonous when taken internally. However, some people still use it sparingly in medicines for application to the human body and to animals. This and the use of small quantities of tansy oil, distilled from the tops and leaves, in toilet waters from time to time, represent tansy outside of the ornamental garden. It has been used in teas and puddings.

The plant is a native of southern Europe and, unlike most herbs, it likes heavy soils. However, it does well in any good garden soil. Remember, too, that tansy likes plenty of sun. In the United States, Michigan produces far more tansy than any other state.

Tansy stands for truly sense-pleasing fragrance and beauty and it should be in your garden.

TARRAGON
Artemisia
dracunculus
of the Compositae
Artemisia family

Tarragon is a fairly hardy perennial that is supposed to be a native of southern Russia, Siberia, and Tartary. It is estimated that tarragon has been cultivated for about five hundred years, and this relatively new herb is becoming more and more prominent in America. There are two reasons for its popularity: tarragon leaves are widely used with steaks, chops, in salads, fish sauce, preserves, pickles, mustard, mayonnaise, and of course in tarragon vinegar; tarragon leafy tops go into the commercial markets to flavor confectionery and to make perfumes and toilet waters.

It is one of the few herbs that is not known to set seed, which means, of course, that propagation is by cuttings or root division. It is a graceful plant when full grown, and the leaves seem to have a fragrance and flavor about them similar to that of anise. The plant has a great number of branching stems on which are found lance-shaped leaves and white flowers that are sterile.

In tarragon you have another wonderful specimen for your herb garden. It has the beauty and the fragrance required outside and it most certainly has the fragrance and flavor required inside. This is another herb that will be of interest to the flower arranger because of its convenient height range.

TARRAGON TASTYS

6 *slices bread*
3 *tablespoons melted butter*
1 *cup grated or spreading cheese*
1 *teaspoon tarragon, chopped*
6 *slices boiled ham*

Brush a slice of bread with melted butter, spread generously with cheese, sprinkle with tarragon, and top with a slice of boiled ham. Continue until you have 6 tarragon tastys. Place on cooky sheet and broil in the oven until cheese is golden brown. Serve with broiled tomatoes on the side. Pass bread and butter pickles. Serves 3.

THYME
Thymus vulgaris
of the mint family

This famous, beautiful, versatile herb could well be referred to as "Old Father Thyme" since it seems to have been with us almost as long as the real Father Time. Since very early days, it has been cultivated for culinary uses, but, like all of the better-known herbs, it was once grown and used on a large scale for its supposed medicinal value. It is cultivated now almost entirely for cookery and, next to sage, is probably the most widely used herb.

The name is from the Greek word *thymon*, or sacrifice; it was used as an incense to perfume the temples. The Romans used thyme both in cookery and as a bee forage. If you have garden space for only a few herbs, be sure to include thyme. It is an ideal ornament for use as a dwarf facer or a border planting. It generally grows to a height of about eight inches, with slender wood stems and oblong tapering leaves that are deep green on top and gray underneath. The flowers, which generally appear in June, form whorls and leafy spikes of lavender-pink in the upper leaves.

Thyme is a native of dry, stony places along the coasts of the Mediterranean but has been naturalized in most civilized countries, regardless of climate. It seems to thrive best in rather poor but limy soil; at least it can be said that some of the wonderful fragrance is missing when it is grown in heavy soils. Seeds should be planted in April or May in a special seed bed that can be kept partially shaded and moist (even though the plant likes full sun when once started). Transplanting can be done when the plants are well out of the soil; they may be set in the field during June or even as late as July, preferably just before or just after a shower. Although thyme is a perennial, it becomes less aromatic after the first two years of growth, so it is suggested that a new sowing be made every second year.

All parts of the thyme plant are fragrant because of its wonderful aromatic, volatile oil, which makes up about one per cent of the total plant. The oil is extracted on a commercial scale, primarily in France, and it is used extensively in perfumery. The fresh tops are used as a garnish, the leaves, either fresh or dried, are chopped and used in flavoring a wide variety of cooked foods. There is scarcely a cook who does not use it almost every day. The dried form of thyme as obtained in the markets does an excellent job of putting zest into our foods, but you are in for a thrill in fragrance the first time you use fresh thyme and experience its very pleasant, bitter tang. The many uses of thyme are listed in the Herb Chart in Chapter 11.

There is a related plant, lemon thyme, with lemon-scented foliage. It is carried by dealers under the name *Thymus serpyllum canadense.*

ENGLISH THYME STUFFING
For 2 2-pound broilers

> 3 *tablespoons minced onion*
> 3 *tablespoons butter*
> ½ *cup chopped mushrooms*
> ½ *pound chicken livers*
> ½ *teaspoon salt*
> ¼ *teaspoon pepper*
> ½ *teaspoon marjoram*
> ½ *teaspoon thyme*

Sauté minced onion in butter, add mushrooms, cook slowly until tender. Add diced chicken livers, salt, pepper, marjoram, and thyme. Cook over low heat until chicken livers are tender. Force through a potato ricer until well blended. Split broilers that have been broiled and stuff each half with thyme stuffing. Cover with buttered crumbs, return to broiler until buttered crumbs are a golden brown. Place on platter, garnish with parsley. Serves 4.

WINTER-
GREEN
*Gaultheria
procumbens*
of the heath family

Once this tiny and bountiful wonder of nature has been seen in the shady woodland, peeping proudly from its leafy perch, one cannot resist the impulse to provide space for it in the herb garden—or at least in the wild flower area of the herb garden. It is somewhat particular about its home site, as it cannot be enjoyed everywhere. But if it can be given a home site based on an acid-type soil with a litter of pine needles or oak leaves, and a bit of sunlight filtered through open woods, you will find it to be a happy little plant and it will share its happiness with you.

The wintergreen is a perennial and a native of America. This hardy little plant has always been a joy to children fortunate enough to have had the opportunity to go mountain "tea" picking, or searching for the tender, spicy leaves of the wintergreen. When a patch was found, they would chew some of the young yellowish-green leaves tinted with red on the spot and gather some to take home for tea making. The location was always marked so that they could be certain of finding their way back in October for teaberry picking. The delicious red "teaberry," which has a mealy taste on the tongue, is loved by woods creatures as much as by the children. Bobwhites, quail, pheasant, and deer nibble on the berries and leaves to acquire a little spiciness in their diet.

Wintergreen usually will grow from two to six inches in height and the plants seem to like to gather together in groups. The stems push upward from the underground scaly bark stems. They are smooth below and downy and crowned with leaves above. The leaves, which are quite large for the size of the plant, are oval and, when young, are a combination of yellow, green, and red. The older leaves are green above and yellow-green below. When the young leaves are crushed between the fingers, they swell as though you had peppermint candy in your hand. The flowers are small, and bloom from June to September. Brilliant red berries come in October. They are delicious when eaten in the coolness of the woods.

Early Americans used the leaves of wintergreen to make tea during the Revolution and many Americans enjoy this tea today. For more than two hundred years the wintergreen plant was our only source of oil of wintergreen, but now it can be produced chemically more cheaply. Its beauty and uniqueness, however, make it more than eligible for your garden. I have transplanted the creeping wintergreen to the wild flower area in my herb garden and there it is growing happily beside the wild ginger and the May apples.

YARROW
Achillea
millefolium
of the Compositae
family

Here is one of the very oldest known herbs or, rather, weeds, as it is known today. Actually all over the world it is called the commonest of common weeds. It is so prevalent everywhere that one wonders at the marvelous scheme it employs to overrun the earth. It has been given broad coverage in the mythology, folklore, medicine, and literature of many peoples. Achilles learned of the virtues of yarrow from Chiron, the Centaur, in order that he might make an ointment that would heal his Myrmidons (Thessalian warriors) who were wounded in the siege of Troy. Divers properties have been attributed to it: it has been used as a love charm and as an herb tea brewed by old crones to cure anything from loss of hair to the ague. It has also been mentioned as an ingredient of an especially intoxicating beer made by the Swedes. Another use was yarrow's supposed ability to induce nosebleed for relief of congestive headache.

Yarrow is a pleasant-looking plant, despite its classification as the "commonest of all common weeds." Actually it has the lacy-looking structure and form of Gothic architecture and detail. Flower arrangers who have not worked with it will be pleasantly surprised at the charm, beauty, and unusualness it will add to any church arrangement. A very leafy plant, it has erect stems that usually grow to a height of one to two feet. The leaves are really a very pretty shade of green. Its flowering season is from June to November, one of the longest of any of the plants. The flowers are pink or grayish white, depending somewhat upon growing conditions.

Although yarrow now finds practically no way into the culinary field, it is definitely a part of the "Big Herb Picture" and the herb gardener should have some knowledge of it, if only for history's sake. With its lacelike foliage pattern, yarrow gives the appearance of being made up of feathery masses. And there is nothing more pleasing in a quiet, hushed way than to catch a breath of the wholesome, autumnal, nutty odor of its flowers.

11. Herb chart:

how the herbs are used

AMBROSIA	Romantic and fragrant ambrosia has been used by the ancients for flavoring and fragrance since recorded history. Use for fruit cups, beverages, salads, preserves, jellies, and potpourri.
ANGELICA	This herb with its lovely-sounding name has many uses, from candies to cordials to a boiled salad. The muscatel flavor is good in custards and desserts.
ANISE	Seeds used for liqueurs, cordials, fruit salads, vegetable salads, coffeecake, baked apples, rolls, shellfish, sea-food salads.
BALM	Fresh leaves used for pleasing, stimulating teas and beverages. Fragrant and dainty in finger bowls.

BERGAMOT	Fresh leaves used in fruit cups, punch, teas, beverages, for fragrant potpourri, and for color in the herb garden. Nice in flower arrangements.
BETONY	Refreshing teas and beverages; a conversation piece in the herb or wild flower garden.
BORAGE	Prettiest of all herbs, with lovely gray leaves and sky-blue flowers. Select the tender green leaves to use with fish, potatoes, cottage cheese, new peas. Use flowers to garnish punch, fruit salads, and beverages.
BURNET	Fresh leaves used for teas and beverages, cooked salads, green salads, in cottage cheese, and for garnishes.
CALAMUS	Use to flavor creams, puddings, and custards, also for color and fragrance in the garden.
CAMOMILE	Use for teas and beverages made to keep the grower well and beautiful, as it is said to be good for indigestion and complexion! To make the hair soft after shampoos, one should always rinse the hair with a solution of camomile. The ancients say, Grow camomile about the herb garden to keep all other plants happy.
CARAWAY	Use for French dressing, cottage cheese, herb breads, cakes, and salads.
CATNIP	Fresh leaves used for teas and garnishes as you would use mint leaves. A little "nip" of the fresh leaves is especially pleasing to your cats and kittens.

CHERVIL	Said to be the most delicately flavored of all the herbs. Use the leaves fresh or dried. Perfect in cheese dishes, butter sauces with baked chicken, and green salads.
CHICORY	Roots are used, cooked with butter, as a green vegetable. Roasted, roots can be added to coffee or used as a coffee substitute. The stalks, blanched, may be used like celery.
CHIVES	Use for salads and salad dressing, liver, creamed beef, cottage cheese, cream cheese, hot buttered popcorn, new potatoes, baby green peas, corn, scrambled eggs, deviled eggs, broiled tomatoes.
CLARY	Sometimes called muscatel sage. Try with baked chicken, omelets, beverages, and teas. Use flowers and leaves for garnishes.
CORIANDER	Seeds are used in broth, or mashed and used for poultry, pickles, bread, and cookies.
COSTMARY	Has a lovely mild flavor—nice with veal or chicken. Fresh or dried leaves make a very pleasant tea.
CRESSES	Upland: cooked green salads, tossed green salads. Water: sandwiches, garnishes, and salads. Especially good with sardines and cream cheese. Garden: cooked like spinach, mixed with greens for salads.

CUMIN

Use seed or fruit when you want a highly seasoned stimulating flavor for sauces, gravies, spaghetti, chili dishes, deviled eggs, pork or tamale pie. Perfect for pizza pies.

DANDELION

Use young leaves for cooked green salad or fresh salad; use blossoms for wine.

DILL

Use for cucumber pickles, fish, chopped steak, potatoes, roast duck, potato salad.

FENNEL and FENNEL FLOWER

Use for salads, soups, sauces, apple pie, garnishes. The stems and bulbs are served raw like celery.

FEVERFEW

Good for medicinal teas, wonderful as a background plant, and lovely in flower arrangements.

GARLIC

Always use cutting boards so other foods do not pick up flavors. Good for baked beans, ripe olives, vegetables, salads, sauces, French dressing, Swiss steak, hamburgers, spaghetti, potato salad, cheese spreads, French bread, lamb roasts, and cooked spinach.

GERANIUM

Beautiful fragrant leaves are used in custards, puddings, jellies, and desserts, as garnish for jellied salads and desserts. Nice for table arrangements.

GERMANDER

Mostly used for ornamental border planting in the herb garden. Mint-flavored leaves used for fragrance, sometimes for flavor.

HOP	The flower buds are cooked for salads. Tea made from buds. Liquid put into breads to make them lighter.
HOREHOUND	Grow for candies and old-fashioned teas.
HORSE-RADISH	Use for beef dishes, oysters, shrimp, crab cakes, sauces, and dips.
HYSSOP	Use in beverages, soups, and salads.
LAVENDER	Grown mostly for fragrance and beauty in the garden, it has been used for flavoring. At your next garden club luncheon, use the flowers to garnish your fruit cups.
LEEK	Use in salads, soups, and stews or for fresh tidbit trays.
LEMON VERBENA	Use for fragrant, fresh-looking finger bowls. For beverages and teas, use to garnish fruit salads and for a conversation piece. Place leaves on a crystal plate, set honeydew wedge on leaves, top with a paper-thin slice of pink ham.
LOVAGE	Seeds are used to flavor desserts and confections. The stems can be candied. The stalks can be blanched and eaten like celery.
POT MARIGOLD	Buds can be cooked in oil and used in salads and as food coloring. Best as a color interest in the herb garden.
MARJORAMS	Can be used fresh or dried. Use for eggs, stuffings, poultry, cheese, meat stews, lamb, beef, pork, veal, baked fish, Swiss steak, cream sauces, gravies, soups, vegetables: lima beans, string beans, and even spinach!

MAY APPLE — Decorative in the garden. Apples can be eaten when ripe for an unusual flavor.

MINTS — Apple: leaves used fresh for beverages, teas, and garnishes, also decorative in the herb garden. Lovely in flower arrangements in pewter containers.
Peppermint: dried fresh or extract is used for jellies, sauces, fruit cups, fresh drinks, salads, confections, meat, vegetables, and vinegars. Peppermint is delightful added to new green peas.
Spearmint: use the cool refreshing fragrant leaves to garnish beverages and teas. Crush leaves to extract oils for sherbets and ices. Use for mint sauces, coleslaw, fruit cups, salads, mint jellies, and flower arrangements. Especially lovely dried for winter bouquets.

MUSTARDS — Leaves for cooked salad greens, seeds for seasonings and flavoring. Prepared mustard sauce.

NASTURTIUM — Flowers for luncheon table arrangements. Leaves for salads and garnishes, pods or seeds for pickles and sauces.

ORÉGANO — Use either dried or fresh for soups, sauces, omelets, crown roast pork, potatoes, pizza, veal, chili con carne, beef, rabbit, lamb, chicken, pheasant, sea food, frankfurters, stuffings, salads, all tomato dishes, stews, cabbage, broccoli.

PARSLEY — Use either fresh or dried for garnishes, cheese, eggs, meat, fish, poultry, salads, sauces, vegetables, such as new potatoes, soups.

PENNYROYAL — Use as you would mints for teas, beverages, and garnishes, also for fragrance in potpourri.

PEPPERS — Tabasco: use for pizza pies, sausage, soups, and stews.
Chili: Mexican dishes, spaghetti, beans, and cauliflower.
Ornamental and colorful in the herb garden.

POPPY — Seeds used to flavor breads, cakes, pie crust, vegetables, German and English boiled dinners. Try decorating open-face cheese sandwiches or hors d'oeuvres.

RHUBARB — Lovely for punches, pies, sauces and combines nicely with fresh strawberries. Wonderful for large flower arrangements.

ROCAMBOLE — Use like garlic. Has a much milder flavor.

ROSEMARY — Use either fresh or dried for fruit cups, fruit salads, sauces, stews, soups, veal, pork, lamb, chicken, fish, duck, beans, cauliflower.

ROSES — Damask: for lovely fragrance in sachets, potpourri, and flavorings.
Provence: candied rose petals, cakes, and jellies.
Eglantine: seed pods eaten as tasty little apples.

RUE — Use for stimulating sandwiches and tasty salads.

SAGE

Use either dry or fresh in sausage, roast pork, turkey dressing, chicken, sardine sandwiches, chicken dumplings, scalloped bananas, biscuits or meat pie topping, cottage cheese, tomatoes, baked beans.

SANTOLINAS

For ornamental beauty and lovely fragrance use for sachets, potpourri, or clothes closets. Try a fresh bouquet in your tub for a refreshing fragrance!

SAVORY

Use either dry or fresh in green salad, eggs, stuffings, or vegetables. Especially delightful piquant flavor for tossed salads. Use to season when cooking with dry wines.
Winter savory is available all winter and is one of the most used of all the herbs. Use for soups, salads, stews, fried chicken, pork chops, veal, and beef.

SESAME

The small oval seeds have a fine crisp taste. Good when used in cookies, candies, cakes, and rolls. Wonderful when used in pastry for fruit pies.

SHALLOT

The green blades are sometimes used in a cooked green salad. Has a mild onion flavor.

SORREL

Cook like spinach, or use tender green leaves for salads. Little wood sorrel is a dainty garnish.

SWEET BASIL

Use for tomatoes, green peas, spaghetti sauce, vegetable juice cocktail, stews, soups, eggplant, cheese, fish sauce, shrimp and lobster. Fresh basil can be added to new potatoes, green peas, sauces.

SWEET CICELY The seeds can be eaten fresh and green. This little herb is said to give all other herbs a better flavor when combined with others. Especially good in beverages and cordials, fruit salads and fruit cups. Leaves can be used when you want a mild anise flavor.

SWEET WOODRUFF Use for May Day drinks and teas. Lovely for sachets and potpourri.

TANSY Mostly used for ornamental effect and cutting greens for flower arrangements. Also used for puddings and cakes.

TARRAGON Use either dry or fresh for sweetbreads, chicken, meat, fish, sauces, salad dressings (French and Russian), eggs, poultry, game, pickles, preserves, roast beef, cabbage, sauerkraut, slaw, stews, soups, mushrooms, lobster (broiled or stuffed).

THYME Use either dry or fresh for stuffings, soups, chowders, meat loaves, creamed chipped beef, pork, veal, chicken, turkey, fish, potatoes, onions, eggplant, beets.

WILD GINGER A beautiful plant in the herb garden. The leaves are used for garnishes. The aromatic roots were used by the Indians to add spiciness to Indian corn puddings, grits, and hominy.

WINTERGREEN Use fresh new leaves for tea. Lovely little red teaberries may be used for garnishes and decorations.

YARROW   Teas were made from the fresh yarrow leaves by the ancients to cure all ills, from headaches to falling hair. Today, it is a must in the herb garden for the flower arranger because of its color range from off-white to pastel pinks.

CHIEF HERBS USED IN COOKERY
ARRANGED IN ORDER OF THEIR APPROXIMATE IMPORTANCE

Sage	Mint	Winter Savory
Thyme	Chervil	Cumin
Parsley	Rosemary	Fennel
Basil	Tarragon	Coriander
Summer Savory	Pot Marjoram	Anise
Sweet Marjoram	Caraway	Dill
Chives		

OUTSTANDING ROBUST HERBS FOR COOKERY

Sage	Summer Savory	Sweet Marjoram
Dill	Winter Savory	Pot Marjoram
Caraway	Horse-radish	Coriander
Fennel	Mint	Anise

MOST COMMONLY USED
COMBINATIONS OF FINES HERBES

Thyme, chervil, and basil	Chives, basil, and parsley
Chervil, parsley, and chives	Parsley, rosemary, and tarragon

12. Some facts about growing herbs

Oh, Adam was a gardener, and God who made him sees,
  That half a proper gardener's work is done upon his knees,
So when your work is finished, you can wash your hands and
      pray
For the Glory of the Garden that it may not pass away!
And the Glory of the Garden it shall never pass away.

RUDYARD KIPLING

There are two lists, one of the perennials and one of the annuals and biennials. Best wishes for good growing, good cooking, and good eating, which, when combined properly, mean "pleasurable living."

PERENNIALS

Ambrosia	Chicory
Angelica	Chives
Balm, Lemon	Costmary
Bergamot	Cress: Upland,
Betony: Wood,	Water
Paul's	Dandelion
Burnet	Feverfew
Calamus	Garlic
Camomile	Germander
Catnip	Hop

Horehound
Horse-radish
Hyssop
Lavender
Leek
Lemon Verbena
Lovage
Marjoram, Pot
May Apple
Mint: Apple, Peppermint, Spearmint
Orégano
Pennyroyal
Rhubarb
Rocambole
Rosemary
Roses: Damask, Provence, Eglantine

Rue
Sage
Santolina: Lavender Cotton, Emerald Green
Savory, Winter
Shallot
Sorrel, Wood
Sweet Cicely
Sweet Woodruff
Tansy
Tarragon
Thyme
Wild Ginger
Wintergreen
Yarrow

ANNUALS AND BIENNIALS
OR BEST GROWN AS SUCH

Anise
Borage
Caraway
Chervil
Clary
Coriander
Cress, Garden
Cumin
Dill
Fennels
Fennel Flower
Geranium: Rose, Lemon
Marigold

Marjoram, Sweet
Mustards: Black, White
Nasturtium
Parsley
Peppers: Tabasco, Red Chili
Poppy
Savory, Summer
Sesame
Sorrel: French, Garden
Sweet Basil

HERB GROWING CHART

NAME	FORM USED	CULTIVATION – GROWTH – HABITS						TYPE OF PLANT
		When to plant	Depth to sow seed	Spacing of plants	Germination time	Color of blossom	Height (inches)	
AMBROSIA *Oke of Cappadocia*	Fresh flower heads	Best to get plants from herb grower		12 inches		Yellowish	24 to 36	Perennial
ANGELICA *Archangelica officindis*	Fresh tips; stems, and seeds	Sow seed early spring, transplant seedlings early summer, permanently in autumn	¼ to ½ inch loose soil	36 inches	Slow	White to yellow or green	up to 48	Perennial
ANISE *Pimpinella anisum*	Leaves—fresh; seeds—dried	Sow seeds in early spring	½ inch	8 to 12 inches	14 to 18 days	Yellowish white	18 to 24	Annual
BALM, LEMON *Melissa officinalis*	Leaves—fresh; leaves—dried for potpourri	Propagation by root division or cuttings spring or fall		18 inches		White or purple	18 to 24	Perennial
BERGAMOT *Monarda didyma*	Flowers for arrangements; leaves—fresh	Early spring root division		18 inches		Red	24 to 36	Perennial
BETONY *Betonica officinalis*	Leaves—fresh	Sow seeds or set plants in spring	¼ inch	6 to 8 inches	Slow	White, purple or red	6 to 18	Perennial
BETONY (WOOD) *Pedicularis canadensis*	Ornamental flowers	Sow seeds or set plants in spring	¼ inch	6 to 8 inches	Slow	Greenish yellow, purplish red	6 to 18	Perennial

HERB GROWING CHART

NAME	FORM USED	CULTIVATION – GROWTH – HABITS						GROWTH – HABITS		TYPE OF PLANT
		When to plant	Depth to sow seed	Spacing of plants	Germina-tion time	Color of blossom	Height (inches)			
BETONY (PAUL'S) *Veronia officinalis*	Ornamental flowers and seeds	Sow seeds or set plants in spring	¼ inch	6 to 8 inches	Slow	Pale blue	3 to 10		Perennial
BORAGE *Borago officinalis*	Fresh leaves; also flowers	Sow seeds in early spring	¼ inch fine soil	1 foot	Fast	Sky blue	18 to 24		Annual
BURNET *Poterium sanguisorba*	Fresh leaves	Best to sow every year in early spring	¼ inch	15 inches	Slow	Bronze-red	Keep cut to 5 or 6 inches		Perennial
CALAMUS *Acorus calamus*	Flower, foliage, and roots	Fall from rhizomes or plants		1 foot		Purplish blue	3 to 5 feet		Perennial
CAMOMILE *Anthemis nobilis*	Flower heads; fresh leaves	Sow seeds or set plants in spring or fall	¼ inch	6 inches	Slow	Yellow center with white rays	15		Perennial
CARAWAY *Carum carvi*	Leaves and roots—fresh; seeds—dried	Sow seeds May or June	¼ inch	8 to 12 inches	Slow	White	12 to 24		Annual or Biennial
CATNIP *Nepeta cataria*	Fresh or dried	Sow seeds or set plants in spring or fall	¼ inch	6 to 8 inches	Slow	White	18 to 36		Perennial

HERB GROWING CHART

| NAME | FORM USED | CULTIVATION | | | | GROWTH-HABITS | | TYPE OF PLANT |
		When to plant	Depth to sow seed	Spacing of plants	Germination time	Color of blossom	Height (inches)	
CHERVIL *Anthriscus cerefolium*	Fresh or dried	Sow seeds in spring or fall, preferably fall; do not transplant	1/4 inch	6 to 8 inches	Slow	White	18 to 21	Annual
CHICORY *Cichorium intybus*	Flowers for colorful backgrounds; roots	Sow seed in early spring	1/4 inch	8 to 12 inches		Bright blue	12 to 36	Perennial
CHIVES *Allium schoenoprasum*	Fresh tops	Set bulblets spring or fall	Set bulblets about 3 inches deep	5 inches	Slow	Lavender	6 to 8	Perennial
CLARY *Salvia sclarea*	Fresh flowers and leaves	Sow seeds in early spring	1/4 inch	18 inches	Slow	White or lilac	24	Annual
CORIANDER *Coriandrum sativum*	Seeds dried	Sow seeds in spring or fall	1/4 inch	8 to 12 inches	Slow	Whitish	24 to 30	Annual
COSTMARY *Chrysanthemum balsamita*	Fresh leaves	Set plants early spring		10 to 12 inches		Yellow	36 to 48	Perennial

HERB GROWING CHART

NAME	FORM USED	CULTIVATION – GROWTH – HABITS						TYPE OF PLANT
		When to plant	*Depth to sow seed*	*Spacing of plants*	*Germina-tion time*	*Color of blossom*	*Height (inches)*	
CRESSES								
UPLAND *Barbarea verna*	Fresh leaves	Start seeds in pots; transplant to streams			About 50 days			Perennial
WATER *Nasturtium officinalis*	Fresh leaves	Early spring	⅛ inch		Fast		2½	Perennial
GARDEN *Lepidium sativum*	Fresh leaves	Early spring	⅛ inch		Fast		2½	Annual
CUMIN *Cuminum cyminum*	Seeds	Sow seeds in spring	¼ inch	8 to 10 inches	Slow	Lilac	6	Annual
DANDELION *Taraxacum officinale*	Leaves; fresh blooms	Sow seeds in March or April	¼ inch	1 to 2 feet	Fast	Yellow	12 to 18	Perennial
DILL *Anethum graveolens*	Green branches; fresh seeds; dried seeds	Sow seeds or set plants in early spring	¼ inch fine soil	1 foot	Medium	Yellow	24 to 36	Annual
FENNELS *Foeniculum*	Fresh stalks; fresh leaves; dried leaves	May or June	¼ inch	18 inches	Reasonably fast	Yellow	24 to 48	Annual

HERB GROWING CHART

NAME	FORM USED	CULTIVATION				GROWTH – HABITS		TYPE OF PLANT
		When to plant	Depth to sow seed	Spacing of plants	Germination time	Color of blossom	Height (inches)	
FENNEL FLOWER *Nigella sativa*	Dried seeds	Sow seed in spring	¼ inch	12 to 18 inches	Slow	Grayish blue	Small low branches	Annual
FEVERFEW *Chrysanthemum parthenium*	Flowers for background planting and arrangements	Early spring root division		12 to 18 inches		White	24	Perennial
GARLIC *Allium sativum*	Cloves or dried sets	Set bulblets early spring	Set each bulb separately	4 to 6 inches		White	6	Perennial
GERANIUMS								
ROSE *Pelargonium graveolens*	Green leaves for flavor and fragrance	Set plants in spring	3 feet			Lavender-pink	Varies	Perennial— treat as Annual
LEMON *Pelargonium limonseum*	Green leaves for flavor and fragrance	Set plants in spring	3 feet					Perennial— treat as Annual
GERMANDER *Teucrium chamaedrys*	Fresh leaves	Set seeds or plants in early spring	¼ inch	Good edging plant; 12 inches	Fast	Rosy	6 to 12	Perennial
HOP *Humulus lupulus*	Fresh seed; pods and dried pods							Perennial

HERB GROWING CHART

NAME	FORM USED	CULTIVATION – GROWTH – HABITS						TYPE OF PLANT
		When to plant	*Depth to sow seed*	*Spacing of plants*	*Germination time*	*Color of blossom*	*Height (inches)*	
HOREHOUND *Marrubium vulgare*	Fresh leaves and flowering tops	Sow seed in early spring	¼ inch	12 to 15 inches	Slow	White	12 to 24	Perennial
HORSE-RADISH *Armoracia rusticana*	Fresh roots	Plant roots in early spring or fall	Cover top of roots with 2 inch soil	15 to 18 inches		White	24 to 36	Perennial
HYSSOP *Hyssopus officinalis*	Fresh or dried leaves and stalks for flavor	Sow seed early spring or get seedlings from herb grower	¼ inch	6 inches	Slow	Blue, pink, or white	24	Perennial
LAVENDER *Lavandula spica*	Fresh or dried leaves and flowers for fragrance	Early spring	⅛ to ¼ inches	8 inches	14 to 18 days	Lavender	24 to 36	Perennial
LEEK *Allium porrum*	Fresh leaves and bulbs for flavor—very ornamental flower and leaf	Start seeds in specially prepared bed in early spring	Cover with ¼ inch fine soil	4 to 6 inches	Fast	Lavender, white	30 to 36	Perennial
LEMON VERBENA *Lippia citriodora*	Fresh leaves for fragrance and flavor	Start new plants from seedlings in early spring		Good mature plants 2 feet		Light lavender	6 to 8 feet	Perennial

HERB GROWING CHART

| NAME | FORM USED | CULTIVATION | | | | GROWTH – HABITS | | TYPE OF PLANT |
		When to plant	Depth to sow seed	Spacing of plants	Germination time	Color of blossom	Height (inches)	
LOVAGE *Levisticum officinale*	Stalks and stems fresh; leaves and seeds; rhizome	Sow seeds in late summer	¼ inch	3 to 4 feet	Slow	Yellowish green	5 to 7 feet	Perennial
MARIGOLD, POT *Calendula officinalis*	Buds and pods	Sow seeds in early spring or get plants from herb grower	¼ inch	8 to 10 inches	Slow	Yellow-orange	12 to 18	Annual
MARJORAMS								
POT MARJORAM *Origanum vulgaris*	Fresh flower buds	Sow seeds in April	¼ inch	10 inches	Slow	Pinkish white	24	Perennial
SWEET MARJORAM *Marjorana hortensis*	Fresh or dried leaves	Sow seeds in early spring	¼ inch	8 to 12 inches	70 days	Off-white	10 to 24	Annual
MAY APPLE *Podophyllum peltatum*	Ripe fruit; foliage for ornamental effect	Get plants from herb grower or woodsides		6 to 8 inches		White	12 to 18	Perennial
MINTS								
APPLE MINT *Mentha rotundifolia*	Fresh leaves	Best to get plants from herb grower		Best to grow in beds		Lilac	18 to 36	Perennial

HERB GROWING CHART

| NAME | FORM USED | CULTIVATION – GROWTH – HABITS | | | | | | TYPE OF PLANT |
		When to plant	Depth to sow seed	Spacing of plants	Germina-tion time	Color of blossom	Height (inches)	
PEPPERMINT *Mentha piperita*	Fresh leaves and stalks	Best to get plants from herb grower		6 to 8 inches		Reddish violet	24	Perennial
SPEARMINT *Mentha spicata*	Fresh for flavor; dried for arrangements	Early spring or fall		Best to grow in moist soil		Pinkish lavender	10 to 14	Perennial
MUSTARD								
BLACK *Brassica nigra*	Leaves—fresh; seeds—dried	Sow seeds in early spring	¼ inch	12 inches	Fast	Yellow	18 inches	Annual
WHITE *Brassica alba*	Leaves—fresh; seeds—dried	Sow seeds in early spring	¼ inch	12 inches	Fast	Yellow	18 inches	Annual
NASTURTIUM *Tropaeolum minus*	Leaves—fresh; seeds—green	Plant seeds in early spring	1 inch	6 to 8 inches	Fast	Yellow, orange to dark red	1 to 8	Annual or Biennial
OREGANO *Origanum vulgare virens*	Leaves—fresh or dried	Best to get plants from herb grower		12 to 15 inches		Lavender	18 to 24	Perennial
PARSLEY *Petroselinum crispum*	Fresh leaves	Sow seeds in spring or fall	⅛ inch	Good border plant	Slow		6 to 8	Annual or Biennial
PENNYROYAL *Mentha pulegium*	Leaves—fresh or dried	Set plants early spring		5 to 6 inches		Lilac-blue	10 to 12	Perennial

HERB GROWING CHART

NAME	FORM USED	CULTIVATION			GROWTH – HABITS			TYPE OF PLANT
		When to plant	*Depth to sow seed*	*Spacing of plants*	*Germination time*	*Color of blossom*	*Height (inches)*	
PEPPERS								
PEPPER TABASCO *Capsicum frutescens*	Crushed or powdered	Best to get plants from herb grower		12 inches		Red pods	18	Annual
SMALL RED CHILI PEPPERS	Mexican chili pods, crushed or powdered	Best to get plants from herb grower		12 inches		Bright red pods	18	Annual
POPPY *Papaver somniferum*	Flowers for border; seeds for flavor	Sow seeds in spring	¼ inch sifted soil	8 to 10 inches	Slow	White to light blue	24 to 36	Annual
RHUBARB *Rheum rhaponticum*	Stalk and leaf for arrangements; stalk fresh for flavor	Roots from herb grower spring and fall		12 to 15 inches			10 to 12	Perennial
ROCAMBOLE *Allium scorodoprasum*	Seeds or cloves; later—the new growth leaves	Plant sets in early spring	Cover with 1 inch of soil	6 to 8 inches		Rose-colored	36	Perennial
ROSEMARY *Rosmarinus officinalis*	Fresh leaves	Sow seeds in early spring	¼ inch	18 inches	Fast	Pale blue	24 to 36	Perennial

HERB GROWING CHART

NAME	FORM USED	CULTIVATION – GROWTH – HABITS						TYPE OF PLANT
		When to plant	*Depth to sow seed*	*Spacing of plants*	*Germina-tion time*	*Color of blossom*	*Height (inches)*	
ROSES								
DAMASK *Rosa damascena*	Bushes for or-namental effect; petals for flavor and fragrance	Spring or fall				Pink or cream		Perennial
PROVENCE *Rosa gallica*	Petals for flavor and fragrance	Spring or fall				Red	3 to 5 feet	Perennial
EGLANTINE *Rosa eglanteria*	Petals for flavor and fragrance	Spring or fall				Pink	3 to 5 feet	Perennial
RUE *Ruta graveolens*	Ornamental shrub—fresh and dried	Sow in spring	¼ inch	18 inches	Slow	Greenish yellow	18 to 24	Perennial
SAGE *Salvia officinalis*	Fresh or dried leaves	Plants from herb grower		6 to 8 inches		Violet-blue	18 to 24	Perennial
SANTOLINAS *S. chamaecyparissus; S. virens*	Fresh and dried leaves; lovely for use in arrangements	Plants from herb grower		3 feet		Yellow	Lavender Cotton, 18 Emerald Green, 24	Perennial
SAVORY								
SUMMER *Satureia hortensis*	Fresh and dried	Sow seeds in early spring	¼ inch	6 to 8 inches	Medium	Dainty pink	12 to 18	Annual

HERB GROWING CHART

NAME	FORM USED	CULTIVATION — GROWTH — HABITS						TYPE OF PLANT
		When to plant	Depth to sow seed	Spacing of plants	Germination time	Color of blossom	Height (inches)	
WINTER *Satureia montana*	Fresh or dried leaves	Root division in September and early spring; sow seed in early spring		10 to 12 inches	Slow	White or purplish	15 to 18	Perennial
SESAME *Sesamum orientale*	Ornamental effect; dried seeds for flavor; fresh leaves for teas	Sow seeds in spring	¼ inch	8 inches		Pink-lavender		Annual
SHALLOT *Allium ascalonicum*	Fresh or dried bulb	Set bulbs in spring and fall		16 inches		Seldom flower	8 to 10	Perennial
SORREL FRENCH *R. scutatus*	Fresh leaves	Early spring		1 foot	About 60 days		3 to 4	Perennial
GARDEN *R. acetosa*	Fresh leaves					Pinkish lavender or magenta		
WOOD *Oxalis viclacea*	Beauty of leaf and blossom	Bulblets in spring					4 to 9	Perennial
SWEET BASIL *Ocimum basilicum*	Fresh or dried leaves for flavor	Sow seeds in early spring; transplant when 3″ tall	⅛ to ¼ inch fine soil	12 inches (seedling)	Slow	Pink	12 to 24	Annual

HERB GROWING CHART

NAME	FORM USED	CULTIVATION – GROWTH – HABITS						TYPE OF PLANT
		When to plant	Depth to sow seed	Spacing of plants	Germination time	Color of blossom	Height (inches)	
SWEET CICELY *Myrrhis odorata*	Ornamental or fresh leaves for flavor	Sow seeds in the fall or root in the spring	¼ inch	18 inches	Very slow	White	24	Perennial
SWEET WOODRUFF *Asperula odorata*	Fresh flowers for arrangements; fresh leaves for fragrance and flavor	Best to get plants from herb grower				White	1 to 2 (low growing ground cover)	Perennial
TANSY *Tanacetum vulgare*	Fresh or dried for flower arrangements; fresh foliage	Early spring; best from root division		For border or 2 to 3 feet		Yellow	36	Perennial
TARRAGON *Artemisia dracunculus*	Fresh or dried leaves	Best to get plants from herb grower		18 inches		White		Perennial
THYME *Thymus vulgaris*	Leaves and stems	Sow seeds when weather is thoroughly settled	Barely covered with sifted soil	12 inches	Slow	Lavender	12 to 18	Perennial
WILD GINGER *Asarum canadense*	Foliage for ornamental effect; roots for flavor	Spring		8 to 10 inches		Reddish brown	8 to 10	Perennial

HERB GROWING CHART

| NAME | FORM USED | CULTIVATION – GROWTH – HABITS | | | | | | TYPE OF PLANT |
		When to plant	Depth to sow seed	Spacing of plants	Germina-tion time	Color of blossom	Height (inches)	
WINTERGREEN *Gaultheria procumbens*	Fresh leaves; ripe berries	Spring		Set in beds or patches		White	2 to 6	Perennial
YARROW *Achillea millefolium*	Flower stalks for arrange-ments; leaves for teas	Best to get plants from herb grower		10 to 12 inches		White or pink	24 to 36	Perennial

SUGGESTED PATTERNS FOR GROWING

MODEL PERENNIAL HERB GARDEN

Supplies a family of six or more with plenty of fresh herbs for summer use, as well as dried herbs for winter use.

Rear of garden—north or west. Building, fence, or hedge should be here.

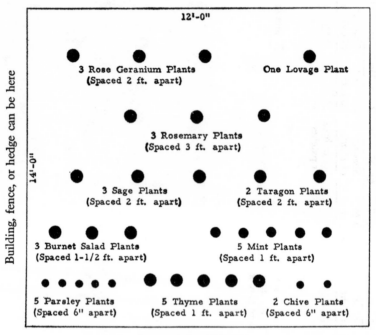

South or east should be open

Furnished through the courtesy of Farmer Seed and Nursery Company, Faribault, Minnesota.

PERENNIAL HERB GARDEN COLLECTION

3 Burnet Salad Plants	2 Clumps Chives	3 Rose Geranium Plants
1 Lovage Plant	5 Parsley Plants	5 Thyme Plants
3 Sage Plants	2 Tarragon Plants	3 Rosemary Plants
	5 Mint Plants	

MODEL ANNUAL HERB GARDEN

To supply the average family.

Rear of garden—north or west. Building, fence, or hedge should be here.

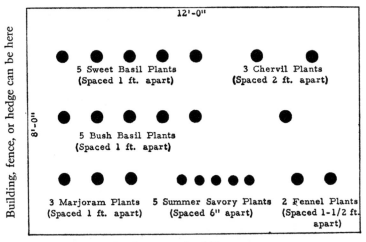

South or east should be open

Furnished through the courtesy of Farmer Seed and Nursery Company, Faribault, Minnesota.

ANNUAL HERB GARDEN COLLECTION

3 Chervil Plants	3 Marjoram Plants	5 Bush Basil Plants
2 Fennel Plants	5 Summer Savory Plants	5 Sweet Basil Plants

Courtesy of Breck's of Boston

SMALL HERB GARDEN
(6 feet in diameter)

Can be made from a three terrace garden pyramid.

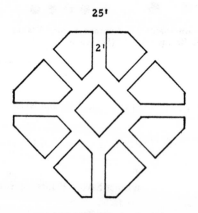

SMALL HERB GARDEN

Can be made from aluminum grass barrier,
discarded bricks, or solite concrete blocks.

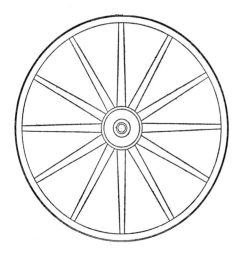

SMALL HERB GARDEN

Can be made from a discarded wagon wheel.

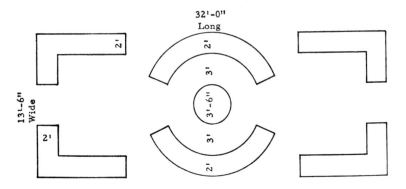

Courtesy of Wayside Gardens, Mentor, Ohio

SEMI-FORMAL "WAYSIDE" HERB GARDEN

Would be nice bordering driveways.

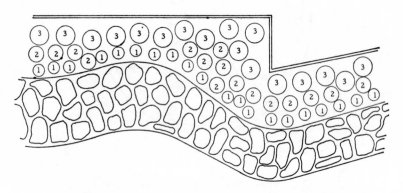

HERB BEAUTY FOR TERRACES AND BORDERS

No. 1. Low-growing herbs for edging borders.
No. 2. Medium-growing herbs for blooms and ornamental foliage.
No. 3. Tall-growing herbs for background planting.
      (Please see growing chart.)

Brighten garage or garden wall with
herb planted window boxes

A plant or two of rose geranium, sage, or chives taken up from the herb garden and reset in a pot of good soil will do well all winter if kept watered and in a sunny window. Parsley for seasoning can also be kept in this manner. This is one herb whose appearance, fragrance, and flavor are welcome through the drab winter months.

45'

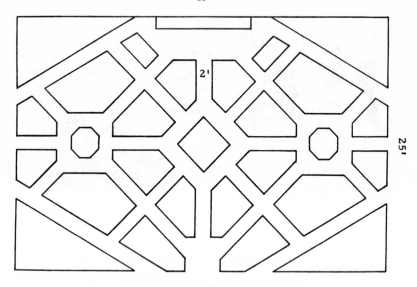

25'

ENLARGED HERB GARDEN

Can be made from aluminum grass barrier,
discarded bricks, or solite concrete blocks

13. *Yesterday, today, and*

tomorrow

HINTS FOR PREPARING
AND DRYING HERBS

DRYING: Select choice new growth when it's at the peak of perfection. Cut herbs in the early morning; tie in bunches and hang over
a stretched wire in a dark airy room, after sun-drying. While leaves
are being dried, spread them thinly on a screen and place screen in
dark airy room. Leaves will dry in color. When herbs are dry place in
airtight jars.

When drying herbs, flowers for fragrance, and flowers for winter
bouquets, cut just when they come into bloom. Tie in bunches, hang
upside down in dark, airy room to dry in color.

HINTS FOR FREEZING
AND THAWING HERBS

FREEZING: May be packed without blanching. Cut only the finest and nicest leaves and stems, wash carefully under spigot, drain
dry in a wire basket. Then dry-pack in plastic bags. Label with cards
or foil placed inside bag. Make bag airtight and place in freezer
immediately.

THAWING: Keep herbs in their original containers while thawing if possible. Place on table in room, allow thirty to forty minutes to thaw. A watertight package may be thawed in cold running water in twenty minutes. The package should be removed from the water as soon as thawing is complete. For best flavor use immediately. Use like fresh herbs, if possible.

14. Rules for judging herb exhibits

For garden club members, listed below are "Rules for Judging Herb Exhibits." This has been furnished through the courtesy of the Herb Society of America, 300 Massachusetts Avenue, Boston 15, Massachusetts.

(A) HORTICULTURAL CLASSES OF HERBS, SINGLE SPECIMEN HERB PLANTS

SUGGESTED CLASSES:
1. Greenhouse culture
2. Garden culture
3. House culture

IN JUDGING HORTICULTURAL CLASSES CONSIDER:
1. Correct labeling
2. Condition of bloom, stem, and foliage
3. Rarity
4. Substance

(B) COLLECTION OF HERBS FOR FLOWER SHOW ARRANGEMENT OR EXHIBITION CLASSES

SUGGESTED CLASSES:
1. Culinary herbs arranged in a wooden container, stoneware, or basket
2. Fragrant herbs arranged in pewter, colored glass, pottery
3. Medicinal herbs arranged in old mortar, apothecary jar, or other suitable container
4. Arrangement of mixed herbs in a copper or tin container
5. Tussie Mussies

IN JUDGING ARRANGEMENT CLASSES USING THOSE LISTED ABOVE CONSIDER:
1. Originality of arrangement
2. Condition of material
3. Color combination
4. Labeling

(C) HERBS AND/OR FLOWER ARRANGEMENT CLASSES

SUGGESTED CLASSES:
1. Design through color
2. Design through line
3. Massed arrangement of dried herbs and/or flowers

IN JUDGING AN ARRANGEMENT OF HERBS AND/OR FLOWERS, CONSIDER:
1. Design
2. Color
3. Balance
   a. Proportion of plant material to container
   b. Proportion of arrangement to space in schedule

4. Condition of plant material
5. Distinction

All plant material used to be listed by exhibitor and presented at entry desk before show.

(D)   MODERN HERB GARDENS

IN JUDGING THIS GROUP CONSIDER:
1. Simplicity in garden design or over-all design
2. Planting design—proper proportion of plants, height, and spacing to conform to design
3. Color
4. Condition of plant material
5. Proper use of garden accessories
6. Correct labeling

(E)   TRADITIONAL HERB GARDENS

SUGGESTED GARDENS TO CONSIDER IN JUDGING:
1. Early Medieval or Physic Garden. Consider simplicity of design, showing knowledge of herbs for the medieval household.
2. Late Medieval or Tudor Garden. In judging consider adaptation of traditional design, planting, proper accessories.
3. Knot Garden. Consider well-patterned design, proper edgings, showing knowledge of herbs for use as/or in knots.
4. Culinary Garden. Consider salad and flavoring plants.
5. Bee Garden. Consider herb plants for bee fodder, water source, suitable garden accessories.

(F) SPECIAL GARDENS

1. Fragrant Herb Gardens or Herb Walk for the Blind.
   Consider in judging raised beds of fragrant herbs, in-
   terestingly textured herbs, information in Braille on
   handrail, garden accessories such as dripping water,
   benches, etc.
2. Hospital Herb Garden. Consider simple design, correct
   and suitable planting, color, harmony, restful atmosphere.

The Committee has assigned no points to the above suggested Herb
Exhibits, the final decision to be arrived at by experienced, qualified
Judges.

Compiled by the Committee
on Revision of Rules for Judging Herb Exhibits.
MRS. HARRY BROKAW SMITH, *Chairman*
MRS. PAUL STURTEVANT, *Co-Chairman*

15. Tussie mussies

Our great-grandmothers carried tussie mussies when they had
to sit in long religious meetings. The crushed scent helped when
they felt faint. They also thought the aromatic, pungent aroma pre-
vented infection. These quaint little nosegays were made up of
several different flowers, mostly herbs. They were loved for their
sweet-smelling oils and antiseptic virtues. The Southern debutante
often carried them at coming-out parties, and the superstitious bride
liked some of the sweet-smelling little flowers tucked in her old-
fashioned wedding bouquet.

Take the tiny sweetheart rose for the center and surround it
with heliotrope, which in the language of flowers is "Eternal Love
and Devotion." Marjoram comes next, for it means "Joy and Happiness." Violets, third, are the symbol of "Modesty, Chastity, and
Loyalty." Sweet-smelling lavender comes next for "Lovers True, and
Strength of Heart." Rosemary, the most significant herb of all, has

been used since time immemorial for weddings. Rosemary is the sweet spicy herb for "Remembrance."

As the assembly with the delightful blessings of the gardens around the world comes to a close, I would like to remind the reader that gardening, the greatest of all hobbies, is waiting for you to pursue for a wonderful world of fragrance. The poem below, from an unknown writer, seems to have been written for the closing of this book.

> *Help us to plant and not destroy*
> *The beauties others should enjoy.*
> *Let us pass by and leave behind*
> *A part of each, of every kind*
> *Of scenery fair and birds in air,*
> *Of fish in streams and blossoms fair,*
> *So that ones who come our way*
> *In some far distant day,*
> *May say that we have guarded well*
> *The treasures among which they dwell.*

ACKNOWLEDGMENTS

Inspiration and encouragement in the work that has gone into the writing and compiling of this book have come from many friends. The writer wishes to express her gratitude to all of them, in particular to those listed below:

My daughter Betty, Mrs. Frank S. Doyle of Baltimore, Maryland, who helped so much in the home to make more time available to me for browsing, planting, and growing.

Frank B. Cox, Roanoke, Virginia, who lent me his cherished Gerard's *Herball* and acted as adviser and counselor.

Raymond G. Rhodes, Kroger Company, Roanoke, Virginia, who located many of the hard-to-find spices and herbs.

James Jongerneel, Rye, New York, whose tremendous background of growing up in the Far Eastern countries and sitting on the Spice Exchange in London, was of much firsthand help.

Mrs. John G. Berry, Garden Therapy Chairman—1954 National Council of State Garden Clubs, Goldthwaite, Texas.

Harold Lang, Roanoke, Virginia, a scholar and good friend.

Marie Johnston Fort, Griffin, Georgia, for her advice and encouragement.

T. C. Cheng, Washington, D.C., who told me of tea and the spices, especially ginger, and the curries of China.

Miss Emily and Miss Rory Cross, Richmond, Virginia, who shared flowering herbs from their Memory Garden.

Mrs. Harry Brokaw Smith, American Herb Society, New York Unit.

Clarence S. Brigham, Director of American Antiquarian Society, Worcester, Massachusetts.

Marshall W. Neale, American Spice Trade Association, New York, New York.

L. G. Schermerhorn, Jr., W. Atlee Burpee Co., Philadelphia, Pennsylvania.

Wayside Gardens, Mentor, Ohio.

Breck's of Boston, Boston, Massachusetts.

Kennett E. Relyea, Farmer Seed and Nursery Company, Faribault, Minnesota.

Ellen Saltonstall, Pan-American Coffee Bureau, New York, New York.

R. H. Shumway, Rockford, Illinois.

Mittie Arnold and Margaret Thomas, Greene Herb Gardens, Greene, Rhode Island.

Albert S. Beecher, Associate Horticulturist, Virginia Polytechnic Institute, Blacksburg, Virginia.

Mrs. J. W. Montgomery, Roanoke, Virginia, for her sincere interest and assistance in proofreading and editing.

Mrs. John P. Kelly, Arlington, Virginia; Mrs. Ted M. Jones, Bradenton, Florida; Mrs. Henry Glasgow, Salem, Virginia; Mrs. Edgar W. Smith, Akron, Ohio; Mrs. John Carper, Salem, Virginia; Mrs. W. W. Graves, Salem, Virginia; Mrs. Tracy Loyd, Roanoke, Virginia; Mrs. Gordon Brooks, Roanoke, Virginia; Mrs. Howard Creasy, Roanoke, Virginia; Mrs. Ella M. Smith, Tampa, Florida; Mrs. Fina Horner, Roanoke, Virginia; Mrs. Charles Dawson, Salem, Virginia; Mrs. Hazel K. Marshall, Roanoke, Virginia; Raymond Gene Kelso, Roanoke, Virginia; Mrs. Henry Grady Moore, Washington, D.C.; Miss Eleanor M. Rankin, Washington, D.C.; Mrs. Charles Farrelly, Roanoke, Virginia; Mrs. Virginia P. Miller, Roanoke, Virginia; Miss Ellen Goodwin, Salem, Virginia; Mrs. W. B. Adams, Roanoke, Virginia; LiliAnn Loubetta, Marseilles, France.

The various garden clubs who asked for programs and kept me searching for legend, lore, and modern uses.

Betty Bond, WSLS Television, Roanoke, Virginia, who wanted her many viewers to share knowledge of our heritage of fragrance, flavor, and beauty, and to be encouraged to plant and grow.

AND

Special thanks to my husband and son, who were my official critics, sounding board, and food tasters. They always showed joy and appreciation when a delightful aroma from the kitchen met them as they entered the house. The dishes were fragrant and flavorful, coming up to their expectations and they would beam with a happiness that is indescribable.

BIBLIOGRAPHY

A book is a garden, an orchard,
a storehouse, a party,
a company by the way,
a counsellor, a multitude of counsellors.

A GARDEN, AN ORCHARD

Gerard's Herball	1597–1633
Brothers of the Spade	
Correspondence of Peter Collinson of London and	1734–1746
John Custis of Williamsburg, Virginia . . . Swem	1948
Practical Floriculture . . . . Henderson	1889
Little Nature Library—Trees . . . . Rodgers	1917
Little Nature Library—Wild Flowers . . . . Blanchan	1923
Colonial Williamsburg: Its Buildings and Gardens . . .	
. . . . Kocher and Dearstyne	1949
Taylor's Encyclopedia of Gardening	1936
The Years in My Garden . . . . Fox	1933
10,000 Garden Questions	
. . . . . . Rockwell, Free, Everett, Grayson	1950
Wild Flowers of America . . . . Rickett	1953
The Vine and Its Fruit . . . . Denman	1875
Garden Gossip	
Recording the Activities of Gardening in the Mid-	
South	1950–1958
Spices . . . . American Spice Trade Association, Inc.	1956
The Primer for Herb Growing . Herb Society of America	1952–1954
Herbs, Their Culture and Uses . . . . . . Clarkson	1942

W. Atlee Burpee Co., Philadelphia (Catalogue) . . .   1948–1959
Savory Herbs Culture and Use . . . .
. . . . U. S. Department of Agriculture
Greene Herb Gardens . . . . Greene, R.I.
R. H. Shumway, Rockford, Ill. (Catalogue) . . . . .
Handbook on Herbs . . . . Brooklyn Botanic Gardens

A STOREHOUSE, A PARTY

The Medical Herbalist . . . . Yemm   1935–1937
The Historical and Scientific American Miscellany . . .   1867
Choicest Productions of English Authors   1853
The World and Its People
    A Comprehensive Tour of All Lands   1934
Compton's Pictured Encyclopedia   1949
The National Geographic Magazines   1948–1959
Herbs for the Kitchen . . . . Mazza   1947
The Tasting Spoon . . . . Troup   1955
Culinary Herbs . . . . Kains   1920
Esquire's Handbook for Hosts   1949

A COMPANY BY THE WAY

The Old and New Testaments . . . .
Shakespeare Complete . . . . Irving   1943
Flowers from Old Gardens . . . . Trovillion   1951
Siftings, the Major Portions of the Clearing and Collected
    Writings . . . . Jen Jensen   1956
The Garden of the Bellflowers . . . . Baily   1953
The World in Your Garden . . . .
    . . . . National Geographic Society   1957
The Illustrated London News   1952

A COUNSELLOR, A MULTITUDE OF COUNSELLORS

WEBSTER'S ENCYCLOPEDIA DICTIONARY
    LIBRARY OF ESSENTIAL KNOWLEDGE . . . . . .
        . . . . Meine, Hopkins, Jr., Michaelis

. . . . . . McDonal Leiper, Jr., Koffer, Graham   1943
THE AMERICAN COLLEGE DICTIONARY . . .
. . . . Barnhart   1949
EUROPE—A JOURNEY WITH PICTURES. Fremantle, Holme   1954
Nature Encyclopedia of America . . . . . . Jordon   1956
Story of Nations . . . . . . Rodgers, Adams, Brown   1955
Rand McNally World Guide . . . .
This Is America's Story . . . .
. . . . . . Wilder, Ludlum, Brown, Anderson   1954
Hammond's World Atlas   1950
Webster's New Twentieth Century Dictionary . . . .
. . . . McKechnie   1958
USEFUL QUOTATIONS—A CYCLOPEDIA OF QUOTATIONS .   1933
. . . . Edwards   1933

List of Suppliers

Your local herb shop or nursery probably carries the ingredients, seeds and plants discussed in this book. In addition, the following suppliers furnish herbs, spices and seeds through the mail. When making inquiries, it's always a good idea to enclose a stamped, self-addressed envelope.

APHRODISIA
28 Carmine Street
New York, NY 10014

BURPEE SEED COMPANY
300 Park Avenue
Warminster, PA 18991

CAPRILAND'S HERB FARM
Silver Street
Coventry, CT 06238

LEODAR NURSERIES
7206 Belvedere Road
West Palm Beach, FL 33406

Index

Aji. *See* Capsicum
Allspice, 33–36; Beth's spice cake, 35; blueberry pie, 36; ground: uses, 60; tree, 34; wassail bowl, 34–35; whole: uses, 60
Ambrosia, 99–100; anisette ambrosia, 100; growing, 227; uses, 99–100, 215
American Herbal, 147, 171
Angelica, 101–2, 155; candy, 102; growing, 227; uses, 215
Anise, 103–5; apple-anisette, 105; growing, 227; plant, 101, uses of, 104; uses, 215
Anisette ambrosia, 100
Annuals (herbs), 226
Apple ale, 164–65
Apple-anisette, 105
Apple mint, 164–65; apple ale, 164–65; growing, 233; uses, 220
Apple pie, old-fashioned, 138
Attar of roses, 186, 187

Balm (lemon balm), 105–6; growing, 227; uses, 215
Basil: bush, 204, sweet, 203–4
Bay, 37–39; -flavored chowder of lamb kidneys, 38–39; tree, 37–38; uses, 38, 60
Beau Brummell pomanders, 25
Bee balm. *See* Bergamot
Beef: chili, accent on, 178; savory tamale pie, 194–95
Bergamot, 106–7, 109; growing, 227; uses, 216
Beth's spice cake, 35
Betony, 107–8; growing, 227; Paul's,

109–10, growing, 228; uses, 216; wood, 108–9, growing, 227
Beverages, 65–82; allspice wassail bowl, 33–34; apple ale, 164–65; catnip in, 116; chart, 82; cocoa, 79–82. *See also* Cocoa; coffee, 65–73, *see also* Coffee; dandelion wine, 132; eggnog, 32; ginger and, 40; hot buttered rum, 29; rhubarb punch, ruby-red, 182; tea, 73–78, *see also* Tea; water, 65
Biennials (herbs), 226
"Big four," 24
Black ginger, 40
Black mustard, 166; growing, 234
Black pepper, 21–22
Black-seeded simpson salad, 23
Black tea, 75
Blueberry pie, all-spiced, 36
Borage, 110–11; growing, 228; uses, 216
Boston Tea Party, 76–77
Bouquet garni, 98
Brewing, hop in, 146
Brothers of the Spade, 95, 117
Brown mustard, 166
Burnet, 111; growing, 228; uses, 216
Bush basil, 204
Butter: nutmeg, 31; paprika, 57

Café au lait, 69
Café brûlot diabolique, 71
Cake icing, mocha, 35
Cakes: Christmas cardamom, 44; cocoa, quickie, 81–82; ginger 'n' honey crumb, 42; mace Mexican wedding, 33; orange jiffy gems, 48–

Cakes (*cont'd*)
  49; spice, Beth's, 35; sugar torte, Margaret's, 88; vanilla icebox, 47. *See also* Desserts *and* Ice cream
Calamus, 112–13; growing, 228; uses, 216
Cambric tea, 114
Camomile, 113–14; growing, 228; tea, 114; uses, 216
Camphor tree, 38
Candy: angelica, 102; horehound, 147
Capers, 54–55; crab meat salad, 54–55; uses, 61
Capsicum, 55–56; ground: uses, 61; whole: uses, 61; yam crisps, 56
Caraway, 114–16; growing, 228; seed, 115; uses, 216
Cardamom, 43–45; Christmas cake, 44; coffee, 44, 69; -flavored grape pie, 45; ground: uses, 61; whole: uses, 61
Catnip, 116; growing, 228; uses, 216
Cayenne pepper, 55, 56
Celery salt, 97
Charcoal-broiled steak à la Ed and Betty, 141–42
Chartreuse, sweet cicely and, 205
Charts: beverages, 82; herbs, 215–24; growing, 227–39; spices, 59–62
Chervil, 117–18; growing, 229; uses, 217
Chicken: English thyme stuffing, 211; rosemary Mediterranean soup, 185; saffron rice and, 53
Chicory, 118–19; growing, 229; uses, 217
Chili, accent on, 178
Chili peppers, uses, 221
Chilies. *See* Capsicum
Chives, 120–21; growing, 229; iceberg salad, 121; uses, 217
Chocolate: sauce, 81; uses, 82
Chowder, bay-flavored lamb kidneys, 38–39
Christmas cardamom cake, 44
Cinnamon, 27–30, 33, 97; "big four," 24; in cocoa, 80; in coffee, 69; crème debanane, 29–30; ground: uses, 60; hot buttered rum, 29; in tea, 76; tree, 17, 28–29; uses, 29;

whole: uses, 59
Clam crisps, de blanche, garlic, 141
Clary, 122–23; growing, 229; uses, 217
Cloves, 24–27, 33, 97; Beau Brummell pomanders, 26; in coffee, 69; "island plant," 28; pickle, watermelon rind, 26–27; tree, 17, 25; uses, 25–26, 59
Cocoa, 79–82; cake, quickie, 81–82; chocolate sauce, 81; hot chocolate à la Mexicano, 80; hot mocha java, 70; houses, 79; pot de crème, 81; tree, 80; types, 80; uses, 82
Coffee, 65–73; alexander, 71; Arabian, 66; café au lait, 69; café brûlot diabolique, 71; cardamom, 44; chicory and, 119; consumption, 67–68; dandelions and, 132; discovery, 65; glaze, 72; -glazed ham loaf, 72; growing regions, 66; hot mocha java, 70; houses, 66; Irish, 70; with liqueurs, 70; with meat, 73; orchard, 67; plant, 66; preparation, 68–69; royale, 70; saffron in, 69; spicy iced, 71–72; uses, 73, 82
Coffeehouses, 66
Conserves, minted cucumber, 165
Cookies, "open sesame," 198
Cordials, 97
Coriander, 123–25; growing, 229; seeds, 123–24; uses, 217
Costmary, 125–26; growing, 229; uses, 217
Crab meat salad, capers, 54–55
Crème debanane, 29–30
Cress: garden, 129; growing, 230; upland, 127; uses, 217; water, 128; winter. *See* Upland cress
Cumin, 129–30; growing, 230; sauce of enchiladas, 130–31; uses, 218
Curried lamb with macaroni, 50
Curry, uses of, 61. *See also* Turmeric
Curry powder, 50, 56; anise, 104; coriander, 124; cumin, 130

Damask rose, 186; growing, 236; uses, 221
Dandelion, 131–32; growing, 230; uses, 218; wine, 132

Desserts: anisette ambrosia, 100; apple-anisette, 105; cinnamon crème debanane, 29–30; floating island, 48; torte, Margaret's sugar, 88. *See also* Cakes and Pies

Dill, 133–35; growing, 230; potato and egg salad, 135; sauce de luxe, 135; seeds, 133; in tithing, 129; uses, 218

Eggnog, 32
Eglantine rose, 187–88; growing, 236; uses, 221
Emerald green santolina, 192
Enchiladas: cumin sauce for, 130–31; Kelsaz, 175–76
Eschallot. *See* Shallot

Fazenda. *See* Coffee, orchard
Fennel flower, 138–39; growing, 231; uses, 218
Fennels, 136–38; growing, 230; Italian, 137; old-fashioned apple pie, 138; ordinary, 136; sweet, 136; uses, 218
Feverfew, 139; growing, 231; uses, 218
Fines herbes, 98, 117, 193; combinations, 224; summer savory, 193
Fish, parsley broiled fillets, 172
Floating island, 48
Flower exhibits, rules for judging, 250–51
Flowers: tussie mussies, 253–54
French sorrel, 200–1; growing, 237

Garden cress, 129; growing, 230; uses, 217
Garden sorrel, 201–2; growing, 237
Gardens. *See* Herb gardens
Garlic, 97, 140–42; charcoal-broiled steak à la Ed and Betty, 141–42; clam crisps de blanche, 141; growing, 231; lesser-leaved, 183; rocambole, 182; uses, 218
Geranium-scented leaves, 142
Geraniums: growing, 231; uses, 218
German camomile, 114
Germander, 144; growing, 231; uses, 218
Ginger, 39–40; black, 40; candied:

uses, 60; ginseng, 41; ground: uses, 60–61; 'n' honey crumb cake, 42; roots, 49–50; -tomato preserves, 42–43; white, 40; whole: uses, 60. *See also* Wild ginger
Ginseng, 41
Grape pie, cardamom-flavored, 45
Green ginger preserve, 40
Green tea, 75

Ham loaf, coffee-glazed, 72
Henry VI, 188
Herball, 94–95, 155; dedication, 91–93
Herb exhibits, rules for judging, 249–52
Herb garden: for borders, 244; enlarged, 246; model annual, 241; model perennial, 240; modern, judging, 251; semi-formal "wayside," 243; small, 242, 243; special, judging, 252; for terraces, 244; traditional, judging, 251; window boxes, 245
Herbs, 94–98; annuals and biennials, 226; *bouquet garni*, 98; chart, 215–24; chief ones used, 224; dried, 97; drying, 247; exhibits, *see* Herb exhibits; fagot of, 98; *fines herbes*, 98, 117, 193, combinations, 224; flavoring for cordials, 97; freezing, 247; garden, *see* Herb garden; growing, 225–46, chart, 227–39; kinds, 99–214, *see also under* name of herb; measurements, 97; perennials, 225–26; preparing, 97, 247; robust, outstanding, 224; thawing, 248. *See also* Herball
Honey, horehound, 147
Hop, 145–46; growing, 231; uses, 219
Horehound, 146–48; candy, 147; growing, 232; uses, 219
Hors d'oeuvres: garlic clam crisps de blanche, 141
Horse-radish, 148–49; and cheese sandwiches, 149; growing, 232; uses, 219
Hot buttered rum, 29
Hot mocha java, 70
Hyssop, 149–50; growing, 232; uses, 219

Iceberg salad, 121
Ice cream, Deep South, 47
Irish coffee, 70
Italian fennel, 137

Kidneys, lamb, bay-flavored chowder of, 38–39

Lamb, curried, with macaroni, 50
Lavender, 151–52, 253; growing, 232; uses, 219
Lavender cotton santolina, 191–92
Leek, 153–54; growing, 232; uses, 219
Lemon balm, 105–6; growing, 227
Lemon geranium, 143; growing, 231
Lemon thyme, 210
Lemon verbena, 154–55; growing, 232; uses, 219
Lesser-leaved garlic, 183
Liqueurs, coffee with, 70
Liver, parsley party pâté, 172–73
Lovage, 110, 155–56; growing, 233; uses, 219

Mace: ground, uses, 60; Mexican wedding cakes, 33; oil of, 31; sauce for fruit dishes, 32–33; uses, 60. *See also* Nutmeg and mace
Mandrake. *See* May apple
Marigold, pot, growing, 233
Marjoram, 253; growing, 233; pot, 159–60; sweet, 157–59; uses, 219
May apple, 160–61; growing, 233; uses, 220
Meat: coffee with, 73; savory tamale pie, 194–95. *See also under* name of meat
Mint: apple, 164–65; growing, 233–34; minted cucumber conserve, 165; peppermint, 162–63; spearmint, 162–63; in tea, 76; in tithing, 129; universal sauce, 165; uses, 220
Minted cucumber conserve, 165
Mocha icing, 35
Mustard, 97; black or brown, 166; growing, 234; uses, 220; white or yellow, 167

Nasturtium, 167–69; growing, 234; pickled pods, 169; uses, 168, 220
National Standard Dispensary, 207

Nosegays. *See* Tussie mussies
Nutmeg, 33, 97; "big four," 24; butter, 31; in cocoa, 80; eggnog, 32; "island plant," 28; and mace, 30–33; mace Mexican wedding cakes, 33; mace sauce for fruit dishes, 32–33; tree, 17, 30–31; uses, 31, 60

"Open sesame" cookies, 198
Opium poppy. *See* Poppy
Orange jiffy gems, 48–49
Orange syrup, 49
Orégano, 169–70; growing, 234; pork Mexicana, 170; uses, 220

Paella, 52
Pan American Coffee Bureau, 68
Paprika, 56–57, 62; butter, 57; coloring agent, 57
Paraguay tea, 76
Parsley, 171–73; broiled fillets, 172; after garlic, 140, 171; growing, 234; party pâté, 172–73; uses, 220
Party pic-a-unes, 178
Pastry, double-crust, 36
Pâté, parsley party, 172–73
Paul's betony, 109–10; growing, 228
Pennyroyal, 173–74; growing, 234; uses, 221
Pepper, 20–23, 97; "big four," 24; black-seeded simpson salad, 23; cayenne, 55, 56; growing, 235; small red chili, 175–78, *see* Red chili pepper; tabasco, *see* Pepper tabasco; uses, 59, 221; white, potato soup, 22–23
Pepper tabasco, 174–75; growing, 235; uses, 221
Peppermint, 162–63; growing, 234; tea, 163; uses, 220
Perennials (herbs), 225–26
Pickled nasturtium pods, 169
Pies: apple, old-fashioned, 138; blueberry, all-spiced, 36; grape, cardamom-flavored, 45; pastry, double-crust, 36; rhubarb parfait, red, 181
Pomanders, Beau Brummell, 26
Poppy, 179–80; Control Act of 1942, 180; growing, 235; uses, 221
Pork: enchiladas Kelsaz, 175–76; Mexicana, orégano, 170

Pot de crème, 81
Pot marigold, 156–57, 219
Pot marjoram, 159–60; growing, 233
Potatoes: savory, 195; soup, white pepper, 22–23; yam crisps, 56
Preserves: ginger-tomato, 42–43; green ginger, 40; watermelon rind, 26–27
Provence rose, 186–87; growing, 236; uses, 221
Punch: rhubarb, ruby-red, 182; tea as base, 78

Red chili pepper, small, 175–78; accent on chili, 178; enchiladas Kelsaz, 175–76; growing, 235; party pic-a-unes, 178; pot soup, 176–77; red devil squash creole, 177
Rhubarb, 180–82; growing, 235; parfait pie, red, 181; punch, ruby-red, 182; uses, 221
Rice, saffron, and chicken, 53
Richard II, 189
Rocambole, 182–83; growing, 235; uses, 221
Roman camomile, 114
Roman coriander. *See* Fennel flower
Rose geranium, 142–43; growing, 231
Rose petal beads, 85
Roses, 185–88; attar of, 186, 187; damask, 186; eglantine, 187–88; growing, 236; provence, 186–87; uses, 221
Rosemary, 96, 184–85, 189, 253–54; growing, 235; Mediterranean soup, 185; uses, 221
Rue, 188–89; growing, 236; uses, 221
Rum, hot buttered, 29

Saffron: in coffee, 69; coloring agent, 57; pot marigold and, 157; rice and chicken, 53; uses, 61
Saffron crocus, 51–53; cost of, 52; uses, 52
Sage, 189–90, 210; growing, 236; sweet marjoram and, 159; uses, 222
Salad dressing, turmeric, 51
Salads: black-seeded simpson, 23; crab meat, capers, 54–55; dill potato and egg, 135; iceberg, 121;

turmeric garden, 51
Salt, 83–85; beads, quaint perfumed, 85; colored, 84; most famous mines, 84; uses, 84–85
Sandwiches: horse-radish and cheese, 149; tarragon tastys, 209; water cress, 128
Santolinas, 191–92; emerald green, 192; growing, 236; lavender cotton, 191–92; uses, 222
Sassafras tree, 38
Sauces: chocolate, 81; cumin, for enchiladas, 130–31; dill, de luxe, 135; mace, for fruit dishes, 32–33; mint, universal, 165
Savory: growing, 236–37; potatoes, 195; summer, 192–93; tamale pie, 194–95; uses, 222; winter, 193–95, 222, 237
Seasonings: *bouquet garni*, 98; salt, 83–85; sugar, 86–87; sugar beet, 87. *See also* Herbs *and* Spices
Sesame, 196–98; growing, 237; "open" cookies, 198; uses, 222
Shallot, 199; growing, 237; uses, 222
Sicillian fennel. *See* Italian fennel
Snuff, sweet basil and, 204
Sorrel: French, 200–1; garden, 201–2; growing, 237; uses, 222; wood, 202–3
Soups: red pepper pot, 176–77; rosemary Mediterranean, 185; white pepper potato, 22–23. *See also* Chowder
Spearmint, 163; growing, 234; uses, 220
Spice chart, 59–62
Spices, 15–19; chart, 59–62; standard, 97; uses, 19; world's most expensive, 52. *See also under* name of spice
Spicy iced coffee, 71–72
Squash creole, red devil, 177
Steak, charcoal-broiled, à la Ed and Betty, 141–42
Stuffing, English thyme, 211
Sugar, 86–87; torte, Margaret's, 88
Sugar beet, 87
Summer savory, 192–93; growing, 236
Sweet basil, 203–4; growing, 237; uses, 222

Sweet cicely, 205; growing, 238; uses, 223
Sweet fennel, 136
Sweet marjoram, 157–59; growing, 233
Sweet woodruff, 206–7; growing, 238; uses, 223

"Talking leaves" tea, 77–78
Tamale pie, savory, 194–95
Tansy, 207–8; growing, 238; uses, 223
Tarragon, 208–9; growing, 238; tastys, 209; uses, 223
Tea, 73–78; American consumption, 77; from anise, 78; bergamot, 107; black, 75; Boston Tea Party, 76–77; cambric, 114; catnip, 116; ceremony, 75; *Ch'a Ching* or *Tea Classic*, 74; cultivation, 74; Fina's "Talking leaves," 77–78; flavor, 75; green, 75; lemon verbena, 155; "Matilda," 76; Oswego, 107; Paraguay, 76; peppermint, 163; plants, 74; trade names, 74–75; Trinidad, 76; *tsamba*, 76; uses, 82; wintergreen, 212; *yaupon*, 76
Thelma's clove pickle, 26–27
Thyme, 209–11; English stuffing, 211; growing, 238; lemon, 210; uses, 223
Tranquilizers, 116
Trinidad tea, 76
Tsamba, 76
Turmeric, 49–51; curried lamb with macaroni, 50; curry, use of, 61; dressing, 51; garden salad, 51; uses, 49, 50
Tussie mussies, 253–54

Universal mint sauce, 163, 165

Upland cress, 127; growing, 230; uses, 217

Vanilla, 45–49; in cocoa, 80; extract: uses, 61; floating island, 48; icebox cake, 47; ice cream, Deep South, 47; orange jiffy gems, 48–49
Violets, 253

Wassail bowl, allspice, 34–35
Water, 65
Water cress, 128; growing, 230; sandwich, 128; uses, 217
Watermelon rind, 26–27
White ginger, 40
White mustard, 167; growing, 234
White pepper, 21–22; potato soup, 22–23
Wild ginger, 41–43; growing, 238; 'n' honey crumb cake, 42; -tomato preserves, 42–43; uses, 223
Wild marjoram. *See* Pot marjoram
Wine, dandelion, 132
Winter cress. *See* Upland cress
Winter savory, 193–95; growing, 237; uses, 222
Wintergreen, 211–12; growing, 239; tea, 212; uses, 223
Witloof. *See* Chicory
"Wonder drugs," 101, 110, 155
Wood betony, 108–9; growing, 227
Wood sorrel, 202–3; growing, 237
Woodruff, sweet, 206–7

Yam crisps, 56
Yarrow, 213–14; growing, 239; uses, 224
Yaupon, 76
Yellow mustard, 167

A CATALOG OF SELECTED
DOVER BOOKS
IN ALL FIELDS OF INTEREST

A CATALOG OF SELECTED DOVER BOOKS IN ALL FIELDS OF INTEREST

CONCERNING THE SPIRITUAL IN ART, Wassily Kandinsky. Pioneering work by father of abstract art. Thoughts on color theory, nature of art. Analysis of earlier masters. 12 illustrations. 80pp. of text. 5⅜ × 8½. 23411-8 Pa. $2.95

LEONARDO ON THE HUMAN BODY, Leonardo da Vinci. More than 1200 of Leonardo's anatomical drawings on 215 plates. Leonardo's text, which accompanies the drawings, has been translated into English. 506pp. 8⅜ × 11¾. 24483-0 Pa. $11.95

GOBLIN MARKET, Christina Rossetti. Best-known work by poet comparable to Emily Dickinson, Alfred Tennyson. With 46 delightfully grotesque illustrations by Laurence Housman. 64pp. 4 × 6¾. 24516-0 Pa. $2.50

THE HEART OF THOREAU'S JOURNALS, edited by Odell Shepard. Selections from *Journal*, ranging over full gamut of interests. 228pp. 5⅜ × 8½. 20741-2 Pa. $4.50

MR. LINCOLN'S CAMERA MAN: MATHEW B. BRADY, Roy Meredith. Over 300 Brady photos reproduced directly from original negatives, photos. Lively commentary. 368pp. 8⅜ × 11¼. 23021-X Pa. $14.95

PHOTOGRAPHIC VIEWS OF SHERMAN'S CAMPAIGN, George N. Barnard. Reprint of landmark 1866 volume with 61 plates: battlefield of New Hope Church, the Etawah Bridge, the capture of Atlanta, etc. 80pp. 9 × 12. 23445-2 Pa. $6.00

A SHORT HISTORY OF ANATOMY AND PHYSIOLOGY FROM THE GREEKS TO HARVEY, Dr. Charles Singer. Thoroughly engrossing non-technical survey. 270 illustrations. 211pp. 5⅜ × 8½. 20389-1 Pa. $4.95

REDOUTE ROSES IRON-ON TRANSFER PATTERNS, Barbara Christopher. Redouté was botanical painter to the Empress Josephine; transfer his famous roses onto fabric with these 24 transfer patterns. 80pp. 8¼ × 10⅞. 24292-7 Pa. $3.50

THE FIVE BOOKS OF ARCHITECTURE, Sebastiano Serlio. Architectural milestone, first (1611) English translation of Renaissance classic. Unabridged reproduction of original edition includes over 300 woodcut illustrations. 416pp. 9⅜ × 12¼. 24349-4 Pa. $14.95

CARLSON'S GUIDE TO LANDSCAPE PAINTING, John F. Carlson. Authoritative, comprehensive guide covers, every aspect of landscape painting. 34 reproductions of paintings by author; 58 explanatory diagrams. 144pp. 8⅜ × 11. 22927-0 Pa. $5.95

101 PUZZLES IN THOUGHT AND LOGIC, C.R. Wylie, Jr. Solve murders, robberies, see which fishermen are liars—purely by reasoning! 107pp. 5⅜ × 8½. 20367-0 Pa. $2.00

TEST YOUR LOGIC, George J. Summers. 50 more truly new puzzles with new turns of thought, new subtleties of inference. 100pp. 5⅜ × 8½. 22877-0 Pa. $2.50

THE MURDER BOOK OF J.G. REEDER, Edgar Wallace. Eight suspenseful stories by bestselling mystery writer of 20s and 30s. Features the donnish Mr. J.G. Reeder of Public Prosecutor's Office. 128pp. 5⅜ × 8½.

24374-5 Pa. $3.95

ANNE ORR'S CHARTED DESIGNS, Anne Orr. Best designs by premier needlework designer, all on charts: flowers, borders, birds, children, alphabets, etc. Over 100 charts, 10 in color. Total of 40pp. 8¼ × 11.   23704-4 Pa. $2.50

BASIC CONSTRUCTION TECHNIQUES FOR HOUSES AND SMALL BUILDINGS SIMPLY EXPLAINED, U.S. Bureau of Naval Personnel. Grading, masonry, woodworking, floor and wall framing, roof framing, plastering, tile setting, much more. Over 675 illustrations. 568pp. 6½ × 9¼.   20242-9 Pa. $9.95

MATISSE LINE DRAWINGS AND PRINTS, Henri Matisse. Representative collection of female nudes, faces, still lifes, experimental works, etc., from 1898 to 1948. 50 illustrations. 48pp. 8⅜ × 11¼.   23877-6 Pa. $3.50

HOW TO PLAY THE CHESS OPENINGS, Eugene Znosko-Borovsky. Clear, profound examinations of just what each opening is intended to do and how opponent can counter. Many sample games. 147pp. 5⅜ × 8½.   22795-2 Pa. $3.50

DUPLICATE BRIDGE, Alfred Sheinwold. Clear, thorough, easily followed account: rules, etiquette, scoring, strategy, bidding; Goren's point-count system, Blackwood and Gerber conventions, etc. 158pp. 5⅜ × 8½.   22741-3 Pa. $3.50

SARGENT PORTRAIT DRAWINGS, J.S. Sargent. Collection of 42 portraits reveals technical skill and intuitive eye of noted American portrait painter, John Singer Sargent. 48pp. 8¼ × 11⅛.   24524-1 Pa. $3.50

ENTERTAINING SCIENCE EXPERIMENTS WITH EVERYDAY OBJECTS, Martin Gardner. Over 100 experiments for youngsters. Will amuse, astonish, teach, and entertain. Over 100 illustrations. 127pp. 5⅜ × 8½.   24201-3 Pa. $2.50

TEDDY BEAR PAPER DOLLS IN FULL COLOR: A Family of Four Bears and Their Costumes, Crystal Collins. A family of four Teddy Bear paper dolls and nearly 60 cut-out costumes. Full color, printed one side only. 32pp. 9¼ × 12¼.

24550-0 Pa. $3.50

NEW CALLIGRAPHIC ORNAMENTS AND FLOURISHES, Arthur Baker. Unusual, multi-useable material: arrows, pointing hands, brackets and frames, ovals, swirls, birds, etc. Nearly 700 illustrations. 80pp. 8⅜ × 11¼.

24095-9 Pa. $3.75

DINOSAUR DIORAMAS TO CUT & ASSEMBLE, M. Kalmenoff. Two complete three-dimensional scenes in full color, with 31 cut-out animals and plants. Excellent educational toy for youngsters. Instructions; 2 assembly diagrams. 32pp. 9¼ × 12¼.   24541-1 Pa. $4.50

SILHOUETTES: A PICTORIAL ARCHIVE OF VARIED ILLUSTRATIONS, edited by Carol Belanger Grafton. Over 600 silhouettes from the 18th to 20th centuries. Profiles and full figures of men, women, children, birds, animals, groups and scenes, nature, ships, an alphabet. 144pp. 8⅜ × 11¼.   23781-8 Pa. $5.95

25 KITES THAT FLY, Leslie Hunt. Full, easy-to-follow instructions for kites made from inexpensive materials. Many novelties. 70 illustrations. 110pp. 5⅜ × 8½.
22550-X Pa. $2.50

PIANO TUNING, J. Cree Fischer. Clearest, best book for beginner, amateur. Simple repairs, raising dropped notes, tuning by easy method of flattened fifths. No previous skills needed. 4 illustrations. 201pp. 5⅜ × 8½.   23267-0 Pa. $3.50

EARLY AMERICAN IRON-ON TRANSFER PATTERNS, edited by Rita Weiss. 75 designs, borders, alphabets, from traditional American sources. 48pp. 8¼ × 11.
23162-3 Pa. $1.95

CROCHETING EDGINGS, edited by Rita Weiss. Over 100 of the best designs for these lovely trims for a host of household items. Complete instructions, illustrations. 48pp. 8¼ × 11.   24031-2 Pa. $2.95

FINGER PLAYS FOR NURSERY AND KINDERGARTEN, Emilie Poulsson. 18 finger plays with music (voice and piano); entertaining, instructive. Counting, nature lore, etc. Victorian classic. 53 illustrations. 80pp. 6½ × 9¼. 22588-7 Pa. $2.25

BOSTON THEN AND NOW, Peter Vanderwarker. Here in 59 side-by-side views are photographic documentations of the city's past and present. 119 photographs. Full captions. 122pp. 8¼ × 11.   24312-5 Pa. $7.95

CROCHETING BEDSPREADS, edited by Rita Weiss. 22 patterns, originally published in three instruction books 1939-41. 39 photos, 8 charts. Instructions. 48pp. 8¼ × 11.   23610-2 Pa. $2.00

HAWTHORNE ON PAINTING, Charles W. Hawthorne. Collected from notes taken by students at famous Cape Cod School; hundreds of direct, personal *apercus*, ideas, suggestions. 91pp. 5⅜ × 8½.   20653-X Pa. $2.95

THERMODYNAMICS, Enrico Fermi. A classic of modern science. Clear, organized treatment of systems, first and second laws, entropy, thermodynamic potentials, etc. Calculus required. 160pp. 5⅜ × 8½.   60361-X Pa. $4.50

TEN BOOKS ON ARCHITECTURE, Vitruvius. The most important book ever written on architecture. Early Roman aesthetics, technology, classical orders, site selection, all other aspects. Morgan translation. 331pp. 5⅜ × 8½. 20645-9 Pa. $6.95

THE CORNELL BREAD BOOK, Clive M. McCay and Jeanette B. McCay. Famed high-protein recipe incorporated into breads, rolls, buns, coffee cakes, pizza, pie crusts, more. Nearly 50 illustrations. 48pp. 8¼ × 11.   23995-0 Pa. $2.00

THE CRAFTSMAN'S HANDBOOK, Cennino Cennini. 15th-century handbook, school of Giotto, explains applying gold, silver leaf; gesso; fresco painting, grinding pigments, etc. 142pp. 6⅛ × 9¼.   20054-X Pa. $3.95

FRANK LLOYD WRIGHT'S FALLINGWATER, Donald Hoffmann. Full story of Wright's masterwork at Bear Run, Pa. 100 photographs of site, construction, and details of completed structure. 112pp. 9¼ × 10.   23671-4 Pa. $7.95

OVAL STAINED GLASS PATTERN BOOK, C. Eaton. 60 new designs framed in shape of an oval. Greater complexity, challenge with sinuous cats, birds, mandalas framed in antique shape. 64pp. 8¼ × 11.   24519-5 Pa. $3.95

THE BOOK OF WOOD CARVING, Charles Marshall Sayers. Still finest book for beginning student. Fundamentals, technique; gives 34 designs, over 34 projects for panels, bookends, mirrors, etc. 33 photos. 118pp. 7¾ × 10⅝. 23654-4 Pa. $3.95

CARVING COUNTRY CHARACTERS, Bill Higginbotham. Expert advice for beginning, advanced carvers on materials, techniques for creating 18 projects— mirthful panorama of American characters. 105 illustrations. 80pp. 8⅜ × 11. 24135-1 Pa. $2.95

300 ART NOUVEAU DESIGNS AND MOTIFS IN FULL COLOR, C.B. Grafton. 44 full-page plates display swirling lines and muted colors typical of Art Nouveau. Borders, frames, panels, cartouches, dingbats, etc. 48pp. 9⅜ × 12¼. 24354-0 Pa. $6.95

SELF-WORKING CARD TRICKS, Karl Fulves. Editor of *Pallbearer* offers 72 tricks that work automatically through nature of card deck. No sleight of hand needed. Often spectacular. 42 illustrations. 113pp. 5⅜ × 8½. 23334-0 Pa. $3.50

CUT AND ASSEMBLE A WESTERN FRONTIER TOWN, Edmund V. Gillon, Jr. Ten authentic full-color buildings on heavy cardboard stock in H-O scale. Sheriff's Office and Jail, Saloon, Wells Fargo, Opera House, others. 48pp. 9¼ × 12¼. 23736-2 Pa. $4.95

CUT AND ASSEMBLE AN EARLY NEW ENGLAND VILLAGE, Edmund V. Gillon, Jr. Printed in full color on heavy cardboard stock. 12 authentic buildings in H-O scale: Adams home in Quincy, Mass., Oliver Wight house in Sturbridge, smithy, store, church, others. 48pp. 9¼ × 12¼. 23536-X Pa. $4.95

THE TALE OF TWO BAD MICE, Beatrix Potter. Tom Thumb and Hunca Munca squeeze out of their hole and go exploring. 27 full-color Potter illustrations. 59pp. 4¼ × 5½. (Available in U.S. only) 23065-1 Pa. $1.75

CARVING FIGURE CARICATURES IN THE OZARK STYLE, Harold L. Enlow. Instructions and illustrations for ten delightful projects, plus general carving instructions. 22 drawings and 47 photographs altogether. 39pp. 8⅜ × 11. 23151-8 Pa. $2.95

A TREASURY OF FLOWER DESIGNS FOR ARTISTS, EMBROIDERERS AND CRAFTSMEN, Susan Gaber. 100 garden favorites lushly rendered by artist for artists, craftsmen, needleworkers. Many form frames, borders. 80pp. 8¼ × 11. 24096-7 Pa. $3.95

CUT & ASSEMBLE A TOY THEATER/THE NUTCRACKER BALLET, Tom Tierney. Model of a complete, full-color production of Tchaikovsky's classic. 6 backdrops, dozens of characters, familiar dance sequences. 32pp. 9⅜ × 12¼. 24194-7 Pa. $4.50

ANIMALS: 1,419 COPYRIGHT-FREE ILLUSTRATIONS OF MAMMALS, BIRDS, FISH, INSECTS, ETC., edited by Jim Harter. Clear wood engravings present, in extremely lifelike poses, over 1,000 species of animals. 284pp. 9 × 12. 23766-4 Pa. $9.95

MORE HAND SHADOWS, Henry Bursill. For those at their 'finger ends,'' 16 more effects—Shakespeare, a hare, a squirrel, Mr. Punch, and twelve more—each explained by a full-page illustration. Considerable period charm. 30pp. 6½ × 9¼. 21384-6 Pa. $1.95

SURREAL STICKERS AND UNREAL STAMPS, William Rowe. 224 haunting, hilarious stamps on gummed, perforated stock, with images of elephants, geisha girls, George Washington, etc. 16pp. one side. 8¼ × 11.   24371-0 Pa. $3.50

GOURMET KITCHEN LABELS, Ed Sibbett, Jr. 112 full-color labels (4 copies each of 28 designs). Fruit, bread, other culinary motifs. Gummed and perforated. 16pp. 8¼ × 11.   24087-8 Pa. $2.95

PATTERNS AND INSTRUCTIONS FOR CARVING AUTHENTIC BIRDS, H.D. Green. Detailed instructions, 27 diagrams, 85 photographs for carving 15 species of birds so life-like, they'll seem ready to fly! 8¼ × 11.   24222-6 Pa. $3.00

FLATLAND, E.A. Abbott. Science-fiction classic explores life of 2-D being in 3-D world. 16 illustrations. 103pp. 5⅜ × 8.   20001-9 Pa. $2.00

DRIED FLOWERS, Sarah Whitlock and Martha Rankin. Concise, clear, practical guide to dehydration, glycerinizing, pressing plant material, and more. Covers use of silica gel. 12 drawings. 32pp. 5⅜ × 8½.   21802-3 Pa. $1.00

EASY-TO-MAKE CANDLES, Gary V. Guy. Learn how easy it is to make all kinds of decorative candles. Step-by-step instructions. 82 illustrations. 48pp. 8¼ × 11.

     23881-4 Pa. $2.95

SUPER STICKERS FOR KIDS, Carolyn Bracken. 128 gummed and perforated full-color stickers: GIRL WANTED, KEEP OUT, BORED OF EDUCATION, X-RATED, COMBAT ZONE, many others. 16pp. 8¼ × 11.   24092-4 Pa. $3.50

CUT AND COLOR PAPER MASKS, Michael Grater. Clowns, animals, funny faces...simply color them in, cut them out, and put them together, and you have 9 paper masks to play with and enjoy. 32pp. 8¼ × 11.   23171-2 Pa. $2.95

A CHRISTMAS CAROL: THE ORIGINAL MANUSCRIPT, Charles Dickens. Clear facsimile of Dickens manuscript, on facing pages with final printed text. 8 illustrations by John Leech, 4 in color on covers. 144pp. 8⅜ × 11¼.

     20980-6 Pa. $5.95

CARVING SHOREBIRDS, Harry V. Shourds & Anthony Hillman. 16 full-size patterns (all double-page spreads) for 19 North American shorebirds with step-by-step instructions. 72pp. 9¼ × 12¼.   24287-0 Pa. $5.95

THE GENTLE ART OF MATHEMATICS, Dan Pedoe. Mathematical games, probability, the question of infinity, topology, how the laws of algebra work, problems of irrational numbers, and more. 42 figures. 143pp. 5⅜ × 8½.

     22949-1 Pa. $3.50

READY-TO-USE DOLLHOUSE WALLPAPER, Katzenbach & Warren, Inc. Stripe, 2 floral stripes, 2 allover florals, polka dot; all in full color. 4 sheets (350 sq. in.) of each, enough for average room. 48pp. 8¼ × 11.   23495-9 Pa. $2.95

MINIATURE IRON-ON TRANSFER PATTERNS FOR DOLLHOUSES, DOLLS, AND SMALL PROJECTS, Rita Weiss and Frank Fontana. Over 100 miniature patterns: rugs, bedspreads, quilts, chair seats, etc. In standard dollhouse size. 48pp. 8¼ × 11.   23741-9 Pa. $1.95

THE DINOSAUR COLORING BOOK, Anthony Rao. 45 renderings of dinosaurs, fossil birds, turtles, other creatures of Mesozoic Era. Scientifically accurate. Captions. 48pp. 8¼ × 11.   24022-3 Pa. $2.50

JAPANESE DESIGN MOTIFS, Matsuya Co. Mon, or heraldic designs. Over 4000 typical, beautiful designs: birds, animals, flowers, swords, fans, geometrics; all beautifully stylized. 213pp. 11⅜ × 8¼.   22874-6 Pa. $7.95

THE TALE OF BENJAMIN BUNNY, Beatrix Potter. Peter Rabbit's cousin coaxes him back into Mr. McGregor's garden for a whole new set of adventures. All 27 full-color illustrations. 59pp. 4¼ × 5½. (Available in U.S. only)   21102-9 Pa. $1.75

THE TALE OF PETER RABBIT AND OTHER FAVORITE STORIES BOXED SET, Beatrix Potter. Seven of Beatrix Potter's best-loved tales including Peter Rabbit in a specially designed, durable boxed set. 4¼ × 5½. Total of 447pp. 158 color illustrations. (Available in U.S. only)   23903-9 Pa. $12.25

PRACTICAL MENTAL MAGIC, Theodore Annemann. Nearly 200 astonishing feats of mental magic revealed in step-by-step detail. Complete advice on staging, patter, etc. Illustrated. 320pp. 5⅜ × 8½.   24426-1 Pa. $5.95

CELEBRATED CASES OF JUDGE DEE (DEE GOONG AN), translated by Robert Van Gulik. Authentic 18th-century Chinese detective novel; Dee and associates solve three interlocked cases. Led to van Gulik's own stories with same characters. Extensive introduction. 9 illustrations. 237pp. 5⅜ × 8½.
23337-5 Pa. $4.95

CUT & FOLD EXTRATERRESTRIAL INVADERS THAT FLY, M. Grater. Stage your own lilliputian space battles.By following the step-by-step instructions and explanatory diagrams you can launch 22 full-color fliers into space. 36pp. 8¼ × 11.   24478-4 Pa. $2.95

CUT & ASSEMBLE VICTORIAN HOUSES, Edmund V. Gillon, Jr. Printed in full color on heavy cardboard stock, 4 authentic Victorian houses in H-O scale: Italian-style Villa, Octagon, Second Empire, Stick Style. 48pp. 9¼ × 12¼.
23849-0 Pa. $4.95

BEST SCIENCE FICTION STORIES OF H.G. WELLS, H.G. Wells. Full novel The Invisible Man, plus 17 short stories: "The Crystal Egg," "Aepyornis Island," "The Strange Orchid," etc. 303pp. 5⅜ × 8½. (Available in U.S. only)
21531-8 Pa. $4.95

TRADEMARK DESIGNS OF THE WORLD, Yusaku Kamekura. A lavish collection of nearly 700 trademarks, the work of Wright, Loewy, Klee, Binder, hundreds of others. 160pp. 8¾ × 8.   (EJ) 24191-2 Pa. $5.95

THE ARTIST'S AND CRAFTSMAN'S GUIDE TO REDUCING, ENLARGING AND TRANSFERRING DESIGNS, Rita Weiss. Discover, reduce, enlarge, transfer designs from any objects to any craft project. 12pp. plus 16 sheets special graph paper. 8¼ × 11.   24142-4 Pa. $3.95

TREASURY OF JAPANESE DESIGNS AND MOTIFS FOR ARTISTS AND CRAFTSMEN, edited by Carol Belanger Grafton. Indispensable collection of 360 traditional Japanese designs and motifs redrawn in clean, crisp black-and-white, copyright-free illustrations. 96pp. 8¼ × 11.   24435-0 Pa. $4.50

CATALOG OF DOVER BOOKS

CHANCERY CURSIVE STROKE BY STROKE, Arthur Baker. Instructions and illustrations for each stroke of each letter (upper and lower case) and numerals. 54 full-page plates. 64pp. 8¼ × 11.　　　　24278-1 Pa. $2.50

THE ENJOYMENT AND USE OF COLOR, Walter Sargent. Color relationships, values, intensities; complementary colors, illumination, similar topics. Color in nature and art. 7 color plates, 29 illustrations. 274pp. 5⅜ × 8½.　20944-X Pa. $4.95

SCULPTURE PRINCIPLES AND PRACTICE, Louis Slobodkin. Step-by-step approach to clay, plaster, metals, stone; classical and modern. 253 drawings, photos. 255pp. 8⅛ × 11.　　　　22960-2 Pa. $7.50

VICTORIAN FASHION PAPER DOLLS FROM HARPER'S BAZAR, 1867-1898, Theodore Menten. Four female dolls with 28 elegant high fashion costumes, printed in full color. 32pp. 9¼ × 12¼.　　　　23453-3 Pa. $3.95

FLOPSY, MOPSY AND COTTONTAIL: A Little Book of Paper Dolls in Full Color, Susan LaBelle. Three dolls and 21 costumes (7 for each doll) show Peter Rabbit's siblings dressed for holidays, gardening, hiking, etc. Charming borders, captions. 48pp. 4¼ × 5½. (USCO)　　　　24376-1 Pa. $2.50

NATIONAL LEAGUE BASEBALL CARD CLASSICS, Bert Randolph Sugar. 83 big-leaguers from 1909-69 on facsimile cards. Hubbell, Dean, Spahn, Brock plus advertising, info, no duplications. Perforated, detachable. 16pp. 8¼ × 11.
24308-7 Pa. $3.50

THE LOGICAL APPROACH TO CHESS, Dr. Max Euwe, et al. First-rate text of comprehensive strategy, tactics, theory for the amateur. No gambits to memorize, just a clear, logical approach. 224pp. 5⅜ × 8½.　　　24353-2 Pa. $4.50

MAGICK IN THEORY AND PRACTICE, Aleister Crowley. The summation of the thought and practice of the century's most famous necromancer, long hard to find. Crowley's best book. 436pp. 5⅜ × 8½. (Available in U.S. only)
23295-6 Pa. $6.95

THE HAUNTED HOTEL, Wilkie Collins. Collins' last great tale; doom and destiny in a Venetian palace. Praised by T.S. Eliot. 127pp. 5⅜ × 8½.
24333-8 Pa. $3.00

ART DECO DISPLAY ALPHABETS, Dan X. Solo. Wide variety of bold yet elegant lettering in handsome Art Deco styles. 100 complete fonts, with numerals, punctuation, more. 104pp. 8⅛ × 11.　　　　24372-9 Pa. $4.50

CALLIGRAPHIC ALPHABETS, Arthur Baker. Nearly 150 complete alphabets by outstanding contemporary. Stimulating ideas; useful source for unique effects. 154 plates. 157pp. 8⅜ × 11¼.　　　　21045-6 Pa. $5.95

ARTHUR BAKER'S HISTORIC CALLIGRAPHIC ALPHABETS, Arthur Baker. From monumental capitals of first-century Rome to humanistic cursive of 16th century, 33 alphabets in fresh interpretations. 88 plates. 96pp. 9 × 12.
24054-1 Pa. $4.50

LETTIE LANE PAPER DOLLS, Sheila Young. Genteel turn-of-the-century family very popular then and now. 24 paper dolls. 16 plates in full color. 32pp. 9¼ × 12¼.　　　　24089-4 Pa. $3.95

KEYBOARD WORKS FOR SOLO INSTRUMENTS, G.F. Handel. 35 neglected works from Handel's vast oeuvre, originally jotted down as improvisations. Includes Eight Great Suites, others. New sequence. 174pp. 9⅜ × 12¼.
24338-9 Pa. $7.50

AMERICAN LEAGUE BASEBALL CARD CLASSICS, Bert Randolph Sugar. 82 stars from 1900s to 60s on facsimile cards. Ruth, Cobb, Mantle, Williams, plus advertising, info, no duplications. Perforated, detachable. 16pp. 8¼ × 11.
24286-2 Pa. $3.50

A TREASURY OF CHARTED DESIGNS FOR NEEDLEWORKERS, Georgia Gorham and Jeanne Warth. 141 charted designs: owl, cat with yarn, tulips, piano, spinning wheel, covered bridge, Victorian house and many others. 48pp. 8¼ × 11.
23558-0 Pa. $1.95

DANISH FLORAL CHARTED DESIGNS, Gerda Bengtsson. Exquisite collection of over 40 different florals: anemone, Iceland poppy, wild fruit, pansies, many others. 45 illustrations. 48pp. 8¼ × 11. 23957-8 Pa. $2.50

OLD PHILADELPHIA IN EARLY PHOTOGRAPHS 1839-1914, Robert F. Looney. 215 photographs: panoramas, street scenes, landmarks, President-elect Lincoln's visit, 1876 Centennial Exposition, much more. 230pp. 8⅞ × 11¾.
23345-6 Pa. $9.95

PRELUDE TO MATHEMATICS, W.W. Sawyer. Noted mathematician's lively, stimulating account of non-Euclidean geometry, matrices, determinants, group theory, other topics. Emphasis on novel, striking aspects. 224pp. 5⅜ × 8½.
24401-6 Pa. $4.50

ADVENTURES WITH A MICROSCOPE, Richard Headstrom. 59 adventures with clothing fibers, protozoa, ferns and lichens, roots and leaves, much more. 142 illustrations. 232pp. 5⅜ × 8½. 23471-1 Pa. $3.95

IDENTIFYING ANIMAL TRACKS: MAMMALS, BIRDS, AND OTHER ANIMALS OF THE EASTERN UNITED STATES, Richard Headstrom. For hunters, naturalists, scouts, nature-lovers. Diagrams of tracks, tips on identification. 128pp. 5⅜ × 8. 24442-3 Pa. $3.50

VICTORIAN FASHIONS AND COSTUMES FROM HARPER'S BAZAR, 1867-1898, edited by Stella Blum. Day costumes, evening wear, sports clothes, shoes, hats, other accessories in over 1,000 detailed engravings. 320pp. 9⅜ × 12¼.
22990-4 Pa. $10.95

EVERYDAY FASHIONS OF THE TWENTIES AS PICTURED IN SEARS AND OTHER CATALOGS, edited by Stella Blum. Actual dress of the Roaring Twenties, with text by Stella Blum. Over 750 illustrations, captions. 156pp. 9 × 12.
24134-3 Pa. $8.95

HALL OF FAME BASEBALL CARDS, edited by Bert Randolph Sugar. Cy Young, Ted Williams, Lou Gehrig, and many other Hall of Fame greats on 92 full-color, detachable reprints of early baseball cards. No duplication of cards with *Classic Baseball Cards*. 16pp. 8¼ × 11. 23624-2 Pa. $3.50

THE ART OF HAND LETTERING, Helm Wotzkow. Course in hand lettering, Roman, Gothic, Italic, Block, Script. Tools, proportions, optical aspects, individual variation. Very quality conscious. Hundreds of specimens. 320pp. 5⅜ × 8½.
21797-3 Pa. $5.95

HOW THE OTHER HALF LIVES, Jacob A. Riis. Journalistic record of filth, degradation, upward drive in New York immigrant slums, shops, around 1900. New edition includes 100 original Riis photos, monuments of early photography. 233pp. 10 × 7⅞. 22012-5 Pa. $9.95

CHINA AND ITS PEOPLE IN EARLY PHOTOGRAPHS, John Thomson. In 200 black-and-white photographs of exceptional quality photographic pioneer Thomson captures the mountains, dwellings, monuments and people of 19th-century China. 272pp. 9⅜ × 12¼. 24393-1 Pa. $13.95

GODEY COSTUME PLATES IN COLOR FOR DECOUPAGE AND FRAMING, edited by Eleanor Hasbrouk Rawlings. 24 full-color engravings depicting 19th-century Parisian haute couture. Printed on one side only. 56pp. 8¼ × 11. 23879-2 Pa. $3.95

ART NOUVEAU STAINED GLASS PATTERN BOOK, Ed Sibbett, Jr. 104 projects using well-known themes of Art Nouveau: swirling forms, florals, peacocks, and sensuous women. 60pp. 8¼ × 11. 23577-7 Pa. $3.95

QUICK AND EASY PATCHWORK ON THE SEWING MACHINE: Susan Aylsworth Murwin and Suzzy Payne. Instructions, diagrams show exactly how to machine sew 12 quilts. 48pp. of templates. 50 figures. 80pp. 8¼ × 11. 23770-2 Pa. $3.95

THE STANDARD BOOK OF QUILT MAKING AND COLLECTING, Marguerite Ickis. Full information, full-sized patterns for making 46 traditional quilts, also 150 other patterns. 483 illustrations. 273pp. 6⅞ × 9⅝. 20582-7 Pa. $5.95

LETTERING AND ALPHABETS, J. Albert Cavanagh. 85 complete alphabets lettered in various styles; instructions for spacing, roughs, brushwork. 121pp. 8¾ × 8. 20053-1 Pa. $3.95

LETTER FORMS: 110 COMPLETE ALPHABETS, Frederick Lambert. 110 sets of capital letters; 16 lower case alphabets; 70 sets of numbers and other symbols. 110pp. 8⅛ × 11. 22872-X Pa. $4.50

ORCHIDS AS HOUSE PLANTS, Rebecca Tyson Northen. Grow cattleyas and many other kinds of orchids—in a window, in a case, or under artificial light. 63 illustrations. 148pp. 5⅜ × 8½. 23261-1 Pa. $2.95

THE MUSHROOM HANDBOOK, Louis C.C. Krieger. Still the best popular handbook. Full descriptions of 259 species, extremely thorough text, poisons, folklore, etc. 32 color plates; 126 other illustrations. 560pp. 5⅜ × 8½. 21861-9 Pa. $8.50

THE DORÉ BIBLE ILLUSTRATIONS, Gustave Doré. All wonderful, detailed plates: Adam and Eve, Flood, Babylon, life of Jesus, etc. Brief King James text with each plate. 241 plates. 241pp. 9 × 12. 23004-X Pa. $8.95

THE BOOK OF KELLS: Selected Plates in Full Color, edited by Blanche Cirker. 32 full-page plates from greatest manuscript-icon of early Middle Ages. Fantastic, mysterious. Publisher's Note. Captions. 32pp. 9¾ × 12¼. 24345-1 Pa. $4.50

THE PERFECT WAGNERITE, George Bernard Shaw. Brilliant criticism of the Ring Cycle, with provocative interpretation of politics, economic theories behind the Ring. 136pp. 5⅜ × 8½. (EUK) 21707-8 Pa. $3.95

THE RIME OF THE ANCIENT MARINER, Gustave Doré, S.T. Coleridge. Doré's finest work, 34 plates capture moods, subtleties of poem. Full text. 77pp. 9¼ × 12. 22305-1 Pa. $4.95

SONGS OF INNOCENCE, William Blake. The first and most popular of Blake's famous "Illuminated Books," in a facsimile edition reproducing all 31 brightly colored plates. Additional printed text of each poem. 64pp. 5¼ × 7. 22764-2 Pa. $3.50

AN INTRODUCTION TO INFORMATION THEORY, J.R. Pierce. Second (1980) edition of most impressive non-technical account available. Encoding, entropy, noisy channel, related areas, etc. 320pp. 5⅜ × 8½. 24061-4 Pa. $5.95

THE DIVINE PROPORTION: A STUDY IN MATHEMATICAL BEAUTY, H.E. Huntley. "Divine proportion" or "golden ratio" in poetry, Pascal's triangle, philosophy, psychology, music, mathematical figures, etc. Excellent bridge between science and art. 58 figures. 185pp. 5⅜ × 8½. 22254-3 Pa. $4.50

THE DOVER NEW YORK WALKING GUIDE: From the Battery to Wall Street, Mary J. Shapiro. Superb inexpensive guide to historic buildings and locales in lower Manhattan: Trinity Church, Bowling Green, more. Complete Text; maps. 36 illustrations. 48pp. 3⅞ × 9¼. 24225-0 Pa. $2.50

NEW YORK THEN AND NOW, Edward B. Watson, Edmund V. Gillon, Jr. 83 important Manhattan sites: on facing pages early photographs (1875-1925) and 1976 photos by Gillon. 172 illustrations. 171pp. 9¼ × 10. 23361-8 Pa. $9.95

HISTORIC COSTUME IN PICTURES, Braun & Schneider. Over 1450 costumed figures from dawn of civilization to end of 19th century. English captions. 125 plates. 256pp. 8⅜ × 11¼. 23150-X Pa. $7.95

VICTORIAN AND EDWARDIAN FASHION: A Photographic Survey, Alison Gernsheim. First fashion history completely illustrated by contemporary photographs. Full text plus 235 photos, 1840-1914, in which many celebrities appear. 240pp. 6½ × 9¼. 24205-6 Pa. $6.00

CHARTED CHRISTMAS DESIGNS FOR COUNTED CROSS-STITCH AND OTHER NEEDLECRAFTS, Lindberg Press. Charted designs for 45 beautiful needlecraft projects with many yuletide and wintertime motifs. 48pp. 8¼ × 11. (EDNS) 24356-7 Pa. $2.50

101 FOLK DESIGNS FOR COUNTED CROSS-STITCH AND OTHER NEEDLE-CRAFTS, Carter Houck. 101 authentic charted folk designs in a wide array of lovely representations with many suggestions for effective use. 48pp. 8¼ × 11. 24369-9 Pa. $2.25

FIVE ACRES AND INDEPENDENCE, Maurice G. Kains. Great back-to-the-land classic explains basics of self-sufficient farming. The one book to get. 95 illustrations. 397pp. 5⅜ × 8½. 20974-1 Pa. $6.50

A MODERN HERBAL, Margaret Grieve. Much the fullest, most exact, most useful compilation of herbal material. Gigantic alphabetical encyclopedia, from aconite to zedoary, gives botanical information, medical properties, folklore, economic uses, and much else. Indispensable to serious reader. 161 illustrations. 888pp. 6½ × 9¼. (Available in U.S. only) 22798-7, 22799-5 Pa., Two-vol. set $17.00

DECORATIVE NAPKIN FOLDING FOR BEGINNERS, Lillian Oppenheimer and Natalie Epstein. 22 different napkin folds in the shape of a heart, clown's hat, love knot, etc. 63 drawings. 48pp. 8¼ × 11. 23797-4 Pa. $2.25

DECORATIVE LABELS FOR HOME CANNING, PRESERVING, AND OTHER HOUSEHOLD AND GIFT USES, Theodore Menten. 128 gummed, perforated labels, beautifully printed in 2 colors. 12 versions. Adhere to metal, glass, wood, ceramics. 24pp. 8¼ × 11. 23219-0 Pa. $3.50

EARLY AMERICAN STENCILS ON WALLS AND FURNITURE, Janet Waring. Thorough coverage of 19th-century folk art: techniques, artifacts, surviving specimens. 166 illustrations, 7 in color. 147pp. of text. 7⅞ × 10¾. 21906-2 Pa. $9.95

AMERICAN ANTIQUE WEATHERVANES, A.B. & W.T. Westervelt. Extensively illustrated 1883 catalog exhibiting over 550 copper weathervanes and finials. Excellent primary source by one of the principal manufacturers. 104pp. 6⅛ × 9¼. 24396-6 Pa. $3.95

ART STUDENTS' ANATOMY, Edmond J. Farris. Long favorite in art schools. Basic elements, common positions, actions. Full text, 158 illustrations. 159pp. 5⅜ × 8½. 20744-7 Pa. $3.95

BRIDGMAN'S LIFE DRAWING, George B. Bridgman. More than 500 drawings and text teach you to abstract the body into its major masses. Also specific areas of anatomy. 192pp. 6½ × 9¼. 22710-3 Pa. $4.50

COMPLETE PRELUDES AND ETUDES FOR SOLO PIANO, Frederic Chopin. All 26 Preludes, all 27 Etudes by greatest composer of piano music. Authoritative Paderewski edition. 224pp. 9 × 12. (Available in U.S. only) 24052-5 Pa. $7.50

PIANO MUSIC 1888-1905, Claude Debussy. Deux Arabesques, Suite Bergamesque, Masques, 1st series of Images, etc. 9 others, in corrected editions. 175pp. 9⅜ × 12¼. 22771-5 Pa. $6.95

TEDDY BEAR IRON-ON TRANSFER PATTERNS, Ted Menten. 80 iron-on transfer patterns of male and female Teddys in a wide variety of activities, poses, sizes. 48pp. 8¼ × 11. 24596-9 Pa. $2.25

A PICTURE HISTORY OF THE BROOKLYN BRIDGE, M.J. Shapiro. Profusely illustrated account of greatest engineering achievement of 19th century. 167 rare photos & engravings recall construction, human drama. Extensive, detailed text. 122pp. 8¼ × 11. 24403-2 Pa. $7.95

NEW YORK IN THE THIRTIES, Berenice Abbott. Noted photographer's fascinating study shows new buildings that have become famous and old sights that have disappeared forever. 97 photographs. 97pp. 11⅜ × 10. 22967-X Pa. $7.50

MATHEMATICAL TABLES AND FORMULAS, Robert D. Carmichael and Edwin R. Smith. Logarithms, sines, tangents, trig functions, powers, roots, reciprocals, exponential and hyperbolic functions, formulas and theorems. 269pp. 5⅜ × 8½. 60111-0 Pa. $4.95

HANDBOOK OF MATHEMATICAL FUNCTIONS WITH FORMULAS, GRAPHS, AND MATHEMATICAL TABLES, edited by Milton Abramowitz and Irene A. Stegun. Vast compendium: 29 sets of tables, some to as high as 20 places. 1,046pp. 8 × 10½. 61272-4 Pa. $21.95

CATALOG OF DOVER BOOKS

REASON IN ART, George Santayana. Renowned philosopher's provocative, seminal treatment of basis of art in instinct and experience. Volume Four of *The Life of Reason*. 230pp. 5⅜ × 8.   24358-3 Pa. $4.50

LANGUAGE, TRUTH AND LOGIC, Alfred J. Ayer. Famous, clear introduction to Vienna, Cambridge schools of Logical Positivism. Role of philosophy, elimination of metaphysics, nature of analysis, etc. 160pp. 5⅜ × 8½. (USCO)
20010-8 Pa. $2.95

BASIC ELECTRONICS, U.S. Bureau of Naval Personnel. Electron tubes, circuits, antennas, AM, FM, and CW transmission and receiving, etc. 560 illustrations. 567pp. 6½ × 9¼.   21076-6 Pa. $9.95

THE ART DECO STYLE, edited by Theodore Menten. Furniture, jewelry, metalwork, ceramics, fabrics, lighting fixtures, interior decors, exteriors, graphics from pure French sources. Over 400 photographs. 183pp. 8⅜ × 11¼.
22824-X Pa. $7.95

THE FOUR BOOKS OF ARCHITECTURE, Andrea Palladio. 16th-century classic covers classical architectural remains, Renaissance revivals, classical orders, etc. 1738 Ware English edition. 216 plates. 110pp. of text. 9½ × 12¾.
21308-0 Pa. $11.95

THE WIT AND HUMOR OF OSCAR WILDE, edited by Alvin Redman. More than 1000 ripostes, paradoxes, wisecracks: Work is the curse of the drinking classes, I can resist everything except temptations, etc. 258pp. 5⅜ × 8½.
20602-5 Pa. $4.50

THE DEVIL'S DICTIONARY, Ambrose Bierce. Barbed, bitter, brilliant witticisms in the form of a dictionary. Best, most ferocious satire America has produced. 145pp. 5⅜ × 8½.   20487-1 Pa. $2.95

ERTÉ'S FASHION DESIGNS, Erté. 210 black-and-white inventions from *Harper's Bazar*, 1918-32, plus 8pp. full-color covers. Captions. 88pp. 9 × 12.
24203-X Pa. $7.95

ERTÉ GRAPHICS, Erté. Collection of striking color graphics: *Seasons, Alphabet, Numerals, Aces* and *Precious Stones*. 50 plates, including 4 on covers. 48pp. 9⅜ × 12¼.   23580-7 Pa. $6.95

PAPER FOLDING FOR BEGINNERS, William D. Murray and Francis J. Rigney. Clearest book for making origami sail boats, roosters, frogs that move legs, etc. 40 projects. More than 275 illustrations. 94pp. 5⅜ × 8½.   20713-7 Pa. $2.50

ORIGAMI FOR THE ENTHUSIAST, John Montroll. Fish, ostrich, peacock, squirrel, rhinoceros, Pegasus, 19 other intricate subjects. Instructions. Diagrams. 128pp. 9 × 12.   23799-0 Pa. $5.95

CROCHETING NOVELTY POT HOLDERS, edited by Linda Macho. 64 useful, whimsical pot holders feature kitchen themes, animals, flowers, other novelties. Surprisingly easy to crochet. Complete instructions. 48pp. 8¼ × 11.
24296-X Pa. $1.95

CROCHETING DOILIES, edited by Rita Weiss. Irish Crochet, Jewel, Star Wheel, Vanity Fair and more. Also luncheon and console sets, runners and centerpieces. 51 illustrations. 48pp. 8¼ × 11.   23424-X Pa. $2.75

YUCATAN BEFORE AND AFTER THE CONQUEST, Diego de Landa. Only significant account of Yucatan written in the early post-Conquest era. Translated by William Gates. Over 120 illustrations. 162pp. 5⅜ × 8½. 23622-6 Pa. $3.95

ORNATE PICTORIAL CALLIGRAPHY, E.A. Lupfer. Complete instructions, over 150 examples help you create magnificent "flourishes" from which beautiful animals and objects gracefully emerge. 8⅛ × 11. 21957-7 Pa. $3.50

DOLLY DINGLE PAPER DOLLS, Grace Drayton. Cute chubby children by same artist who did Campbell Kids. Rare plates from 1910s. 30 paper dolls and over 100 outfits reproduced in full color. 32pp. 9¼ × 12¼. 23711-7 Pa. $3.50

CURIOUS GEORGE PAPER DOLLS IN FULL COLOR, H. A. Rey, Kathy Allert. Naughty little monkey-hero of children's books in two doll figures, plus 48 full-color costumes: pirate, Indian chief, fireman, more. 32pp. 9¼ × 12¼. 24386-9 Pa. $3.50

GERMAN: HOW TO SPEAK AND WRITE IT, Joseph Rosenberg. Like *French, How to Speak and Write It.* Very rich modern course, with a wealth of pictorial material. 330 illustrations. 384pp. 5⅜ × 8½. 20271-2 Pa. $4.95

CATS AND KITTENS: 24 Ready-to-Mail Color Photo Postcards, D. Holby. Handsome collection; feline in a variety of adorable poses. Identifications. 12pp. on postcard stock. 8¼ × 11. 24469-5 Pa. $2.95

MARILYN MONROE PAPER DOLLS, Tom Tierney. 31 full-color designs on heavy stock, from *The Asphalt Jungle, Gentlemen Prefer Blondes,* 22 others. 1 doll. 16 plates. 32pp. 9⅜ × 12¼. 23769-9 Pa. $3.95

FUNDAMENTALS OF LAYOUT, F.H. Wills. All phases of layout design discussed and illustrated in 121 illustrations. Indispensable as student's text or handbook for professional. 124pp. 8⅛ × 11. 21279-3 Pa. $4.50

FANTASTIC SUPER STICKERS, Ed Sibbett, Jr. 75 colorful pressure-sensitive stickers. Peel off and place for a touch of pizzazz: clowns, penguins, teddy bears, etc. Full color. 16pp. 8¼ × 11. 24471-7 Pa. $3.50

LABELS FOR ALL OCCASIONS, Ed Sibbett, Jr. 6 labels each of 16 different designs—baroque, art nouveau, art deco, Pennsylvania Dutch, etc.—in full color. 24pp. 8¼ × 11. 23688-9 Pa. $3.95

HOW TO CALCULATE QUICKLY: RAPID METHODS IN BASIC MATHEMATICS, Henry Sticker. Addition, subtraction, multiplication, division, checks, etc. More than 8000 problems, solutions. 185pp. 5 × 7¼. 20295-X Pa. $2.95

THE CAT COLORING BOOK, Karen Baldauski. Handsome, realistic renderings of 40 splendid felines, from American shorthair to exotic types. 44 plates. Captions. 48pp. 8¼ × 11. 24011-8 Pa. $2.50

THE TALE OF PETER RABBIT, Beatrix Potter. The inimitable Peter's terrifying adventure in Mr. McGregor's garden, with all 27 wonderful, full-color Potter illustrations. 55pp. 4¼ × 5½. (Available in U.S. only) 22827-4 Pa. $1.75

BASIC ELECTRICITY, U.S. Bureau of Naval Personnel. Batteries, circuits, conductors, AC and DC, inductance and capacitance, generators, motors, transformers, amplifiers, etc. 349 illustrations. 448pp. 6½ × 9¼. 20973-3 Pa. $7.95